Storytelling for Virtual Reality

Storytelling for Virtual Reality serves as a bridge between students of new media and professionals working in the emerging world of VR technology and the art form of classical storytelling. Rather than examining purely the technical, the text focuses on the narrative and how stories can best be structured, created, and then told in virtual immersive spaces. Author John Bucher examines the timeless principles of storytelling and how they are being applied, transformed, and transcended in Virtual Reality. Interviews, conversations, and case studies with both pioneers and innovators in VR storytelling are featured, including industry leaders at LucasFilm, 20th Century Fox, Oculus, Insomniac Games, and Google.

John Bucher is an award-winning writer and narrative consultant based out of Los Angeles, California. He is a regular contributor to VirtualRealityPop.com, LA-Screenwriter.com, HBO.com, and *MovieMaker Magazine*. He cohosts *The Inside Out Story Podcast* and *The Westworld Watch Podcast* and currently teaches at the LA Film Studies Center, where he leads courses in Virtual Reality storytelling and filmmaking. A popular speaker, John has given talks on five continents regarding story, technology, and art. He is completing a Ph.D. in mythology and depth psychology and is the author of books including *Master of the Cinematic Universe: The Secret Code to Writing in the New World of Media, Storytelling by the Numbers*, and *The Inside Out Story*. He can be found online at his site, tellingabetterstory.com, and on social media @johnkbucher.

For more information about story, Virtual Reality, this book, and its author, go to StorytellingforVR.com.

Storytelling for Virtual Reality

Methods and Principles for Crafting Immersive Narratives

John Bucher

Routledge
Taylor & Francis Group

NEW YORK AND LONDON

First published 2018
by Routledge
711 Third Avenue, New York, NY 10017

and by Routledge
2 Park Square, Milton Park, Abingdon, Oxon OX14 4RN

Routledge is an imprint of the Taylor & Francis Group, an informa business

Library of Congress Cataloging-in-Publication Data
Names: Bucher, John K., author.
Title: Storytelling for virtual reality : methods and principles for crafting immersive narratives / John Bucher.
Description: New York and London : Routledge, Taylor & Francis Group, 2018. | Includes bibliographical references and index. | Identifiers: LCCN 2017005830 (print) | LCCN 2017022849 (ebook) | ISBN 9781315210308 (E-book) | ISBN 9781138629653 (hardback) | ISBN 9781138629660 (pbk.)
Subjects: LCSH: Mass media—Authorship. | Virtual reality. | Narration (Rhetoric)
Classification: LCC P96.A86 (ebook) | LCC P96.A86 B835 2018 (print) | DDC 808.06/6302—dc23
LC record available at https://lccn.loc.gov/2017005830

ISBN: 978-1-138-62965-3 (hbk)
ISBN: 978-1-138-62966-0 (pbk)
ISBN: 978-1-315-21030-8 (ebk)

Typeset in Warnock Pro
by Apex CoVantage, LLC

Visit the companion website: StorytellingforVR.com

Contents

Acknowledgments

My editors and the staff at Routledge, Emily McCloskey, Simon Jacobs, and John Makowski for all their help and guidance and for believing in this project. Thanks also to Jack Stenner at University of Florida, Michael Smith at Pepperdine University, and Eric R. Williams at Ohio University for deep insights about the organization, structure, and content of this book.

The LA Film Studies Center and extended alums and friends—Jeremy Casper, Chris Krebsbach, Rebecca Ver Straten-McSparran, Paul Yoder, Nathan White, Alex Swickard, Kris Young, and Sarah Duff.

My friends at The Alliance for giving me my first opportunity to tell stories—Peter Burgo, Bob and Joan Sanford, Miles Reese, Rob McCleland, and Heather Arment helped me greatly. Thanks to John Stumbo, Jordan Christopher, Pam Fogel, and Deb Gregory as well.

My family—Katie, John K. Bucher, Cathie Bucher, Josh Bucher, Matt Bucher, Jordan Bucher, Henry Bucher, Arlo Bucher, Tony Reyes, Luanne Reyes, Aaron Reyes, Alicia Reyes, Caleb Reyes.

Dr. Kim Walker, Dave Anderson, Jim and Ashley Krueger, and all my friends at Pacifica.

Special thanks to those who gave of their time to participate in the book . . .

Chris Milk, Tye Sheridan, Nikola Todorovic, Chris Edwards, Ted Schilowitz, Angela Haddad, Rob Bredow at LucasFilm, Noah Nelson and the No Proscenium Podcast, Annie Lesser, Keight Leighn, Mark Cordell Holmes, Larry Rosenthal, Liz Markman, Jonathan Krusell and Brian Rose at Google, Paul Debevec, Jessica Brillhart, Jess Shamash and Pete Billington at Oculus, Paul Meyhoefer and Kevin Cruz at JK Imaging Ltd., Sarah Hill at StoryUp, Heather Brenners, Matt Celia, Robert Watts, Steve Peters, Adam Orr, Brian Allgeier, Dr. Carolina Cruz-Neira, Doug Liman, Melissa Wallack, Matt Thompson, Robyn Tong Gray, Tai Crosby at SilVR Thread, and the entire crew at Jaunt VR.

Foreword

I am a child of the theme-park world. I grew up in central Florida right around the time Disney World opened. I remember going on the Haunted Mansion ride, and though I couldn't have articulated it at the time, I recognized that when you move people through space while telling them a story, it creates the feeling of traveling on a journey and gives the experience meaning. I was lucky enough to find ways later in life to apply my love of spatial storytelling to the world of technology. I've always innately lived in that world, but this story's not about me, it's about how the recent rise of immersive media will affect our future.

We can reflect on every medium that has been created to tell stories and see that people eventually settle on certain elements that they like, and those elements then become the mainstream definition of what that medium is. Novels, movies, video games, plays, and television shows all have mainstream definitions based on the elements of those mediums that have been successful and lasted. As a medium continues to grow and explore new territory, you have departures and divergent paths off the original idea and methods of that medium. The cinematic language of VR is still developing. But it will only move forward and become more advanced through experimentation and by increasing the volume of stories being told in its space.

Many people have referred to VR as a *new medium,* or at least a new way to tell stories. I would be a contrarian to that idea. I would say that there is nothing fundamentally new about Virtual Reality. It's a new way to experience what I refer to as spatially oriented entertainment—much like that Haunted Mansion ride I rode as a kid. The world of theme parks has been doing this for number of generations now. The world of theater has been doing it even longer. We have plenty to learn from these disciplines and plenty others.

In the world of flat-screen media, a movie theater can be anywhere you want it to be, including on an airplane or in your hands. The one element that doesn't translate well in those environments is the idea of true spatial sense. With spatial storytelling, you get to move around, walk around, and activate. The best and most intriguing attempts to do this thus far, using flat-screen media, have been in the gaming world, where you use certain mechanics to give the impression that you're moving in space, but your body, mind, and brain know that you're looking at a flat screen. We have developed 3D technology, which gives us a pseudo-illusion that there's depth, but depth is different than space. Virtual Reality is more than just adding depth to entertainment, it's adding actual spatial universes.

As someone who focuses on the future for a major movie studio, I reflect into the past to see where the guiding lines and the divining rods are that give us telltale signs to what is ahead. For years now, we've stared into screens. We're fooling our brain. We're fooling our eyes into believing that what we are seeing on the screen is real. But what if we start to wear the screen? We can unbind the restrictions of the display. The creative starts to say, "What could I do if I didn't have to work within the restrictions of a rectangular screen? What if you could literally strap a theme park to your face?" Once we cracked the code of the rectangle, the technology afforded the opportunity to build story all around us. Now we are finding different and unique ways to do this and finding the boundaries that we thought we used to have no longer exist.

We're on a journey, but the promise of something better is here. We've started to crack the code, and now there are technologists, scientists, and storytellers working to see where this medium could take us as human beings. We'll look back on these first waves of VR and one day chuckle, like we look back at our first laptops and our very first cell phones. The best storytellers I've seen thus far in Virtual Reality are the ones that understand how to explore the imagination in such a way that they don't feel restricted anymore by the tools that they used to have.

The nature of storytelling will always remain the same. It's now about how intense of an experience you can create for your participant. These new tools allow a new level of intensity, and the best storytellers will find ways to tap into that intensity that we haven't really even seen yet. I don't think we've seen the best of storytelling in VR at this point. I think that it's going to come from a generation that starts to embrace this technology in different ways than we presently do because of our tendency to lean back into the past.

We're on the cusp of something that will be more powerful than perhaps any medium we've experienced before. I can't wait to see what the future holds and the tales that storytellers will create as a result.

Ted Schilowitz
Futurist
20th Century Fox
Hollywood, CA
2016

1

A New Reality and How We Got Here

For well over 100 years, audiences have looked into rectangular screens, ignoring everything peripheral to the edges of the frame. But in recent times, the edges of the screen have been removed. Narratives now have the potential to play out anywhere we can crane our necks to glance or stare. Like in life, any place we can walk to or journey toward becomes the screen for a story. This breakthrough in storytelling is changing the way audiences engage with the moving image as well as the ways we create content—and this is only just the beginning. Virtual Reality (VR) is one of the latest developments in the remediation process that has come to define digital media. According to theorists Bolter and Grusin, this process of remediation has become integral to the ongoing progress of media, which is now constantly commenting on, reproducing, and eventually replacing itself.[1]

Immersive content is still in its infancy, but after Facebook's $2 billion acquisition of Oculus, VR in the mainstream began marching forward at an entirely new pace. AOL's purchase of RYOT to bring immersive video to *The Huffington Post* is equally significant in the move to bring VR into people's homes. The affordability of Google Cardboard and demand for upcoming releases of Sony PlayStation VR, the HTC Vive, and Oculus Rift have quickly made 360-degree video something most tech manufactures are incorporating into future releases. Vimeo, YouTube, and Facebook are all already capable of 360-degree video upload and display. Samsung, GoPro, and Nokia all have significant VR products on the market as well. The technology is ready and available, and people are enamored with it. But there's one problem. No one has really figured out how to tell a story with it.

Pixar Animation cofounder Ed Catmull famously stated to a reporter with *The Guardian* that Virtual Reality technology may not be the revolution in storytelling that some of its evangelists have claimed. "It's not storytelling. People have been trying to do [Virtual Reality] storytelling for 40 years. They haven't succeeded. Why is that? Because we know that if they succeed then people would jump on it. Linear narrative is an artfully directed telling of a story, where the lighting and the sound is all for a very clear purpose. You're not just wandering around in the world," Catmull said.

Critics have pointed out that Catmull's approach—that storytelling in Virtual Reality would look and be structured like it is in cinematic narratives—is dated and lacks an understanding of the potential of the medium. Catmull has stood his ground, saying, "It's good, but it's not storytelling. The fact that you've changed the technology, and people are excited about it, doesn't change the underlying difficulty of the compelling narrative story. Just like books aren't the same things as movies. They don't have to be," he said.[2]

Media futurists such as Palmer Luckey, founder of Oculus VR, are out to prove Catmull wrong, just as Pixar proved the industry wrong with its 1995 animated feature and cultural juggernaut *Toy Story*. Luckey hailed the potential for VR films at the 2016 Web Conference, stating, "Telling stories in Virtual Reality is very different than telling stories through traditional films or even video games—it's going to be a long time until Virtual Reality storytelling is nearly as refined as film. Decades."[3] John Gaeta, creative director at LucasFilm's ILMxLAB, has agreed with Luckey's sentiments, saying, "Cinema is a master storyteller's art form. Until recently, a "fourth wall" has contained this form. Soon, however, we will break through this fourth wall, and cinema will become a portal leading to new and immersive platforms for expression. ILMxLAB is a platform for this expansion. We want you to *step inside our stories*."

While Catmull, Luckey, and Gaeta lean toward the philosophical, others are making large financial investments that someone will figure out compelling ways to tell stories with VR technology. Investment researchers Piper Jaffray have forecasted that VR will be a major mega tech theme through 2030. "We liken the state of virtual and augmented reality today as similar to the state of mobile phones 15 years ago. It likely will take a decade before mainstream adoption as necessary improvements in displays and applications as well as lower pricing are needed to drive demand," the company stated in 2015.[4]

Piper Jaffray is basing its optimism around consumers' insatiable appetite for new tech experiences. They have suggested that on the virtual side, new immersive worlds will open up, including gaming, live sports, concerts, immersive cinema, and social experiences. They also forecast that eventually users will be able to virtually attend an NFL or NBA live game with a 50-yard-line seat, listen to a live concert of your favorite band with a front-row seat, watch movies optimized for VR, or visit friends in far-away locations. Further, they are predicting that classrooms will be able to virtually (and relatively inexpensively) tour the Great Wall of China, Egyptian pyramids, Stonehenge, the Coliseum, or the inside of a factory or laboratory. They have concluded in their report that Virtual Reality will encompass a $62 billion industry by 2025.[5]

There's little debate that VR technology is here to stay despite the disagreements about if and how stories can be told with the medium, and it will only gain more traction as time goes on. As with any new medium, experimentation and creative thinking are what will push the tools to deeper depths of storytelling. New possibilities and perspectives will continue to arise as filmmakers forge the path ahead and find innovative ways to connect with their audiences.

EARLY CONCEPTUAL IDEAS ABOUT VR

Virtual Reality can be and has been defined in a wide variety of ways. Some have suggested that even panoramic paintings were an early means of creating the illusion that a viewer is somewhere they are not by filling their entire field of vision.[6] Many others agree that stereoscopic viewers, popularized in the early 1800s, were a step forward in creating a three-dimensional experience and somewhat resembled the head-mounted displays (HMDs) we encounter today. A century later, these devices were mass marketed by the View-Master company, and children have enjoyed the technology ever since.

In the 1930s, science fiction author Stanley Weinbaum wrote a story called "Pygmalion's Spectacles" and seemed to foretell the VR we experience today. French poet and playwright Anton Artaud discussed how the props and characters in a play could be seen as *la réalité virtuelle* (Virtual Reality in English) in *Le Théâtre et son double*, a collection of essays he wrote about drama and the theater in 1938.

During the 1950s, Morton Heilig developed *Sensorama*, attempting to stimulate all the senses while audiences watched a movie. In the 1960s, engineers created the first HMDs and quickly added rudimentary motion tracking to the unit. A decade later in the 1970s, Myron Krueger coined the term *artificial reality* to describe his interactive immersive environments. By the end of the decade, MIT had developed the Aspen Movie Map, a *hypermedia* experience that allowed users to "wander" the streets of the Colorado town.

THE ROOTS OF THE MOVEMENT

VR continued to pop up in science fiction, notably in 1982 when Damien Broderick's *The Judas Mandala* was released. Atari founded a development lab for VR research that same year but closed it within two years. Finally, in 1987, Jaron Lanier, founder of the visual programming lab (VPL), popularized the term "Virtual Reality" to a larger audience than had been familiar with the concept before. VPL developed goggles, gloves, and HMDs that began to fully incorporate haptics.

In the early 1990s, VR machines began to turn up in some pop culture conversations. *Brainstorm* and *The Lawnmower Man* introduced a generation of moviegoers to the concept of VR. Video game arcades offered VR experiences, though many were short lived because of low latency, which often caused nausea. Later in the 1990s, both Sega and Nintendo announced VR technologies for their gaming systems. Both were racked with problems and quickly discontinued. Apple introduced QuickTime VR in 1994, a product that was widely available but never quite caught on. However, the end of the decade brought philosophical ideas about VR to the forefront of culture in the immensely popular film series *The Matrix*.

THE MODERN ERA

The 21st century saw massive development in computer technology, graphics, and hand-held devices, all paving the way for where VR has landed presently. In 2007, Alex McDowell coined the phrase "immersive design" in a discussion around the growing field that was emerging around story-based media within the context of digital and virtual technologies.

Companies such as Kaiser and Canon developed progressive HMD and VR technology in the early 2000s, which would usher in the next generation of pioneers. At this point, the focus was still very much on the technology, and few were having conversations about how to tell a story with it.

In 2012, the Oculus Rift prototype was developed, and story conversations began. Smart glasses from Moverio and Google advanced conversations about Augmented Reality (AR) possibilities and affected the conversation surrounding VR as well. In 2014, Google Cardboard entered the public conversation around VR and offered an extremely inexpensive way for the average person to have a VR experience. Samsung, HTC, and Sony all released products that capitalized on VR's progress and made it more desirable and affordable. However, that year is most significantly remembered as the year that Facebook purchased the VR startup, Oculus, for $2 billion. This acquisition is considered to have ushered VR into the mainstream market.

NAVIGATING MEDIATED EXPERIENCES

Theorists have considered the psychology behind the rise of VR since its earliest iterations. Bolter and Grusin discussed the rise in terms of remediation, highlighting the ways that Virtual Reality has incorporated elements and aspects of other previous media forms. They suggest that culture moves toward media where the evidence of a mediated experience is less noticeable. They point to websites as being hypermediated experiences, offering photographs, video clips, hyperlinks, and other elements to guide the user's experience, making users further aware of the force between themselves and the meaning behind the media experience they are engaged in. Bolter and Grusin suggest that users do not want an intervening agency but prefer to go beyond mediation to immediacy.

Technological advances that have led to greater and greater levels of immersion in VR tend to eliminate the evidence of a mediated experience, though one could argue there is an even greater level of mediation actually at work behind the scenes. Viewers in virtual experiences often respond as though they are having the immediacy experienced outside of the virtual world, suggesting that these virtual experiences have lowered the evidence of the mediated experience to levels almost indistinguishable from those they engage in without an HMD.

Further, Bolter and Grusin state that within a mediated experience, the meaning itself is not immediate. In order for it to be so, the viewer must be able to ignore the medium's representational function. This most often occurs when the viewer encounters something from their world outside the virtual space, as opposed to something abstract. Since representational media such as film tend to rely on concepts, participants, and objects from outside virtual space rather than abstractions, such as those that might be found in fine art, it should be no surprise that cinematic VR—the combining of film techniques and principles with immersive media—creates an even greater sense of an unmediated experience and more immediate meanings for the viewer.

CHANGES IN PERSPECTIVE

For decades now, filmmakers have thrown themselves into film schools and other training venues to learn how to tell visual stories. With emerging technologies like VR, however, many of the concrete rules everyone has learned and spent time perfecting go out the window. For example, since the inception of film, we have forced a viewer's perspective on our story by placing and moving the camera where we wanted it. This allowed us to use the edges of the frame to craft a window into the world we were creating for the audience. With 360-degree cameras, the field of vision is opened up to a dimension we've never had to deal with before. In essence, we've lost the edges of the frame and thus the traditional way we've manipulated the viewer's perspective. We've also used lighting and lenses to further direct an audience's attention toward who our protagonist is and what he or she is trying to accomplish.

THE TWO PHILOSOPHIES

Shari Frilot, senior programmer and new frontier curator at the Sundance Film Festival, believes the only way to figure out how to tell stories in this new era is to cultivate artistic and social environments that disarm audiences when they enter the space of VR. "There's not going to be just one way of telling a story," she says emphatically. "There's going to be different artists working in different media figuring out different ways to architect in this space. It's still in a very nascent stage, storytelling in this new medium," Frilot has said.[7]

Currently, there are two dominant philosophical storytelling approaches and perspectives in VR. The first allows the viewer to watch a scene that is played out in the space around them. They are immersed in the scene but not necessarily an active participant. This is engaging for a few moments but can become frustrating to the viewer when they want to more intimately interact with the world around them. Storytelling in Virtual Reality is less about *telling* the viewer a story and more about letting the viewer *discover* the story.

The second philosophical approach allows the viewer to actually become the camera, in a sense. Stories told in this format begin to blur the line with video games. However, VR storytellers are finding that not all gaming theory applies in this format either, as we might assume. *Allumette* from Penrose Studios premiered at the Tribeca Film Festival in 2016 and fully embraced the "viewer as camera" approach. The results were stunning. Most who have experienced the film have raved about it being a game changer for storytelling.

Former Pixar exec Tom Sanocki is creating his Limitless Entertainment brand with the same principles that made his former bosses storytelling giants. Limitless's first film, *Gary the Gull*, is smart and funny and features a great lead character. Sanocki has said that storytelling is about figuring out how people solve problems. Now we have to figure out how they solve them in virtual or augmented realities. Sanocki has compared the process to the early days of filmmaking when experimentation was the key to moving the medium forward.[8]

Cinema's journey began with much less promise than VR holds. Voices from Vaudeville and the more established theater community combined with objections of prominent technologists such as Edison opposed early cinematic storytelling, preferring to keep it confined to the realm of science. Experimentation with the film camera and the projectors that allowed its product to be shown for large groups eventually pushed through the opposition and created a new visual language for communicating, entertaining, and crafting narratives. It would take decades of innovations in both technology and creativity before cinema would arrive fully as the storytelling medium it is today. Sound, color, realistic special effects, and even the ability to edit would not become available until later.

While the development of immersive storytelling benefits from previous art forms, such as the cinema, it still may be some time before the full potential of this new medium is seen. The eyes of new generations and the fresh perspectives they will bring will continue to recraft the path. However, the initial foundation must be laid before bricks can be added to the wall.

SPOTLIGHT ON DIRECTING: Storytelling in VR through Cinematic Directing
Jessica Brillhart, Principal Filmmaker for VR at Google

Jessica Brillhart joined Google's Creative Lab in 2009, where she spearheaded numerous award-winning shorts and documentaries before joining the VR team in 2015. Since directing *WORLD TOUR*— the first VR film made with the Jump ecosystem—Brillhart has continued traveling the world, filming, and experimenting, all in an effort to better understand and help inform others about VR technology. She is currently the principal filmmaker for VR at Google.

John Bucher: I'd love to start with a bit about probabilistic experiential editing in VR, which is a concept a lot of people won't be familiar with. You've spoken about that before, and I'm curious to know how you feel like that affects story design, as creators are beginning to try and sell stories?

Jessica Brillhart: A lot of it has to do with understanding how a visitor engages with the world that she's in. It's the first step in getting an understanding of how it was more of a dialogue and a dance with someone that was in the space instead of it being something that I wanted or I was going to force a person to experience. It embraces the fact that we each have our

---

(Continued)

(Continued)

own agency, even when we're dancing with somebody, we can still do something kind of spontaneous, we can either go with the flow, we can go with someone who's leading. Once you understand the agency of a person and the space that they're in, once you understand that a visitor is basically being dropped onto a world and has the agency to do what she wants, then it's really my job to think about how those worlds interact with the visitor that might be there, interact with the participant, but also, conversely, how do I craft worlds that can kind of interact with the person better, and I think that the craft is really in that connection between those two things.

John Bucher: With your traditional background in a filmic storytelling, can you talk a little bit about the role of characters and props and things that we use in telling traditional cinematic stories when creating in VR space?

Jessica Brillhart: How do you convince somebody that that world actually exists? Which is all really character and props, too. The characters are there as vessels for the story, so that you can better understand the events that happened. You look at live-action VR and there are substantial things, like people with human faces and dogs or various elements of the real world, that we can latch onto and be like, "I know that. I can add context to that because I know what it is." Interaction is a less direct thing. It's not like, "Hey, how are you, I'm so and so. What's your name?" It's a nuanced understanding of how we are around other people, how we build relationships, how we exist in spaces with people and are we compelled to do things when we're

(Continued)

(Continued)

<table>
<tr><td></td><td>around other people, or we're not compelled to do things when we're in that same situation. It's a lot of behavioral science, honestly. It's so much about presence.</td></tr>
<tr><td>John Bucher:</td><td>You said something that I think is really intriguing in a recent TED talk about importance of giving the viewer an identity. Can you speak a little bit more about how that's accomplished?</td></tr>
<tr><td>Jessica Brillhart:</td><td>You need to figure out who you want this person to be, what's their role in all of this? Who are they? We want validation in the real world, right? You do, because you believe what you have has value, and you want to have value in your existence. Not to be too pragmatic, but that's why we all do what we do, right? That transcends, you don't lose that going into a virtual space, you would want the same thing.

It's really just about figuring out what I can give that person that comes in to this world. What is their role in this life that I'm putting them in? It doesn't necessarily have to be the point, it doesn't have to be like, "You are the main event." It changes over time, too. If you think about going to a dinner party, it's a pretty simple example, but in the beginning, you may not know anyone and you may feel a little bit like an outsider, but at the end you may know everyone at the party, you might be the life of the party, you might be the point. Or maybe you get more distant, or more removed. We change. Our roles evolve and change over time. In terms of specific identity, you have to determine, are you a main character that has agency to change the story, or are you someone who doesn't? Are you someone that they acknowledge, or are you someone that they don't? Understanding what this</td></tr>
</table>

(Continued)

(Continued)

person's role is is vital, because that's what actually allows for us to build the worlds that facilitate that.

I feel like identity is a narrative layer as much as everything else. VR is layer upon layer of narrative pipes. It's not narrative in the way that we know it, from this objective, removed position. Once you're in a narrative, suddenly it becomes layered and textured. I think that identity affects everything. It's dependent upon what the rules of the universe are that you would like there to be. If you can't move around and you can't interact with anything, then that's limiting. It also allows you to be a little bit more specific about who that person is. You don't want to give that person an identity where their job is to do something when they can't do anything. It feels weird and suddenly you're taken out of it, because you're like, "I can't push that button. But my job is to push that button." Unless the experience is about frustration, it's not the right thing. You have to ask, "Is it enjoyable? Is the point frustration, is the point anxiety?" If it's not, and it's supposed to be really fun and upbeat, make sure you set that person up for success, not for failure. That just snowballs into a bad experience for anyone who comes in.

John Bucher: You've spoken about the potential of a multiverse approach to structuring a VR experience. Do you think there is a place for traditional story structure approach in VR? Not necessarily three-act structure, but any sort of traditional structure that you think we can carry from traditional storytelling into VR?

Jessica Brillhart: I think you have to unpack traditional three-act structure. I know it's sort of tough to describe, but

(Continued)

(Continued)

for me, I think the easiest way to say it is because you're basically allowing for a storyteller to exist. Normally what we do is we have an experience, if that experience is a success, we leave it. Someone asks, "Hey, what'd you do, what happened?" I think back to the experience and through a bunch of filters say, "Oh, this happened." The thing that I create is that tool to communicate, the way that nugget of info that I give to somebody is story. That's a result of an experience. It's not as though I'm having the experience.

In VR, what we're doing is creating experiences for people to then go into and have their own experiences—to have those experiences affect them, and then they leave and someone asks them, "What happened?" Then they tell the story. Because it's removed, it's more like thinking about it as potential story, instead of kinetic, if you want to get geeky about it. Kinetic story is story as it's happening. Story that is active. Story that I'm telling. That's when we say story in the traditional sense, that's basically what we mean. We're going back to an experience, and we're communicating that to somebody through some kind of medium, like a novel or a song or a play or a movie.

With VR, because it's a magnitude back, what we're really doing is setting up potential story. We're looking to the future. We're saying, "Okay, these are the stories that could potentially come out of this." Or maybe this is the story that I want to tell. I have to work through identity and work through rules of the universe to really get a better understanding of what's the potential here? Go back to that first story that I came up with and say, "Okay,

(Continued)

the likelihood that someone is going to come out of that experience with exactly that story is very unlikely, unless I literally force them to look in a direction the whole time." In which case, I should just make a film and be done with VR.

If you think about fables in the past, it's about a tortoise and a hare, and the tortoise wins and the hare loses, but the core of that story is that slow and steady wins the race, right? Regardless of who you empathize with the most, and if you care about the hare more or the tortoise more. It's very clear that that's the takeaway. There's a gradient of potential experiences there, really. It's thinking about unpacking that story that you want to tell. Is it love? Is it peace? Is it humanity? Is it connecting with another human being? Is it life and death? You start really thinking about the story spirit and then you start to think about how you can create these worlds that help facilitate that. Ultimately, what you're doing is you're setting up the visitor for being able to get something close to the bullseye, but if they're a little off, it's fine, as long as it's in the general area, and as long as you work from the ideas and the philosophies of what you're trying to do, then my guess is that that makes for a successful piece. Because you allow for the gradient of a story to exist.

John Bucher: You've talked about the importance of eye contact and you mentioned that that can feel like a close-up shot, which is a traditional element from the language of cinema. Have you found other methods in your work that mirror our traditional language of cinema, things that feel like close-ups, things that feel like the experiences we have in

(Continued)

(Continued)

	watching conventional cinema that you have been able to reinterpret?
Jessica Brillhart:	Energy is a big thing. That's probably the biggest thing for me. I used to be an editor. I still edit in VR. Editing still has to be possible in this medium. You edit things for energy. Walter Murch did that. He understood that people are going to look at different parts of the screen, and he accounted for that. You edit things for focus. You build in systems to translate feeling and vibe and energy to someone who's not a part of that world. What's interesting is that energy is very palpable in VR. You can basically have a person in a space and can make them feel very awkward very fast. The same kind of quick cuts and the disorientation doesn't really work the same as it does in conventional cinema. Again, it's that whole unpacking idea—where energy means something different in VR. Energy means the way that people relate to you. Energy is the chaos of the space. Is it easy to discern between this and that? Do you know exactly what you should be paying attention to? Are you to accept that, are you supposed to try to focus? What's that like? Energy is a big thing.
	A lot of it's just a behavioral thing. Establishing a hero. You see Clint Eastwood show up and he has sweat on his brow, and he rides in on his horse. You know, "That's our guy! He's the guy that's going to do it." You find in VR that you really need to find a way to connect with someone, because you're in the presence of that person. You need that relationship to build over time. We study how we deal with people around us—how proximity changes our relationship with people and the rest of the

(Continued)

(Continued)

space. It's culturally different from the way that Europe and the U.S. generally deal with things versus what China will do—how they will deal with meeting someone new for the first time versus knowing somebody for a long time.

In terms of the hero, what's interesting is shared experience—having something big happen, some kind of main event. You're there right next to the hero watching it. That creates camaraderie. That creates shared experience. That creates empathy. Additionally, we provide opportunities to discover elements, like owning memories, owning moments, owning the hero. Maybe the first thing you *don't* see is the hero. The hero emerges and you discover her. Suddenly, it's like she's mine now. She's part of me. Shared experience and discovery and having that be two important things actually help establish a stronger connection with whoever your potential main character is are so important.

The other thing, too, is the idea of perception, which I think is a really big thing. Letting the layers of how you perceive the world, how we perceive the world, how other characters might perceive the world help us better understand the story and better understand their positioning. If you think about a way a woman might look at a city street at night versus what a man might see—that change in perception is huge. If you think about the film *Pretty Woman*. You have the female character. What does she see the world as? Then you see the male lead. What does he see the world as? It's different, they come from different worlds. Over time, you see that their worldviews start to become very similar and that's how they fall in love. That's how you

(Continued)

(Continued)

> know that they're in love. It's really exploring the
> differences between characters but thinking more
> mentally about it, deeper about it, than just what's
> on the surface. Which is where some is, which is
> great, but now that we're in the world, surface isn't
> enough.

CONCEPTS TO CONSIDER FROM JESSICA BRILLHART

▶ Engaging with a viewer in VR is more of a dialogue or a dance than
an experience that can be forced upon them.

▶ Characters are vessels for story.

▶ Creating presence is nuanced and can be difficult to achieve.

▶ You must determine what you want the viewer's role to be in the
virtual world and then communicate that to them somehow.

▶ Traditional three-act structure is useful in VR storytelling but must
be unpacked through a kinetic lens.

▶ Creators should leave space for a variety of potential experiences
the user may have—the gradient of a story.

▶ Energy, or the emotional journey of the audience through the
experience, and perception, how the viewer is experiencing the
world, should drive the technical decision making in VR storytelling.

PUTTING IDEAS TOGETHER

Jessica Brillhart introduces concepts and ideas that will be key to understanding and developing new approaches to storytelling in virtual space. The concepts of engagement, presence, and energy will continue to arise and be explored as we delve deeper into the world of immersive narratives, as will story-related ideas such as character and three-act structure. As

Brillhart highlights, the central concern must always be the experience of the audience. If they are not engaged, the novelty of our approach will not be sustainable. Every creative decision involving either narrative or technology must be to that end.

FORCING PERSPECTIVE IN NEW WAYS

The word "perspective" is Latin in origin and comes from the words *per*, which means "through" and *specere*, which means "to look." The rules of perspective in filmmaking are taken from the centuries of development in the arts of drawing and painting. The human form appeared more realistic when certain proportions were considered in relationship to others. Proportions were also considered in relationship to the subject's distance from the viewer. The point of using perspective is to create a sense of depth. In cinematic storytelling, this is true both in a physical sense and in the metaphoric. We are using viewed images, juxtaposed together, to create a greater sense of meaning—a story. We are creating an extension of reality through art.

Forms in filmmaking, be they a person, an object, or a location, consist of three basic characteristics. They have size. They take up space or cover distance. And they extend in different directions. Keeping these ideas from classical art in mind as one begins to consider 360-degree virtual space and how characters and stories will work in it will be helpful. We sometimes refer to the relationship between the viewer and these forms as *depth perspective*.

Understanding how perspective worked in the early artistic disciplines gave us a head start when learning how perspectives would function through the lenses of cameras. While a camera is capable of reproducing an image faithfully, we are also able to manipulate the image and thus the perspective based on the movement of those lenses through spatial distance and time.

Manipulations of lenses affecting depth of field, focus, brightness, and contrast have long served as methods for forcing a viewer's perspective on significant characters, themes, or moments in cinematic narratives. However, those tools are not as accessible in the world of VR filmmaking. Forcing perspective has allowed us to make certain characters seem larger in the frame and thus more dominant. Characters can be positioned below the viewer's eye line or "down their nose" and thus made to feel looked down upon.

Regardless of our methods, the forcing of perspective is all about attempting to communicate a photographable subject to an audience, a baseline necessity in telling a story through filmmaking. In establishing their perspective, we are creating the audience's eyes in the world of the story. Stories in the VR world are often quite simple, as the public's VR literacy is just beginning. As their experience grows, the complexity of the narratives is likely to grow as well.

EDGES OF THE FRAME AND THE GAMING EXPANSION

Maintaining the rule of thirds, creating headspace, and establishing a 180-degree line have been standards of cinematic storytelling for decades. The goal in using these techniques has been to keep the audience immersed in the story. When the filmmaking process becomes visible to the audience, they are quickly taken out of the narrative and reminded that they are just observing technology. Their investment in the characters and the theme lessens.

In many ways, the edges of the frame have been convenient tools for filmmakers to rely on, knowing that they can hide what's "behind the scenes" in the story they are telling. As the camera moves in a fashion motivated by the story, the viewer's eyes and attention move along with it. The peripheral world to the edges of the frame is not visible and thus not important in the viewer's mind.

Early efforts in video games resemble the structural and static nature of paintings more than that of great cinematic art. However, as gaming continued to develop, the technical rules experientially crafted by filmmakers began to appear more often. Eventually, games gave the player realistic first-person challenges. The user's sense of presence and immersion increased as interactivity increased. The ability to control space inside a virtual world had not previously been experienced in any technology. This technique has proved to be important in the development of VR, as many early immersive experiences have duplicated the style and language of video games. VR experiences in gaming continue to be one of the most popular and effective uses of the technology, providing a canvas for storytelling that is still advanced beyond what can be achieved with cameras at this point in our technological development.

As visuals expanded in the world of gaming, the quality of and techniques for employing the accompanying audio expanded as well. Serious gamers invested in surround-sound audio systems or quality headphones that further immersed them in the virtual world. Advances in fields such as binaural audio provided further opportunities to bring users into the experience they found themselves in. All these developments would be useful in establishing the specs and guidelines for the best available VR experiences.

THE ULTIMATE EMPATHY MACHINE

In a TED talk he delivered in 2015, filmmaker Chris Milk heralded VR as "the ultimate empathy machine." Scientists are beginning to study VR and its relationship with emotions and even depression, believing that Milk may be correct.[9] "Every time we build something new, more of my questions get answered, even if a few more questions come up. It feels like we're getting better at it each time, and this is an evolving medium and an evolving process. In the long term, we do need to create a library of things that is not just about having 500 *Citizen Kanes*, because not everybody wants to watch *Citizen Kane*, and the people that do, don't want to watch it all the time," Milk says in his talk. "They want to watch *Scream* or whatever. Sometimes people want to watch things other than high art," he concludes.[10]

Milk is pointing toward a potentially altered state of human consciousness being on the horizon. "Right now we're still in the darkness of night, poking around with flashlights and trying to find our way there," he has said.[11] As he suggests, VR storytelling and filmmaking will only progress as creators continue to experiment and share what they have learned to work. As with any new medium, learning what does *not* work will be just as significant as learning what does.

Elia Petridis, a VR filmmaking pioneer who founded the experimental filmmaking company Filmatics, believes he is seeing shards of light in the technological darkness surrounding VR storytelling. "There's this element with VR of, 'I don't want to stand on a spaceship, I want to stand on the *Millennium Falcon* because that has meaning to me,'" he says. "It is the emotional connection, that something that was hanging on your walls is now right in front of you. As a storyteller, I find that aspect really crucial," Petridis has said.[12] Other creators are also finding that establishing meaning leads to an emotional connection for the viewer in VR worlds. If the technology is indeed to fill this role as "ultimate empathy machine," building this sort of connection will be crucial.

SPOTLIGHT ON CAMERAS: Storytelling in VR through the Lens
Paul Meyhoefer, VP JK Imaging/Kodak

Paul Meyhoefer is a vice president with JK Imaging/Kodak. The Kodak SP360 4K camera rig is being used to create VR experiences.

John Bucher: Tell us a little about yourself and how you fit into the world of VR.

Paul Meyhoefer: JK Imaging is who we are. We are a company that was formed just after Kodak had basically filed for Chapter Eleven in their digital camera business. The company was created with the idea of creating a license for the Kodak brand. We had a relationship with the ODM manufacturer of digital cameras and the idea was to pick up on the Kodak brand and create digital point-and-shoot cameras. Everything from $59 to $350-type cameras. The company was formed and actually the negotiations worked out with Kodak that we are actually now the sole licensee for all digital cameras for Kodak worldwide. That's JK Imaging.

Over the past few years, the digital camera business actually decreased at a much more rapid pace than we expected before. We knew it was declining but we also thought at the entry-level position, with a lot of retail customers, we'd be able to sustain, maybe it's double-digit declines but then it went flat. Early on, we were very interested in the video side of things. We were very interested in what GoPro was doing. We've watched them from day one. The expertise that we had was really the optical lens. What could we do to create the next generation of video that's just not point and shoot? The obvious things were there. Wider aspect ratio, 4K resolution, higher frame rates, all those kinds

(Continued)

(Continued)

of things. That didn't interest us as much as looking at a wide-angle lens. Just really pushing the envelope of how far we can go. We actually created the first one which was the SP360—the original. There was a video camera before this that had a 240-degree lens—Our SP1. But it was just a 16 × 9 HD video camera with a super-wide-angle lens.

From that technology, we realized if instead of an aspherical lens, we made a spherical lens, we could actually capture a 360-degree image. We could go beyond 180 degrees and create this circular image. We started the development of this SP360. In the beginning, there was no software. All of our images were round. We had our own software that we started working with, which now you see has evolved into Stitch. We also had an app that we started working with on the SP360 development, because we knew we had to create a format to unwrap this video into something that was usable for people. We started development work on that and it took us 6 months or so to get some pieces of software out there that people could actually use.

We did stuff that you normally see for surveillance-type cameras—split screen, left/right images. One of our most popular was a front and back split screen which was 180 degrees forward and 180 degrees back. You could really see people couldn't get their head around the idea that their video now captures not only what I see but what's behind me or if you are in video, how do I get out of a scene where normally I'm focused on creating a shot for my storytelling or whatever it is?

We forged some relationships with YouTube. We got involved with their efforts to create the format that

(Continued)

(Continued)

would allow their users to interact with 360-degree video. We knew that that was the ticket for us. We continued immediately to start to develop our 4K, next generation of cameras. We paid attention to our customers. What were they doing with this yellow SP1, one of the SP360 cameras? They were taping them together. They were putting them on their helmets. They were putting three of them together. They were making goggles out of them. That's proven to be very successful for us so far. We implemented certain features. Facebook got involved with 360-degree videos, so we supported them. We like Facebook because they pushed us to support not only video but photos. Now we do both.

John Bucher: For filmmakers and storytellers, you have the ability to shoot one direction and have all your equipment and gear behind you and then turn around, and shoot the other direction and then stitch those together, with your rig. Do you think at some point, we will have possibilities besides a single fixed-lens option, where we can use traditional cinematography methods?

Paul Meyhoefer: I think content creators and cinematographers want to create a more immersive virtual experience. In order to do so, you need to split the lens because then you can put it, for example, on a helmet. You have a front and back. Your body is in the shot but your head is actually the lenses. You'd actually feel like you are this person walking around or playing a game. You can then take that and, with augmented reality, transpose that experience into wherever your imagination will take you.

We see that as a very important tool for a lot of the developers. Also, like in the case of drones,

(Continued)

for example, we don't want the drone in the shot. We want to give you the feel of being Superman and you are flying. You want to make that as fluid as possible, because then the emotional aspect will kick in. Somebody will actually feel like, "I'm there." In reality you are sitting in your office with your feet up. We do see that as a critical thing. We also think it's important for creating. There are a lot of stereoscopic-type applications that are starting to evolve as well. Being able to have multiple lenses integrated into a point of view is very critical for the future.

If it's fused into one optical lens, it's very difficult to create that without the other camera getting in the way of the lens. It's all optical tricks. One of the things I hope is that some of the hardware manufacturers will develop actual sensors and capabilities to take spherical lenses and create images from that, because right now the technology that a lot of people are using, other than the optical technology, are standard photo optic sensors and standard microprocessors and technology that flat digital cameras use. They are not optimized for spherical or 360-degree video. Hopefully, they are seeing the market evolve and will start investing in that direction so that the development teams and others can start creating products like this. Eventually, I think it could end up in the phones, to tell you the truth. It's probably a couple of years away. There is no reason why it wouldn't. Like we've seen everything else go in the phone.

CONCEPTS TO CONSIDER FROM PAUL MEYHOEFER

▶ Some VR experiences are captured through one or more spherical lenses that produce a 360-degree spherical image.

▶ Software is required to interpret and manipulate these spherical images.

▶ 360-degree video is not the same as Virtual Reality, though it can be used to create VR experiences.

▶ Technical challenges exist with using 360-degree and VR cameras, such as keeping lighting and sound equipment out of the shot.

PUTTING IDEAS TOGETHER

Paul Meyhoefer mentions creators wishing to create more *immersive* virtual experiences. This idea will be unpacked in a variety of ways throughout the text. While technology provides the immersion for the viewer in VR, one of the chief concerns of and challenges to the technology is not breaking the immersion that it is providing. It is important to recall from the earlier interview with Jessica Brillhart that the emotional experience of the audience must remain at the pinnacle of our goals as creators. Breaking the immersion breaks the emotional journey and thus defeats the purpose of the experience we are creating. Technology must remain the tools we are using to tell our stories rather than the focus of the stories themselves.

MOVING BACKWARD TOWARD THE FUTURE

Virtual Reality and its cousins, Augmented Reality and Mixed Reality, have not and will not only be used for the purpose of storytelling. However, the potential for storytelling in these mediums will be a significant factor in its long-term success. Film cameras and the accompanying technology would have continued to have uses, even if Edison and the theater community had gotten their way. However, film and later video would have likely not become the communications media they are today had we not figured out ways to tell stories with them. Even when these visual tools are used for purposes outside of the realm of narrative, the techniques and methods that storytellers created are still often used to employ them. Whatever technologies lie beyond us in visual communications, it is likely that immersive technologies and storytelling methods will be key to reaching them.

As our technologies have advanced, voices from Huxley to Postman have suggested that our mythologies have diminished. It is the opinion of this author that VR holds the potential for providing a platform for recreating them. Early mythologies were surrounded by rituals. These rituals had lasting impact because they provided those involved with experiences that not only resembled real-life mysteries and events but seemed to offer some connection to them that transcended the verbal languages people had come to rely on. The effect these rituals, and thus mythologies, had was visceral. It is entertaining to watch YouTube videos of those experiencing VR for the first time. The reactions could easily be described with the same term—visceral. The donning of an HMD headset and waving one's hands about, reaching for objects that simply aren't there, would certainly have appeared to be ritualistic, even cultic activity to the ancients.

The classic Greek myth of Demeter and Persephone is no longer familiar to the average citizen, as it was in ancient Greece. In the tale, Persephone is out gathering flowers one day when she is nabbed by Hades, god of the underworld. Her mother, Demeter, is crushed by the kidnapping. Persephone refuses to eat during her time in the underworld, having heard if one eats there, she can never leave. Eventually she succumbs when offered a few pomegranate seeds. Demeter convinced Zeus to send Hermes to negotiate a deal with Hades for the return of her daughter. The compromise required that Persephone would marry Hades and return to the underworld for a season every year. In the remaining months, she was free to live above ground, returning to her previous life. Demeter mourned every year when her daughter returned to the underworld. Being the goddess of the harvest, she used her power to keep the crops from growing, and all plantation died. She caused flowers to sprout again and plant life to return when her daughter arrived home each year. Several versions of the myth record that Persephone grew to love her time in the underworld, eventually preferring her time in the darkness to her time in the light. The experiences she had there offered powers she was unable to recreate anywhere else.

Entering virtual space through a VR headset is not unlike a trip to the underground. The virtual world holds possibilities beyond our natural landscape. It very well may make achievements possible that would never have been conceived in previous eras. Its dangers are equally real. Like Persephone, there may be those who begin to prefer the new world to the old, causing problems we can only imagine at this point. Still, virtual experiences may hold answers beyond those we've been able to grasp thus far in human development. VR has allowed scientists to view data in ways that have unleashed fresh insights and interpretations. The technology has allowed disabled veterans to visit war memorials, allowing emotional experiences they would have never had otherwise. The wonder seen embodied in those experiencing VR for the first time is reminiscent of the ecstasy those early rituals and mythological experiences provided according to ancient writings.

The myth of Demeter and Persephone allowed the Greeks to explain why seasons on the earth mysteriously came and went. It allowed them to make better sense of the world around them. It allowed them to have deeper insight into what it meant to be a human being on this earth. These are the things mythologies are capable of providing. Could there be any greater hope for what VR might offer us? Immersive experiences will not lead us to mythological insights about who we are unless they are accompanied by stories. Stories allow us to work in the language of metaphor, not necessarily allowing us to articulate the nuances of life as much as allowing us to experience insights into them in ways that seem to transcend language. But before we can transcend the language of VR storytelling, we must understand what others have discovered about it and how to speak it ourselves.

NOTES

1 Bolter, Jay David and Richard Grusin. *Remediation: Understanding New Media.* Cambridge, MA: MIT Press, 2000. p. 55. Print.
2 Stuart Dredge, Pixar co-founder warns virtual-reality moviemakers: "It's not storytelling." www.theguardian.com/technology/2015/dec/03/pixar-virtual-rea lity-storytelling-ed-catmull
3 Stuart Dredge, Oculus VR: "Classrooms are broken. Kids don't learn the best by reading books." www.theguardian.com/technology/2015/nov/03/oculus-vr-founder-classrooms-are-broken
4 Munster, Gene, Travis Jakel, Doug Clinton, and Erinn Murphy. "Next Mega Tech Theme is Virtual Reality." https://piper2.bluematrix.com/sellside/Email DocViewer?encrypt=052665f6-3484-40b7-b972-bf9f38a57149&mime=pdf&co= Piper&id=reseqonly@pjc.com&source=mail
5 Munster, Gene, Travis Jakel, Doug Clinton, and Erinn Murphy. "Next Mega Tech Theme Is Virtual Reality." https://piper2.bluematrix.com/sellside/Email DocViewer?encrypt=052665f6-3484-40b7-b972-bf9f38a57149&mime=pdf&co= Piper&id=reseqonly@pjc.com&source=mail
6 The Virtual Reality Society in the UK. www.vrs.org.uk/virtual-reality/history.html
7 Voynar, Kim. "Future Tense: Sifting Through the Patterns of VR Storytelling at Sundance." www.indiewire.com/article/future-tense-sifting-through-the-patterns-of-vr-storytelling-at-sundance-20160201
8 Ibid.
9 Falconer, Caroline, J., Aitor Rovira, John A. King, Paul Gilbert, Angus Antley, Pasco Fearon, Neil Ralph, Mel Slater, Chris R. Brewin. "Embodying self-compassion

within virtual reality and its effects on patients with depression." http://bjpo.
rcpsych.org/content/2/1/74
10 "Chris Milk: How virtual reality can create the ultimate empathy machine." www.
youtube.com/watch?v=iXHil1TPxvA
11 Ibid.
12 Hill, Jessica. "Eying the future of storytelling using virtual reality." www.then
ational.ae/arts-life/film/eyeing-the-future-of-storytelling-using-virtual-reality

2

A Stone Bridge Covered in Microchips

THE PURPOSE AND GOALS OF THIS BOOK

New fields and disciplines take time to develop. The only way that we eventually stop wandering around in the dark is when someone begins to create a map around the area they have found and someone else shines a light on it. Early developers and storytellers in VR have begun to create those maps. The purpose of this book is to shine a light on their discoveries and then draw a few conclusions as to what those discoveries might mean.

There has been some distrust between classical thinkers and technology proponents. Heidegger wrote in 1977, "Everywhere we remain unfree and chained to technology."[1] Those who find deep value in the philosophies, methods, and truths of the ancients can be dismissive of ideas that seem to go viral overnight while ironically ranting about it on their smartphones. Those who spend their time pushing forward our technological capacities found an interest in doing so often because the ways and thinking of the past either didn't make sense or simply weren't working for them. What we will explore here is the desperate need that each camp has for the other in order to progress their work. There has long been a stone bridge covered in microchips that led the way to the future.

Interestingly, in technological fields that rely on principles of good story-telling, such as video game development and design and 3D animation, the quantity of training or discussion around the timeless truths that have long been taught about constructing narratives is minor compared to the techni-cal training. A quick scan of the syllabi of the top three academic programs in these fields confirms this to be the case. It is sometimes assumed that since the platform is new, all narrative methods should be new as well. This occurs at the expense of effectiveness in storytelling. While exceptions certainly exist, and many developers have solid instincts for crafting stories, many more examples fall flat and do not resonate with their intended audience simply because the stories are ineffective. Creators scratch their heads and wonder why, failing to realize that while the world they have built and the characters in it resonate with them, they lack the universal elements necessary for a nar-rative to maintain longevity and engagement on a mass scale. Understanding what has endeared stories to audiences for millennia psychologically, philo-sophically, neuroscientifically, and even unconsciously is essential, especially when developing experiences on the scale that VR, AR, and Mixed Reality (MR) offer. These technologies may be often compared with the Wild West. However, it is important to remember that this is simply the season they pres-ently exist in. Even the Wild West was eventually tamed with laws, structure, and form. Doing so is exactly what allowed our society to develop into a cul-ture that would eventually produce the sorts of technology we all enjoy today.

In order to tame the Wild West of alternate realities, it is important that we look at the principles that have governed narratives since the days of Aristotle and perhaps before. Examining the architecture behind good sto-rytelling gives the understanding we need in order to discuss how we move forward in crafting audience experiences that are successful. Understanding how stories work, what makes them effective, and the ways that they can be created will give us the materials to take into new realities in order to build new narrative structures and methods for new mediums and platforms.

WHAT MAKES A GOOD STORY?

Revered author Flannery O'Conner once said that everyone seems to know what a story is until they sit down to write one. Understanding what makes a story good first requires that we define a few terms, namely "story" and "good." As with most words, there are multiple definitions that can be applied to the terms, all of which help us get the words' use and the applications we may have for such an expression. Story is derived from the Middle English word *storie*, which likely came from the Latin *historia* or the Anglo-French *estorie*. We see these terms as early as the 13th century. However, our word story doesn't come into popular use until the 15th century.[2]

The meanings of the word today can range from the unit of measure used to describe the space in adjacent floor levels in a building to a widely told rumor. The definitions that Merriam-Webster offers, such as a narrative, a report about incidents or events, and a short, often amusing tale get us closer to the use we will apply but still lack precision. While we will eventually land on a definition that can be used for applications in VR, it may be helpful to further deconstruct the term "story" in terms of the elements used to construct stories. Stories often consist of the following features, which will be unpacked in greater detail later in the text.

Characters

It would be difficult, if not impossible, to convey a story without at least one character. Later, we will examine all the various characters found in stories, including essentials such as the protagonist, the antagonist, and a plethora of other archetypes.

External Goals

While various types of stories work with internal journeys and abstract expressive forms, visual storytelling usually requires a photographable goal that at least one character or protagonistic force is trying to achieve. While the protagonist in a story is often a single individual, a protagonistic force can include a duo or group of individuals that share the same external mission. It is important that the goal they share is something that can be seen. Finding love is an abstract concept that occurs inside a character. We cannot photograph the act of finding love; therefore it lacks the visuals required to stand on its own in visual storytelling. Finding a date to a dance, however, is a photographable external goal that would work well as evidence of a protagonist trying to find love.

Internal Goals

Seeing a character accomplish something is fundamental in a visual story. However, we also desire to know that they have accomplished something internally. The internal goal of a protagonist is also unique from the external goal in that the character is rarely aware of their own internal goal. It is clear to the audience but greatly resides in the character's subconscious. An example of an internal goal might be to prove a character's worth to his or her father.

Conflict

This is perhaps the most significant element found in stories. Without conflict, we merely have a scenario. Conflict can be built in a number of arenas within the story world. The conflict can come from the great odds the protagonist faces in accomplishing their goals. The conflict can come from another character, such as the antagonist, who wishes to accomplish the exact same goal. The conflict can also come from within the character in the form of self-doubt and insecurity.

Resolution

Stories resolve in a wide variety of ways. However, in order to feel some sense of satisfaction with the story, the audience needs to experience resolution of the conflict. The only exception would be if the goal of the story is to leave the audience unresolved. However, this can be risky and should only be executed in a precise fashion by experienced storytellers.

STORIES IN ALTERNATE REALITIES

While there are certainly nuances to the stories told in alternate realities, for the purpose of this book, we will hold the following definition for a story told in VR, AR, or MR.

A story is a sequence of events or scenarios that demonstrate characters trying to resolve conflict by accomplishing goals.

This definition will leave us space to expand the uses of the term "story" to fit most if not all applications of VR, AR, and MR technologies. The events or scenarios might be fiction, nonfiction, or taking place in real time as the viewer is navigating space. They might be for the purpose of entertainment or education or purely informational. The sequence of events used in the alternate reality story might be linear or nonlinear. There may be a single protagonist or multiple protagonistic forces. That protagonist might be the viewer or another character the viewer is observing. The resolution might be through the viewer accomplishing a clear external goal or through the feeling experienced when viewing another accomplish that goal. The resolution, as well as the goals, may be internal or external. All of these various combinations of applications we can experience in alternate reality space can qualify as stories.

FORMS VERSUS FORMULAS

This book is not a collection of formulas for how to tell stories in VR but instead a way of seeing VR so that you might tell stories in it. In essence, we will be attempting to highlight the establishment of a form or a language that seems to be emerging for telling stories in this new medium. Ironically, the narrative arts seem to be the lone resistant art form when it comes to form.

Courses in painting and in drawing all begin with rigorous exercises walking students through forms. Learning how shapes and colors affect audiences is a time-honored part of the discipline. When learning music, fundamental elements such as notes and scales are offered long before complex arrangements. In architecture, understanding how load-bearing walls, pitched roofs, and foundations work is essential before choosing how many windows will be in a given structure. All disciplines accept that structure is a key part of how their art form works. One cannot imagine a musician trying to invent a new note or chord. Architects never attempt to build a new home without walls or a floor. Yet storytellers try to ignore the forms and structural principles of the medium on a regular basis, often to their own detriment. This is usually because form is confused with formulae. In his book *Story Proof: The Science Behind the Startling Power of Story*, Kendall Haven states, "Story is not the information, the content. Story is a way of structuring information, a system of informational elements that most effectively create the essential context and relevance that engage receivers and enhance memory and the creation of meaning."[3]

Even in narrative endeavors, formulas do work—if they are hidden well. There's an old adage in Hollywood storytelling that says, "Give me the same thing—only different." Though they might deny it, a large segment of audiences enjoys the experience of familiarity in a story. There's a reward triggered in the brain when we see a pattern we recognize. The key is to then surprise the brain with a bit of irony. Even without this element, however, audiences often return to films they have seen dozens of times simply because they have a similar emotional experience even when they are aware of the structure and ending of a narrative. The power of narrative is in the journey.

STORY OPPORTUNITIES WITH VR AND HOW VR LENDS ITSELF TO CERTAIN TYPES OF STORIES

Every medium has its advantages and disadvantages when it comes to storytelling. Graphic novels offer visuals that tell stories in a way that novels are incapable of. However, novels can provide depth and internal insights that graphic novels are unable to replicate. Determining the advantages and disadvantages of VR can assist us in crafting stories that lean in to the medium instead of searching for workarounds. Current VR experiences require the use of an HMD. While there will likely come a time when virtual experiences can be had without a headset, this element is a necessary component of the VR experience presently. This provides advantages and disadvantages for the viewer as well as the storyteller. The advantage is that the viewer has their eyes sealed in darkness, save for the light emitted through the lens of the HMD. This quickly transports the viewer into an immersive experience. When headphones are added to the HMD, the sound further immerses the viewer by covering their ear canals. This disadvantage is, of course, that headsets can be heavy and, with their very presence, remind the viewer that what they are experiencing is manufactured and not real. While ineffective in most story worlds, stories that journey the viewer through an experience in which they might be hearing a similar headset in real life, such as with a spacecraft simulator, become much more effective.

Stories that take place in worlds outside our own immediately lend themselves to VR storytelling, allowing the viewer to be immersed in a land they have never or could never experience in real life is unique to the medium of VR. This includes created worlds as well as existing worlds and landscapes. Even stories that take place in familiar environments such as a domestic kitchen can be turned into new worlds with creative camera placement. While we could easily observe a couple having an argument in a kitchen in reality, we would never likely be allowed to stand between the couple and experience the tension held in that space. We could also never experience the same scenario from the perspective of a mouse on the floor. VR, of course, also affords us the ability to experience this argument in first-person form with someone we are not familiar with in reality in an unfamiliar space we have never stood in before. Our immediate response to VR storytelling might be to only craft narratives that take full advantage of the 360-degree landscape that we now have access to, which can be an effective strategy. However, we must also remember that many other experiences will be successful in VR space simply because of access we now have to locations and scenarios. Every narrative has the potential to be made interesting in virtual space.

THE ROLE OF GAMING AND GAME THEORY IN VR

While being a fairly recent addition to the potential storytelling canon, video games have become a major cultural force in a short amount of time. There is solid evidence that human beings have enjoyed games since times before language was a part of the human experience. Anyone who has played peek-a-boo with a baby understands this reality. There is additional evidence that games may even stretch beyond human activity into other forms of consciousness, as there is research that suggests certain species of animals participate in games as well. Throwing a ball for a dog to retrieve has become a common experience across cultures that would indicate this to be true. Games are part of the human experience. It should be no surprise that they will be part of our virtual experience as well.

Game theory is the study of how people behave in certain interactions, usually social and economic, and how they make decisions when immersed in these settings. It is an area of study originally developed by economists that has widened to other disciplines. A game in game theory is not just what traditionally has been described as games (soccer, chess, roulette, Monopoly, or tennis) but is any interaction between individuals or social groups. Essentially, it is the study of how these parties make decisions during interactions. When dealing with *games*, the participants are usually called *players*. Players must make decisions that display behaviors, usually called *actions*. The behavior leads to *payoffs* for the players. This, of course, closely resembles aspects of *narrative structure*, where we have *characters*, who make *decisions* and take *action* that cause *setups*, leading to eventual *payoffs*.

Game theory is usually approached with one of three lenses or sometimes a combination of the three. The social science approach explores how games affect viewers, both individually and on group and society levels. The humanities approach explores what meanings and philosophies are expressed through games. The industrial and engineering approach explores the technical aspects of the discipline including elements such as computer graphics, artificial intelligence, and networking. Often, theories evolve as the discoveries in one of these areas affect our understandings of the others. Selmer Bringsjord of the Rensselaer Polytechnic Institute (RPI) has looked at game theory through a narrative lens. He suggests that while many games are compelling, they may not be *dramatically* compelling in the same way that Dante's *Inferno, Hamlet,* Gibson's *Neuromancer,* and the plays of Ibsen are compelling. Bringsjord goes on to ask if it is even possible to build dramatically compelling interactive digital entertainment in the form of computer games.[4] He suggests that doing so will require seminal advances in the intersection of artificial intelligence (AI) and narrative. "Since interactive digital narrative will need to be crafted and massaged *as the story is unfolding,* computers, not slow-by-comparison humans, will need to be enlisted as at least decent dramatists—but getting a computer to be a dramatist requires remarkable AI," he states.[5] This level of AI and narrative capability, however, seems to be quickly approaching.

LUDOLOGY VERSUS NARRATOLOGY IN GAME STUDIES

The most heated debate in game studies since the 1990s has been around this topic of the unfolding story and what philosophies and approaches apply to it. While the intensity of the debate has subsided, neither philosophy has become dominant. One group of theorists, called ludologists, support that stories are only a subset of games and that games should not be analyzed primarily in terms of narrative. Another group, called narratologists, insists that games are a subset of stories and thus subject to primarily narrative analysis. Still others offer that this binary approach is altogether the wrong path.[6] There is value to both approaches for VR, and ludologists do concede that there are, without question, narrative elements found in video games.[7] Some VR experiences would tend to favor the case for ludology, building the world of the user as he or she progresses in the experience, free from any narrative traditions or constraints. Other experiences clearly employ an underlying philosophy of narratology, assuring the user that every decision and element of agency they experience fits into a larger planned narrative. The title of this book likely gives the reader an indication of where the author falls on this spectrum. However, since VR is an emerging medium, not a video game and not cinema, considerations from every philosophical approach should be welcome. Some immersive creators will gravitate toward an approach that favors the entire experience that he or she creates to feel as an overarching narrative. Others will prefer only to see minor narrative elements in the work they create. As VR continues to progress, there should remain room for both types of creators.

THEORETICAL LESSONS IN 3D SPACE

The origins of how objects work in three-dimensional space and the basic study of geometry go back to ancient times. As technology has advanced, the representations of objects and shapes in 3D space has become of greater interest, especially to those in the computing industry. Most recently, the orientation of these objects and the "camera view" through which the viewer sees them have become important aspects of storytelling in virtual three-dimensional space. While the approaches and methods behind these ideas come from earlier disciplines of painting, photography, and filmmaking, nuances have risen specific to computerized versions of these representations. While painters took advantage of and crafted with natural light, photographers and filmmakers used technology to achieve effects with lighting. Now VR creators have the ability not only to tell stories with shadow and light but also to create those elements themselves from scratch. In addition, they have the ability to craft the textures on the objects that will respond to the light. While a greater degree of control has been handed to the creators, the way that human beings react to shadow and light has not changed since the early painters were working with these elements. The most dedicated artists in virtual world building still go back and refer to the lessons and discoveries of early artists, as the basic principles have not changed. What has changed is that viewers experience a greater sense of entering the space of the virtual third dimension rather than simply letting their brains only imagine that process. The irony is that it is still the brain imagining the process, but the realization of the mediation is less opaque. Perhaps the most repeated anecdotal lesson from those designing in three-dimensional space is that every angle must be considered in terms of the viewer's experience. If you are going to allow a viewer to pick an object up or enter through a doorway, the entirety of the experience must be considered as each option is presented. In other words, the larger narrative must be held in one hand while holding every angle of every detail in the other.

SPOTLIGHT ON GAMING: Storytelling in VR through Video Games
Brian Allgeier, VR Game Designer, Insomniac Games

Brian Allgeier is a video game designer, best known for his work as lead designer and creative director on the *Ratchet & Clank* series developed by Insomniac Games for Sony PlayStation. He began working in video games in 1991 as an artist and animator on *Hanna Barbera's Cartoon Carnival*. Most recently, he served as lead designer and creative director for Insomniac's VR game *Edge of Nowhere*.

John Bucher: You are someone with a very rich history in telling stories in this media of gaming. Let's talk about some of your most recent work, especially your work in the VR space with *Edge of Nowhere*. Can you talk about where the initial ideas for telling this story came from?

Brian Allgeier: I think, early on in 2015, we started talking to Oculus about making this third-person adventure game. We liked the idea of playing with the theme of the main protagonist unclear on what is real and what is not. We'd originally started working on this more surreal, dream-like world, where the hero is questioning if they were still alive, if they were dead, and if everything represented in this dream world all tied back to their normal life before they'd entered it. We explored that for a while, and as we started developing the story, we realized that on a very practical level, we couldn't create the number of assets that people expect from a dream world, where just anything you can imagine can be conjured up. We also didn't like the idea that the story didn't feel very grounded. We wanted the sense of reality to mix and contrast with what is unreal and dreamlike.

I was reading a lot of HP Lovecraft short stories, because we also wanted to pursue horror. I always

(Continued)

(Continued)

	liked the fact that when you put on a VR headset, you immediately feel vulnerable. You're cutting off your sight and sound, and the primitive brain kicks in and you start to get really, truly nervous about what is in this experience. I really wanted to delve deeper into that genre (horror), and VR just seemed like the perfect medium to do it.
John Bucher:	The environmental storytelling in this game is really impressive. When you read a Lovecraft story or you begin to imagine these things, at some point in time, somebody's going to have to actually lay code to these things to actually make it appear. How do you go from taking a story, an environmental story that's in your head, and translating that to someone who's going to do the technical labor of bringing it to the screen?
Brian Allgeier:	It's a pretty lengthy process. We typically start with prototyping early on, with just the great moments we know we want to see, and we work best under deadlines. With *Edge of Nowhere*, we had an initial demo that we had to create for the E3 Convention and had 2 months to do it. We only had ideas about running through Antarctica, and at the end you run into a rundown ship and it turns out it's a library or it's like a study and tentacles wrap around you. We had no idea how any of that stuff fit into any story whatsoever. We just thought that would be a great demo. Through brainstorming, trial, and error, we developed a document that became like the bible for the game, and all of the creatives use it. Once that happens, everyone has a good image and target for what to shoot for, and the whole team can start developing for it.
John Bucher:	The topic of magic comes up quite a bit when I'm talking with narrative designers and those who are

(Continued)

(Continued)

	trying to take these 2D stories they've traditionally been working in and bring them into VR space. I often hear comparisons about magicians and sleight-of-hand artists that use similar methods of getting the audience to look where they want. How can you let the audience explore the environment that's all around them but, at the same time, guide their journey through this story in VR?
Brian Allgeier:	That's something I've been thinking about a lot recently. I'd say we can learn a lot from magic acts, in terms of directing attention, and also from live theater, in terms of how to create these 360-degree environments, where we want to make sure that people tend to be looking where we want them to look. There are a lot of tricks for doing it. Some of them are even solved on more conventional games, like the *BioShock* series. I think they're pretty brilliant in how they direct your attention.
	Typically, people will always look to the brightest spot in the room. They're like moths to a flame, so whatever is brightest, people will tend to go to it. Another great trick for Virtual Reality, and it's same with live theater, is spatialized audio. The fact that we can place audio in locations and have people automatically turn to look where the sound is coming from is really powerful. Something we used quite extensively in *Edge of Nowhere* was moving objects to draw the viewer's eye. Another great trick that you see is using a trail of breadcrumbs, in a figurative sense. So, if there's blood that's dripping along the ground, you want to know where it's leading to. You'll follow that trail and then see the end results.
John Bucher:	Let's zoom out for a second and look at VR as a storytelling medium in general. *Edge of Nowhere* is a

(Continued)

(Continued)

third-person experience. Obviously, there are those who are crafting first-person experiences, where the viewer is the protagonist. Can you talk a little bit about what you bring from the world of traditional storytelling into VR space that absolutely applies and then what we may have to throw out of the window?

Brian Allgeier: I think from traditional storytelling, one thing that will always persist is three-act structure. It's in our DNA—the monomyth or hero's journey. We expect there to be a beginning, middle, and end and inciting incidents and the course, with the hero facing various enemies and allies and then having that finale where the hero is transformed and overcomes the major conflict of the story. I think that's something that all storytellers should continually be learning and developing.

In terms of VR, I think a lot of it comes down to the techniques that are used to tell the story. With traditional filmmaking, of course, we're accustomed to doing cuts, having camera angles, and that's something we can no longer do in all instances. The more cuts we do, the less immersive it becomes, because you're always reminded that we're shifting your viewpoint and you're not really there. There has to be very elegant ways of transitioning from one shot or one scene to the next, though. A lot of it comes down to just relying on the performance and the movement of the actors and the world around you and less on what the director is trying to make you see. We just can't get too specific guiding people's attention.

John Bucher: Let's build on that by talking about the role of characters in VR. You're someone who has been responsible for crafting amazing characters. Can you talk

(Continued)

	a little bit about your approach and if you approach say, *Ratchet & Clank* differently than you approached Victor in *Edge of Nowhere*? Has your approach to character changed with this new medium?
Brian Allgeier:	It's an interesting question. They are two very different story styles. With *Ratchet & Clank*, it's certainly more traditional, where we would figure out what our characters wanted and we were shifting perspectives between Ratchet and Clank and the Crack in Time. Both of them were trying to figure out where they belong in this universe, and we were learning more about their history and the trajectory of what they were meant to be or what they thought they were meant to be. Then they ultimately have to make a decision whether or not they want to fulfill what seems to have been predestined for them or not.
	With *Edge of Nowhere*, we were trying to tell a story through the perspective of one character, one hero—Victor Howard. We really could only show it from two angles. One when you were floating behind him in this detached, disembodied head as he's travelling through Antarctica. With the second angle, we had these head-space moments where you felt like you were really inside of his head and you'd see everything from a first-person POV. That was how we managed to both support the idea of a third-person adventure game, where we could travel through these worlds and see the hero, but then really cause you to feel like you were present *as* him, when he was thinking through these head-space moments.
	There were minimal camera cuts. We might cut to a close-up moment in gameplay, and then we would try to smooth the transition from the game world to the head-space world by doing a fade to black or

(Continued)

(Continued)

	something that would help smooth it out. Whereas with *Ratchet & Clank*, we'd get away with a lot more cutting and traditional cinematic scenes.
John Bucher:	This particular story, *Edge of Nowhere*, speaks to people's current desires for adventure, and it certainly provides some interesting worlds that we really haven't seen before. What would you say were the major themes that you were trying to hit on or allow a player to experience?
Brian Allgeier:	I'd say one of the big ones is perception. Oftentimes, what we believe is real is not real. I think that's a theme throughout a lot of Lovecraft. If only we could see behind the veil of reality, we would all go mad. I think there's an aspect of it in this story— that everything comes down to our own perception. I think that in life we have a lot of regrets and we're always wrestling with them and reconcile them with our perception of the world.
John Bucher:	You're speaking to themes of the human condition with Victor. I imagine he's exploring what it means to be human, while he's searching for his fiancée.
Brian Allgeier:	We tried not to explain everything. It was ambiguous, so that a lot of people could read their own interpretation of what they believe the story was about. I think you're right, though, a lot of it is about the human condition. What drives us? What keeps us going? What we believe in can be everything to us. That's what we hold onto.

CONCEPTS TO CONSIDER FROM BRIAN ALLGEIER

▶ Practical aspects of VR lend themselves to certain genres such as horror.

▶ Environmental storytelling is a key part of VR gaming narratives.

▶ Older art forms such as sleight of hand offer principles that still work in directing an audience's attention.

▶ Three-act structure persists in many immersive VR experiences.

▶ Transitions between narrative scenes are important and can break the immersion for the viewer.

▶ Perception continues to be an important part of the VR user experience.

PUTTING IDEAS TOGETHER

Brian Allgeier reinforces the concept of story structure in VR experiences, allowing for modifications that suit emerging immersive technologies, such as the redefining of scene transitions. He also reminds us that other, older methods, such as those used in the world of stage magic, may be worth our consideration as we continue to seek ways to tell stories, in which the audience becomes unaware of the medium with which they are being communicated to. His suggestions prompt us to consider the necessity of the creator's invisibility as we strive to create immersive experiences. It can be tempting to call attention to novelty or cleverness when designing an experience. The most effective hard work, however, seeks to disguise itself, allowing the audience to become caught up in the narrative—their minds convinced that the experience is their own and not only that of a character they encounter in the virtual world.

THE LAND BEYOND THE BRIDGE

We began this chapter by looking at the metaphor of a stone bridge covered in microchips. But what lies beyond the bridge once we have crossed it? In 1902, a French magician named Georges Méliès created a film called *Le Voyage dans la Lune* (*A Trip to the Moon*). It is a story about a group of scientists, who bear a strong resemblance to the wizards of Harry Potter lore, that successfully launch a manned rocket to the moon. While there, the explorers encounter aliens, battle them, and even find a way to destroy them. They safely return to Earth by pushing their spacecraft back off a cliff, where it falls back to the earth. The film is widely credited as one of the first pieces of cinema that told a coherent story. While the practical effects used by Méliès get the majority of the attention, one factor that rarely receives discussion is what the filmmaker got right and completely missed the mark on when it came to actually embarking on a trip to the moon. It is hard for modern audiences to appreciate the fact that when the story was told, humankind had never been to the moon before. Our technology was far from being capable of such endeavors. From a purely scientific perspective, we can appreciate that Méliès correctly identified one of the key factors that would keep us from making such a voyage in real life for decades—power to blast a craft that distance against the forces of gravity. The first act of his film explores this problem. Méliès also correctly assumed the atmosphere of space would not be welcoming to humans. He costumed his characters in space suits with helmets that would assist with their breathing. His ideas about our encountering alien life forms, necessitating a battle, is still a common trope used in storytelling today. However, there are a vast number of assumptions Méliès got wrong—things he just could have never known or anticipated. No historians fault him for such errors; we instead celebrate his forward thinking and the creative vision. History will likely look back at modern creators with the same grace. We must not be afraid to push the boundaries and explore this new medium of storytelling. We should embrace the principles from the past that still serve us well. We should seek innovation and modification of those that do not. There are unfathomable stories that lie beyond that stone bridge covered in microchips. Let us move forward into the new world that awaits.

NOTES

1 Heidegger, Martin. *The Question Concerning Technology*. New York: Harper Perennial Modern Classics, 2013.
2 Merriam-Webster Dictionary Online. www.merriam-webster.com/dictionary/story
3 Haven, Kendall. *Story Proof: The Science Behind the Startling Power of Story*. Westport, CT: Libraries Unlimited, 2007.
4 Bringsjord, Selmer. "Is it possible to build dramatically compelling interactive digital entertainment (in the form, e.g., of computer games)?" www.gamestudies.org/0101/bringsjord/
5 Ibid.
6 Murray, Janet. "The Last Word on Ludology v Narratology in Game Studies." Delivered as a preface to keynote talk at DiGRA 2005, Vancouver, Canada, June 17, 2005.
7 Frasca, Gonzalo. "Ludologists love stories, too: notes from a debate that never took place." www.ludology.org/articles/frasca_levelUP2003.pdf

3

Science and Technology behind Storytelling

Though stories have been around since the beginning of human communications, scientific research into the particulars of the field is still relatively new. In his book looking at the science behind the power of story, Kendall Haven says that our minds were evolutionarily hardwired long before birth to think in specific story terms—that these internal neural *story maps* are not stored in our conscious mind but in the subconscious.[1] Beyond these concepts, children are read stories before they are old enough to grasp the words being said to well beyond the formative years. We never reach a point of maturity at which we stop telling each other stories. All this storytelling has mass effect on our brains and our lives.

STORY AND THE ESSENCE OF THE BRAIN

Brian Boyd contends that humans are "hyper-intelligent and hyper-social animals."[2] By combining factors of intelligence, pattern seeking, alliance making, cooperation, and the understanding that others have beliefs and knowledge of their own, stories make us a stronger and more effective species. He suggests a story is "a thing that does" instead of "a thing that is." Perhaps the most significant factor that Boyd mentions is *pattern seeking*. Stories that adhere to even loose structural frameworks are, in a sense, built around patterns. This is certainly a factor in the reason why story and its various narrative elements are attractive to the brain. A recent report in *Frontiers in Neuroscience*, available from the US National Library of Medicine and National Institutes of Health, states that pattern processing is the very essence of the evolved human brain.[3] In light of the earlier discussions around story structure in this book, while nonlinear stories and those that stray further away from traditional patterns humans recognize in their narratives can still have resonance with an audience, those that rely more heavily on pattern-based structure have a neurological advantage when offered to an audience. This concept holds true with different forms of visual narratives, leading us to believe it will hold true for VR as well.[4]

Author Jonathan Gottschall suggests that another field of science in which a great deal of research has been performed might lead us to insights about our relationship with narratives. He states, "Dream researchers define a dream as—this is a quote—'a vivid sensory motor hallucination within a narrative context.' It's a night story. It focuses on the protagonist, usually the dreamer, who has to overcome obstacles to achieve his or her desires."[5] In his book *The Storytelling Animal*, he suggests that people are interested in simulated worlds because they desire to live better in this one. While looking at storytelling in video games, Gottschall interviews one game designer who says that his games give players a daily vacation from the pointlessness of their actual lives, opting instead for the meaning-rich environment the game provides. Most research around narrative games and stories in general suggests that this quest for meaning lies at the base of the human compulsion to engage in these activities.

SCIENCE, STORY, AND THE BODY

The Virtual Human Interaction Lab at Stanford University conducts a wide array of studies around Virtual and Augmented Realities. Many of their studies are focused on issues of embodiment. One recent study asks the question, "Can an avatar's body movements change a person's perception of good and bad?" Specifically, the study looks at whether embodying a character in VR space has the power to change our minds about certain matters. While remaining clear that more research is needed, the study does conclude that VR experiences "may implicitly shape how users form mental representations about their digital experience and those outside the media interactions."[6] Other studies conducted by Stanford state that embodying animals and even nature in VR space can change the way we interact with those elements outside of the digital space.[7,8]

Another area where science seems to be intersecting with story and the body is in how we actually view ongoing activity in the world. A study on the subject revealed that a steady diet of the type of editing used in film production has caused humans to begin to think in terms of *segments* or *scenes*.[9] In other words, we expect a certain continuity in our lives and our activities, even as they unfold in real time. One report describes it as such: "Animal and human movement is integrated in rhythmic and graceful sequences of discreet units of activity, each with their own particular goal-orientation, which are coordinated by the purpose of a higher-order goal or project."[10] Many studies have begun to look at the effects of when human life does not so easily conform to these parameters and expectations, especially in digital environments. Users have documented dissociative feelings they experience since the early days of VR—termed "post-VR sadness."[11]

SPOTLIGHT ON VR SCIENCE AND STORYTELLING:
Storytelling through Data and Neurology
Dr. Carolina Cruz-Neira, Director of the Emerging Analytics
Center, the University of Arkansas, Little Rock

Dr. Carolina Cruz-Neira has been globally recognized as an international pioneer in the areas of Virtual Reality and interactive visualization. The Arkansas Research Alliance (ARA) and Gov. Mike Beebe appointed her as one of two ARA Scholars responsible for sharing their knowledge and research to create new paths for the state's economic success.

John Bucher: Can you begin by giving us some background on your work?

Dr. Carolina Cruz-Neira: I've been around for a long time. My history has been in creating large resource centers for Virtual Reality. The Emerging Analytics Center at the University of Arkansas in Little Rock or EAC is actually

---

(Continued)

(Continued)

the third center that I've directed. I built a very large center at Iowa State University, back in the late '90s. It was called the Virtual Reality Application Center. It's not as visible, perhaps, as it was when I was running it, but they still exist.

I conceived the concept of that center and spent a lot of time doing the fundraising together with a couple of other faculty colleagues. That center was one of the largest centers in the world to do Virtual Reality at the time. There were as many as 35 or 40 professors involved and 200 or 300 graduate students. We had a six-sided VR cave, and a large SGI system. After Hurricane Katrina, the governor of Louisiana wanted to invest the funds to create new technology initiatives in Louisiana, to help the state. I was recruited to be a part of those efforts. I went there and I built my second large-scale Virtual Reality Center. It was called the Louisiana Immersive Technologies Enterprise. It was more like a company than a university, so I was the CEO of that for a while. Then, just recently, here in Arkansas, the previous governor had an initiative to advance research and technology in the state. That was how I came to my present position. The Emerging Analytics Center was created prior to my coming.

We are positioned to be mostly a center of expertise for using Virtual Reality technology for industry—for military and

(Continued)

(Continued)

basically for everything that is not games or entertainment. We are unique in the sense that we do a lot of industry work, which most universities will not do. We do more practical applications.

At the moment, we're being very platform agnostic. If you have looked around, 90% of Virtual Reality today, perhaps more, is perceived through HMDs. Everybody loves the Oculus Rift. Everybody loves the HTC Vive. People are enjoying the HoloLens and so on. A lot of these systems are very single-user systems. For gaming and entertainment, they work fabulously because normally you play a game by yourself with the computer, and your social interactions are through multiplayer games that you never really see who the other person really is. That works very well, but when you're in industry, you work as a group. You sit in conference rooms. We try to focus on the whole spectrum of Virtual Reality platforms and understand what do you need? What are you trying to do? What does your daily life look like? What is the workflow in your company? Based on that, we try to find what's the best platform. We don't have to shovel a platform down your throat just because that's the only one we have in the lab. We're probably the most diverse group right now, as far as VR platforms go.

John Bucher: Let's stay with platforms for a second, because I think that's a conversation

(Continued)

(Continued)

	worth having. Can you talk a little bit about the advantages of a cave or a sphere that allow us to see and do things that we would not be able to experience with a standard HMD? Why use those other platforms? What sorts of applications do they lend themselves to?
Dr. Carolina Cruz-Neira:	I think that like everything, there are good things and not-so-good things about each platform. We all have shoes, but you don't have just one pair. Is it better to have on a stiletto shoe or is it better to have a running shoe? Well, none of them are better. It depends on the context. I'm not going to put on my stiletto shoe and go climb Mt. Everest, because that would be absurd. At the same time, I'm not going to put on my running shoes and go to dinner in the White House, because that would be also kind of absurd. I think with the VR platforms, that's exactly what we're doing. We're telling people, "Get your stiletto shoes and go climb Mt. Everest." For Virtual Reality, there is not a single best platform. It just doesn't make sense to say "the best." When you use a cave, it has many positive points, because again, you can have a team of people that together walk into the virtual space. Together they have the experience in a similar manner as you have experiences in the real world. If you ride a little cart with someone at Disney, that's a shared experience. I'm seeing you and me, and I see your body language, and I see your facial expression, and I see

(Continued)

(Continued)

your finger pointing at things. For those kinds of situations, the cave is very good. It's also good because it doesn't limit your real-world vision. It's extremely important to me that I see myself with respect to the virtual world, so my body is still my frame of reference to understand sizes, to understand distances, to understand front and back, to estimate my physical effort, to reach out for something in the virtual world. Those kinds of things you get when you are not only in a cave but any sort of system that is not attached to your eyeballs, basically.

We have done some experiments over the years and have statistically proven that when you don't have a display directly attached to your eyeballs, the issues related to motion sickness, disorientation, discomfort, all those things are much less. We don't have those situations when people are inside the cave or the dome or with any of the large-scale display formats. Now, there are disadvantages, of course. With the cave and other large-format display systems today, those systems are implemented for one person to have the track-controlled viewpoint, and everybody else sort of rides along with that person. Depending on how far you are from the person holding the point of view, your perception of the virtual world is going to have more or less distortions. It's not going to necessarily be very comfortable on your eyes, and it might be a little

(Continued)

	harder for you to estimate distances or sizes. It's the equivalent to when you go to a movie theater to see a 3D movie and see it in the middle of the theater as opposed to seeing it all the way in the front or all the way to the left. There's also disadvantages depending on how large your group is and how large your cave is.
John Bucher:	Are you able to speak at all to neurology issues in VR? Do you ever work with brain scientists to look at what is going to engage the mind quicker or what's going to draw attention in immersive space?
Dr. Carolina Cruz-Neira:	We've done that in the past. In our current work, we're starting to do that, but we're mostly at the brainstorming stages. In the previous places that I've been, we've done many things related to that. We have a very large project with the Army that had to do with the engagement of the soldiers in training. The scenarios are always the same, so the soldiers train to play the game, but then they don't really learn the skills that they are supposed to be trained on. They just know this particular training environment instead of developing tactical thinking. We were generating dynamic scenarios during training, so the scenarios would randomly create themselves as the training was happening so there was no knowledge of the space. Even the layout of the streets would be completely different every time the soldier goes to the training environment.

(Continued)

(Continued)

That's one example of work that we've done in the past in this area.

Another thing that we did had to do with utilizing Virtual Reality for elderly people. Using it for pre-Alzheimer's memory stimulation, for example. The medical group that we were working with, the psychiatry group, they thought that for elderly people, it's very hard sometimes to have two different activities in their brain at the same time. We were using Virtual Reality to put them in very pleasant environments. The group conducted interviews with their patients, and some of them in their younger years did a lot of scuba diving. Other groups were more into mountain hiking. We then created two or three virtual environments. We had a beautiful underwater scuba-diving world. We had an Alps landscape and a shopping mall. The psychiatrist and the patient would be sitting in the middle of the cave, in this beautiful underwater environment. They were seeing the fish swimming by. There was a sunken galleon that they could go and scuba dive in there, but they were having a conversation about something completely unrelated to this underwater environment. The images triggered unrelated memories in their mind.

They would go away for a week or two, and then the patient would go back to the psychiatrist's office, not to our lab, and they were able to recall that conversation they

(Continued)

(Continued)

	had with the psychiatrist in the VR cave. The doctor would say, "What did we talk about last week?" And the patient would be like, "Oh, I don't know." "Don't you remember? We were sitting underwater watching the fish?" "Oh, yes, that's true. We were talking about something that happened in Germany." They were using the virtual environment as a memory trigger. We are also looking at things related to pain control, which other groups are doing as well, and we have some groups that are interested in posttraumatic stress disorder. We are interested in working with victims of rape, victims of robbery, victims of car accidents—those kinds of things. We're working with some people and having very early preliminary conversations.
John Bucher:	What about the use of narrative elements in VR? Not just using VR to tell cinematic stories but in world building and how narratives affect the human mind? I've heard you talk about your work with using VR in data and data mining as it relates to narrative to create a visual story of sorts. You have said that when data becomes visual, people begin to formulate a story around that data.
Dr. Carolina Cruz-Neira:	John, we could have many hours of conversations about this because there are lots of stories. I'll tell you one of them. When I was fresh from grad school and starting my career as a professor, one of

(Continued)

(Continued)

the big Fortune 500 companies came to me and said, "Hey, Carolina, one of our products that we just put on the market is having trouble. It's having problems. We don't know. We cannot figure it out. My entire engineering team has been looking at the problem. We have gone to the beginning to the earliest stages of design of this product, and we're trying to figure out what's going on in here, and we really can't. Here's your chance. We've heard you say that VR technology is going to help our industry, so help us find this." I said, "Okay. We'll take the challenge."

We got some of their data. Just a bunch of data points, with no particular three-dimensional meaning, and my students and I put together an immersive visualization of all this data. When you look at data on your screen, you look at it from one point of view. If you want to change the point of view, usually you have some sliders or buttons that will give you a Y rotation or a Z rotation or whatever. It is, in a sense, a one-dimensional manipulation of three-dimensional data. Your ability to really see that data from a lot of different angles is quite limited. Much more than people actually realize. Most engineering work and most design work is still being done on computers. Flat monitors. It's sometimes interesting to see how limited the ability to look around is. We put this project together, and once we started visualizing it, we started noticing some

(Continued)

	very weird patterns with the data that you could only see from a very specific point of view. Just a small variation of that point of view. Eventually we found the angle where we could see the problem. We went back to these people, and said, "Hey, guys, we think we found something in your data, but it's really hard to see." We literally brought them into the environment, and we were literally grabbing their heads, like, "Okay. There it is! Right there! Do you see it?" Then once we did that, literally within five seconds, the three or four of them that came, were like, "What in the . . .?" They went nuts. They went bananas with it. They immediately knew what it was. We didn't know what it was. We just saw that there was an irregularity that you could only see from a certain angle. They immediately knew what it was, and they were able to find a solution. That, for us, was wonderful, because this company was one of the first that then developed a very long-term funded engagement with me and my team.
John Bucher:	Story theorists say that the way story structure works is based on how human beings solve problems in their heads. Can you talk a little bit about how VR does allow us to solve problems that we couldn't get at otherwise? The story you just shared is a perfect example of that, but why do you think it is that VR opens up this new space for us to be able to solve problems in ways we haven't before?

(Continued)

Dr. Carolina Cruz-Neira:	Let's say we're trying to resolve a problem because I need to design a new machine that takes care of some process that maybe needs to make the process faster or more efficient. I'm the engineer. I'm not going to be the guy that actually is going to sit down using the machine in the real world. My understanding of the problem is not necessarily the understanding that my final user is going to have. I don't mean the Virtual Reality user. I mean the *user*—the consumer of my product. A lot of engineers think *they* are the users. They're *not*. Their products are going to be utilized by *somebody else*. It's sometimes very hard to see the point of view of *that* user. You don't know what his daily work, his daily job looks like.
John Bucher:	There was a reason that the biggest challenges that faced VR were issues like latency and frame rate. What would you say are now the biggest challenges that we have to overcome to fully be able to utilize this technology in new ways?
Dr. Carolina Cruz-Neira:	At the risk of sounding boring and repetitive, those challenges are still here. We still have issues with latency. We still have issues with frame rates. We still have issues with synchronizing your visuals to whatever is going on. We still have issues that the vast majority of all the Virtual Reality projects that we do right now have almost no computations of any kind other than very simplistic physics. I think that

(Continued)

most of the challenges that I was addressing when I was a grad student are still on the table to be addressed today.

How do we introduce additional sensory experiences beyond visuals? How do we accommodate for individual differences? Right now, we assume all of us have two eyes that are universally located in the same position on everybody's face. That's absolutely not correct. Each one of us have very significant individual variations. Our eyes are not necessarily horizontally properly aligned. You might have one eye that sees a little better than the other one. All those kinds of things. Pretty much every single challenge that you might see mentioned in any kind of VR publication from the '90s is still valid today. There's been some significant improvements, of course. The technology has become incredibly affordable, and that's why we're all so happy about it. It's an exciting moment, but it is also a very fragile moment.

CONCEPTS TO CONSIDER FROM DR. CAROLINA CRUZ-NEIRA

► Every VR platform has its own advantages, disadvantages, and applications.

► There are connections in the study of VR to the study of memory.

► Narrative elements have uses in VR beyond entertainment.

▶ Technical challenges are still steep and must be overcome for VR to advance.

PUTTING IDEAS TOGETHER

As Dr. Cruz-Neira mentions, even those whose work transcends the primary goal of storytelling rely on narrative elements. Understanding these elements and how they can be used gives creators an advantage in the types of work they may choose to involve themselves in. Narrative elements are helpful when constructing methods and applications for solving a problem, be it psychological, physical, or digital in nature. Understanding the way that narrative elements function apart from, alongside, and together with other narrative elements gives a creator insight into world- and structure-building methods that may be most useful in developing a solution for a given issue. The answer may not always rely on developing a new technology to fill a gap but to look at using the existing technology to provide a different narrative.

TECHNOLOGICAL CHALLENGES WITH TRADITIONAL CINEMATIC STORYTELLING TECHNIQUES

We are at a unique point in history where technology has been advancing more rapidly than our methods of production. This is true across the global culture but specifically true in areas of produced entertainment. Cameras were capable of resolutions higher than those that could be edited or displayed for a period. As fast as computer processing power was advancing, the average user is still unable to perform advanced operations with large data files in real time—rendering must still occur, slowing the rate at which content can be produced. VR has not been without its technological challenges as well. In fact, many say the largest tests that face VR are technological, as the human imagination has already dreamed a future far beyond what VR is capable of—for now.

Perhaps the most discussed challenge has been the logistical issue of just where to put all the supporting lights, audio, and grip equipment needed to produce the aesthetically appealing productions that audiences have grown used to. Certainly, YouTube and other online video platforms have diversified audience expectations when it comes to the production quality of video content they enjoy. However, when audiences are asked to *pay* for content, there remains a certain level of expectation that the production quality of what they buy will be at a level they consider professional.

Clever VR creators have already invented a variety of means to hide gear and crew members in plain sight within the VR space. Homemade helmets have been used to mount the camera above the director of photography's head. Monitors have been hidden behind newspapers and disguised as televisions on the wall. Crew members have been disguised as extras in scenes—some with hidden microphones mounted strategically on their bodies. Stories that were originally meant to be told indoors have been moved outside to take advantage of natural light. All represent methods that creators are discovering in order to tell their stories with the technological challenges that presently exist in the medium.

USING PRODUCTION PRACTICES TO TELL BETTER STORIES IN VR

Even with all the challenges, creators must use the production gear that presently exists to produce content in the medium. While eventually VR will likely develop its own tool sets, those used in film, television, theater, and the web must suffice for now. While the camera is likely the only piece of equipment currently on VR sets that is solely and specifically for use in the medium, this will quickly change. While the majority of equipment presently needed to tell VR stories will come from the production worlds of film and television, the discipline of immersive theater has developed tools and techniques that will be helpful as well. Creators in this field have a head start on hiding production elements that tend to break the immersion experienced by the audience.

Before discussing specific production practices, tools, and techniques, it is important to state a few ideas about the philosophical nature of the equipment used to tell the story. Far too often, the *means* of production becomes of higher priority than the *content* being produced. In other words, the production is aesthetically pleasing but the story the crew was telling doesn't hold up to the aesthetics. While there is a certain audience expectation for the quality of content they are paying for, viewers tend to forgive simple and even problematic production elements but are less likely to forgive dissonance, confusion, or plot holes in the narrative. It is of utmost importance that every crew member realize that *they* are a storyteller. This is not solely the domain of the writer or director. Each production element tells a story within the larger narrative being communicated. Directors must combine these smaller stories to craft a larger one, much in the way a conductor combines all the sections of an orchestra to create a symphony. If one section of the musical collective is out of tune, the whole is in jeopardy. Dissonance created by one department can make the entire narrative confusing or difficult. One of the jobs of the director is to make sure that everyone is making the same story. If the lighting department believes the story they are telling is a horror narrative but the sound department believes it is a comedy, the final product will be unlikely to strike a chord in audiences—at least not one they enjoy.

HOW THE CAMERA, THE FRAME, AND ITS EDGES AFFECT YOUR STORY IN VR

As has been discussed, the camera is likely the sole element on the set that has been specifically designed for VR production. This production tool will make or break how the audience experiences the story. Its importance cannot be overstated. Depending on the scale of the production, VR cameras vary greatly in size, shape, and weight. Some cameras feature a single wide-angle lens that shoots up to 180 degrees. Creators then often take two or more of these cameras and tether them together to create immersion. Other cameras have multiple lenses that perform the same task in order to capture 360-degree space. It is worth offering a gentle reminder of a concept presented earlier in the text.

360-DEGREE VIDEO IS NOT THE SAME AS VR

While 360-degree video may be used in VR to help create immersion, they are not, by definition, the same. You may recall this concept being introduced in the Spotlight on Cameras section in Chapter 1. Removing the edges of the square frame does several things in the mind of the audience. The square frame has long acted as a window through which we see the narrative world. When the audience has been repulsed or frightened by what they saw within the frame, they could look away. With the audience placed literally inside the frame, looking away is not an option. A viewer could close their eyes. However, this requires an even greater sacrifice of control on the part of the viewer. Most people would not close their eyes in a situation that frightened them unless they were a child. When scenes within the frame upset a viewer, they had the option of looking over at the person next to them, perhaps even taking their hand. With preset VR experiences, that agency has been taken away, which speaks to the importance of the impending social VR technology. The vulnerability established by the camera, the frame, and its edges affects the viewer's experience of the story a great deal. This must be recognized when crafting narratives. It can be tempting for creators to press the boundaries of how deeply a viewer feels immersed in a world. However, there must also be an innate respect for the audience on the part of the creator—a consideration for the wide variety of audience members that may enter the world. Striking the balance between the deep immersion the audience feels in the experience and the level of comfort and enjoyment a diverse audience is capable of will continue to be of great importance when crafting stories in VR. It is also worth noting that even within the realm of animated VR narratives, the function of the camera is still in play, though there may not be a physical camera used in the creation. Animated worlds in VR remove many of the technological challenges that presently exist in physical production. However, the story challenges remain the same. The cautions mentioned earlier concerning audience immersion are equally important in animated VR stories.

CONNECTING WITH CONCEPTS AND METHODS IN EXPERIMENTAL VR STORYTELLING

Science and technology have become useful in the innovation of many art forms. However, the only way any art form moves forward is through experimentation and pressing the established boundaries. There's a common saying in the film industry: "You need to know the rules before you can break them." However, once one does know the rules, breaking them immediately becomes of interest. Experimental approaches in art rarely get much press. They are often only known to those working *within* the boundaries of the established industry. Those within the industry occasionally get bored with traditional approaches and look to those experimenting with the form for inspiration, taking approaches and techniques they find interesting and incorporating them into largely "safe" works. The original experimental approach often never gets acknowledged and certainly does not become financially successful. This pattern has been repeated over and over again in music, theater, literature, and film. While studied and lauded by academics, the writing and filmmaking of Guy Deboard in the early part of the last century remains unknown to most artists creating interactive and immersive work. In his book *The Society of the Spectacle*, Deboard unpacks spectacle as false representations seen in our real lives. He goes on to state that spectacle is a materialized world view, subjecting humanity to itself. He seemed to suggest that the more art resembled actual reality, the more significant its impact. In attempts to prove his theories, Deboard created films that forced his audiences to interact with the medium rather than remaining passive receivers of information. His methods were often extreme. His first film, *Hurlements en faveur de Sade*, consisted only of black and white screens. When the screen was black, there was no music or dialogue. When it was white, a speaker made a brief comment and quickly turned to black again. The periods between white screens sometimes lasted up to 20 minutes. Needless to say, the film was not a hit with audiences. The theory that Deboard was trying to enforce by breaking the rules, that audiences should interact with the images, remains quite relevant today. In this section, we will examine some of the potential methods of "breaking the rules," as well as methods that reinforce them. These concepts are provided as templates that creators may play within or attempt to transcend while creating their stories.

ABSTRACT VERSUS REALISTIC STORYTELLING

There are a few basic terms and concepts that might be helpful to unpack before looking at the larger field of potential. The first is the tension between *abstract* and *realistic* storytelling. Obviously, visual mediums can be much more than just a "record of drama." Abstract experiences push boundaries, stir emotion, and express the intangible feelings of the artist. They can also showcase specific effects or graphic techniques, explore sounds, emotions, and other more feeling-based ideas. Abstract experiences can push the boundaries of theme and structure in ways that more realistic approaches are unable to. Thematic abstract experiences explore narrative and cinematic *concepts*, whereas realistic narrative experiences usually tackle the specific issues of *story* and *character*. The line between abstract and realism is gray. Abstract films *can* have characters and realistic films *can* have abstract elements. In realistic experiences, audiences expect to see the rules of a certain *genre* adhered to. If that experience is documentary in nature, we wouldn't be comfortable seeing the documentarian step from behind the camera and perform a show tune. If the genre is horror, we have certain forms that we anticipate the creators will maintain. With abstract experiences, the genre rules become less important, and simple feelings become the method of expression. It is important to note that abstract experiences may be created with photo-realistic images and realistic experiences may be created with artistic animation. The terms speak more to the conceptual approach to the work and its relationship with reality than to the technical medium employed to create the piece.

BREAKING THE FOURTH WALL

Traditionally in theatrical experiences, an invisible wall has existed between the viewer and the stage players. The players are unable to see through this wall, and this gives the impression that they are unaware of our presence as an audience. This concept was brought over from traditional theater and employed in film as that medium developed. When a player, or actor, acknowledges the viewer, this is referred to as "breaking the fourth wall." This concept has also relied on the assumption that the audience is only able to peer through one wall—the fourth wall. Even when we change angles or perspectives in film, we are still only looking through a single physical dimension. In immersive experiences, the viewer is placed *inside* the plane of action rather than watching it through an invisible wall. However, the player may still look directly into the camera and, in effect, break the fourth wall. While in a third-person experience, this would likely break the immersion, it actually *heightens* the immersion in a first-person experience.

RETROSPECTIVE STORYTELLING VERSUS REAL-TIME STORYTELLING

Beyond the abstract and realistic, there is another philosophical understanding of story that will be helpful to us in moving forward. *Retrospective storytelling* refers to narratives told from a perspective that looks to the past. In other words, the story being told is not happening at the time the storyteller is describing. There is an underlying assumption with retrospective storytelling that the events will add up to something or lead to a conclusion. Since the story is being told looking backward, the viewer assumes there has been a lesson learned or perspective gained on the narrative events that unfold. Retrospective narratives provide the "why" when we are curious about the present.

Real-time storytelling refers to narratives that are unfolding in the present. The viewer is experiencing them as they actually occur. This can be exhilarating for the viewer. However, it can also be disappointing, as there may or may not be meaning at the end of the experience. There is certainly not meaning while the experience is playing out. With real-time storytelling, sometimes the story simply ends without a dramatic conclusion or lessons learned. Usually, the viewer has the first-person perspective with real-time storytelling.

While meaning may not be readily available in real-time storytelling, the human mind is capable of creating meaning quite quickly, constantly looking back at the events that are playing out in order to retool the meaning that seems to be manifesting. The longer a narrative plays out in real time, the more information the user has to create meaning with. With retrospective storytelling, there is a set meaning to narrative events. With real-time storytelling, meaning is constantly unfolding, changing, and taking on new forms.

THE ROLE OF MEMORY IN RETROSPECTIVE NARRATIVES

Researcher Kate McLean has done significant work in the relationship between the role of memory and retrospective narratives in human psychology.[12] Though her work was with adolescents, she states that there is every reason to believe her findings apply to expanding social networks. McLean suggests that rather than storytelling, we actually participate in *memory telling* after having experiences. This memory telling causes us to create a narrative identity about ourselves. To simplify, when we have experiences, we try to take our *memories* of what has occurred and string them together to try to create a coherent story about what we experienced. These memories *may or may not* have direct connection to *what actually occurred*. Sometimes the memories actually more closely conform to narrative concepts that help us make sense of what happened. Our brains look for stories. We need them to make sense of the world. Actual memories are secondary to story in our minds. For those wishing to delve deeper into these matters, the work of Gary Fireman and Ted McVay is an appropriate starting place.[13] The work of Fivush, Habermas, Waters, and Zaman may also be helpful.[14]

THE ROLE OF THE ENVIRONMENT IN REAL-TIME STORYTELLING

When telling real-time stories, the audience immediately begins searching for information that might be helpful to them in orienting themselves in the new world they have entered. Environmental elements will be some of the first images the audience encounters and begins processing. The term *environmental storytelling* was popularized in the gaming world and refers to the act of "staging player-space with environmental properties that can be interpreted as a meaningful whole, furthering the narrative of the game."[15] Game designers have long stressed the importance of environmental storytelling in creating an immersive experience. According to Henry Jenkins of MIT, "Environmental storytelling creates the preconditions for an immersive narrative experience in at least one of four ways: spatial stories can evoke preexisting narrative associations; they can provide a staging ground where narrative events are enacted; they may embed narrative information within their mise-en-scene; or they provide resources for emergent narratives."[16] Mike Shephard expands on Jenkins's thoughts, saying, "Many games rely heavily on the embedding of narrative information within mise-en-scene, a term used to describe design aspects in production. It examines set design, lighting, costuming, and so on in how they contribute to the narrative."[17]

Creators of VR, AR, and MR experiences must consider the impact of environmental elements in their narratives in order to provide the most realistic and immersive stories. Much has been said about the role of and need for photo-realism in environments, characters, and objects in VR space. This conversation is nuanced by the inclusion of animated and stylized experiences, of course. The key question to ask when designing any environmental element is *why*? Why should the ground be sand as opposed to rock? Why should the story take place at night as opposed to day? Why are there fallen trees that must be climbed over? What caused them to fall? Why would this character not walk around the tree? These are the sorts of questions that open up space for storytelling and narrative design. There are entire volumes exploring the psychology of color, the impact of shapes on the brain, and the emotions associated with various aesthetics. For readers interested in exploring more depth about these issues, *If It's Purple, Someone's Gonna Die: The Power of Color in Visual Storytelling* by Patti Bellantoni is a sufficient starting place for novices and academics alike.

PASSIVE VERSUS ACTIVE STORYTELLING

Another lens we can view interactive and immersive storytelling through is created when we juxtapose passive storytelling and active storytelling. Further, there are a number of approaches when teasing out meaning from those terms. One approach is to leave gaps in the story that the audience fills in with their imagination, taking the narrative from passive to active. This approach is most effective in novels and short stories. When visuals begin to enter the narrative, we fill in many of those gaps for the audience. The more visuals that enter the narrative, the fewer gaps for the audience to fill in. With VR, the potential for the amount of imagery presented to the viewer is more vast than any sort of storytelling experience that has been created thus far. So this approach, if it is to be effective in VR, would need to leave *thematic* and *narrative* gaps as opposed to gaps in *detail*. It is worth noting, however, that strong narratives usually contain both passive and active storytelling elements. Passive elements give the viewer orienting elements. They set up conflicts and allow for later active storytelling elements in the narrative. Active storytelling elements are often what keep the audience engaged over time.

PASSIVE AND ACTIVE STORYTELLING
IN FIRST-PERSON EXPERIENCES

These concepts look slightly different when we consider first-person experiences. When the viewer is the protagonist and at least partially responsible for crafting the narrative, the flow between passive and active storytelling may resemble the dance in which the creator/designer is leading the dance partner but there is still active participation required on the part of the other partner, as referred to earlier in the text. Creator and viewer are truly creating the story together. Passive storytelling elements in many ways become even more important in first-person experiences, giving the viewer rules and railings to keep them on track. They set up the active storytelling choices that the viewer will make. They will drive where they look, what they touch, and how they act in the space.

The balance of active and passive storytelling elements is significant in most narrative approaches. However, the balance takes on even greater significance in experimental story structures and perhaps the most significance in first-person experimental experiences, in which a linear story may be absent. Creators may choose to take away the familiarities of structural narrative from the viewer, but it is important to remember to give them *something* to orient. This could include any of the *narrative shards*, which are basically any of the elements commonly found in narratives that have been previously discussed, or an expression of agency that would allow the viewer to create the types of meaning he or she needs in order to navigate the experience enjoyably.

EMBODIMENT IN PASSIVE AND ACTIVE STORIES

A distinction must be drawn between stories that allow for passivity or activity in the mind and those that allow for these concepts in the body as well as the mind. The incorporation of embodiment into VR, AR, and MR experiences will continue to grow in importance as the technology expands beyond simple room-scale experiences. In the earliest VR experience, viewers only saw through the eyes on one inside virtual space. They were unable to look down and see their own bodies, creating a lesser sense of immersion. Later, viewers were given "wands" or other tools that provided some agency. Eventually, viewers could see and respond with their hands. Technology that brought more aspects of the human body into virtual space was not far behind. The further we immerse users into their own bodies, thus embodying them in virtual space, the more impactful the stories in that space will become. Storytelling in future environments will bring new challenges beyond what we can even conceive of presently. Discussions of risk, ethics, and active storytelling requirements will only become more nuanced as the field expands. As with all other aspects of this emerging field, trial, error, and experimentation will be our only guides for navigation. As the potential for fully embodied experiences grows, what audiences anticipate in the balance between active and passive storytelling will likely change and develop as well.

SPOTLIGHT ON STORY: Storytelling at the Oculus Story Studio
Jessica Shamash, Producer
Pete Billington, Immersive Storyteller

Jessica Shamash has worked as the characters feature film coordinator and the lighting feature film coordinator for Pixar. She is currently a

---

(Continued)

(Continued)

producer at the Oculus Story Studio. Pete Billington has worked for more than 15 years in entertainment design experiences and special effects. He has served as digital supervisor at DreamWorks Animation and now holds the title of immersive storyteller at the Oculus Story Studio.

John Bucher:	Could you both talk about your history with storytelling?
Jessica Shamash:	For me, at least, in terms of why I wanted to get involved with film was that just as a child film had such an impact on me in terms of empathy and being able to relate to characters and feeling different emotions and experiencing different worlds. It was so inspiring. And I felt that if someone could inspire me that much, I wanted to do that for someone else with my life in storytelling. So I got a film degree, and the best part of my degree was studying screenwriting. After school, I got involved at Pixar and was there for 4 years, and Pixar was always a dream job for me mostly because story is king there. About a year ago, I was talking to people at Oculus, and they were looking for someone to help produce and manage their projects. Now I'm working with directors like Pete on developing Virtual Reality films here.
John Bucher:	What about you, Pete?
Pete Billington:	My parents were really good about exposing me to creative processes early on, and my dad was a huge movie enthusiast, so I was always surrounded by great films. We had a LaserDisc player in the late '70s, which was a crazy thing to have at the time. Consuming that content set a precedent for me. I had an affinity for the *Star Wars* universe and set a goal to one day work for George Lucas.

(Continued)

(Continued)

	There was a random path to get there, but one of my early jobs was working at Skywalker Ranch. At the same time, I worked in several high-tech areas including computer graphics, so there was this delta that would ultimately point to VR. I spent a lot of time working with Robert Zemeckis in the early 2000s and watching him craft stories. I spent a little bit of time with Spielberg, so I had these amazing role models to follow in terms of how the stories get built and what their evolutionary process was.
	Finally, I got really motivated to start telling my own stories and had the opportunity to play in visual effects, animation, and live action, and that informed VR too. I learned what VR *really* was. It's not a game. It's not a movie. It's something else that we're trying to figure out. My main motivation is world building, so both narratively building a world with strong characters but also having a universe that supports that and all the intricacy that goes into that is another good opportunity for VR to support the story you're telling.
John Bucher:	What is the relationship between good characters and good story?
Pete Billington:	I think good story is good emotion. We connect to stories through how we empathize with characters, so having someone you can make a deep connection with is that conduit to a story. When you structure a story, you get down to the nuts and bolts of how you're building a story. It's about emotional arc, and emotional arc per beat, and the only way that I know to do that is through how you relate to a particular character or character's circumstances. At the most granular level,

(Continued)

storytelling is emotional reaction to the character. How you observe that, how you see that interplay between multiple characters, and in the context of VR, how you yourself connect to that character's emotion.

Jessica Shamash: I think connecting through characters is so important because that is where you see depth. And the more depth that character has, the more relatable the story will be. In *E.T.*, you have this vulnerable character and you relate to that because you've known someone who was vulnerable or you yourself have felt vulnerable.

John Bucher: There are currently two approaches in VR. There's the approach where the viewer is kind of a ghost in the scene, who's just observing things that are going on. Then there is the approach where the viewer actually is the protagonist in the story, which is something we don't get in cinematic experiences. The characters on movie screens seem to have no idea that people are watching them. With immersive theater, the actors are very aware that you're there as well, yet it's still a story. It's still narrative. It's not just reality. Can you talk about agency and interactivity in immersive storytelling?

Jessica Shamash: I think that will be one of the most amazing things about VR storytelling in the future. You will be a greater participant in the experience. It will be like the immersive theater that we've experienced, where you can have those one-on-one moments where you are changing the narrative, or you're influencing the narrative. That's what you walk away with. That's why you keep going back, because of those moments. You influenced it. That

(Continued)

(Continued)

	is where the real opportunity is right now in VR storytelling.
Pete Billington:	I think some of it's getting back to the roots of storytelling. I keep thinking of how stories were originally told around a campfire. It's much more similar to what we're going to experience with VR in having that connection with a person. Cinema, in terms of that detachment, was a means to an end. We were asking how we tell the biggest possible story. But it has its limitations That intimacy around the campfire, telling a story, getting sucked in and using your imagination to fill in the blanks is even more powerful. There's something very primal about that form of storytelling that we're now just starting to understand. The idea of being a ghost or being a protagonist is one where we're not pushing that far enough yet. We're doing the easy things first because they haven't been done yet. But I think we'll get to a point where it doesn't feel so awkward to not have to put labels on those types of experiences or silo them off as particular genres. We don't want VR to be completely limited just to imaginary-friend experiences or cast-level experiences. I think we'll quickly get past that as we see more people exploring different ideas.
John Bucher:	René Descartes came up with this idea that we call Cartesian Dualism. It involved the separation of the mind and the body. He considered it possible that our mind was completely separate from our body, which led to the idea of consciousness being separate from the body, which gets us thinking about consciousness being able to be downloaded into a computer. In VR space, because of the lack

(Continued)

(Continued)

of a body in some experiences, we still have this consciousness where we can fully be aware of what's going on around us, however. What are your thoughts about the relationship between the mind and the body as it relates to presence in VR?

Pete Billington: We study that a lot. We talk to a lot of people outside of the industry about things like perception and how our hands relate to our body, because that's our first corporeal existence right now. In general, the way I feel about presence is that the more layers that you can put on top of an experience, the deeper you are in that experience. So that can be sensory, because we have our eyes, and we have our ears. But giving you even more agency by giving you things like tasks to do, giving you a sense of the spatial where your hands relate to your body in a human way.

To me there is a heavy reinforcement of a strong conscious body connection in VR, and the more we are aware of that when developing content, the more you will feel a deeper presence. I use the metaphor of plugging into as many ports as you can. Having an ambient track of sound and then a dialogue track of sound and then something happening in the distance which is another indication of something happening off screen—all these layers get you deeper and deeper into the immersed state, into presence, and allow you to block everything else and forget the world that exists outside of the experience. I keep looping back to early questions in older art forms because I think they're interrelated—studying sleight of hand and stagecraft. We want to do things to trick you constantly into thinking you're completely a part of the story.

(Continued)

(Continued)

	I think people need to take more risks with defining the boundaries before we close off things and say this isn't something that we should be doing. I saw the same exact thing happen when we introduced stereoscopic 3D into film and Cameron came up with these seven rules that you can never break and then 5 years later everyone was breaking those rules and it was because at the moment that that technology released, there was this massive paranoia that we were going to see *Jaws 3D* from the '80s again, and everyone thought that was terrible. So the sort of auto-censoring of what's possible and what's not possible, what's good in VR and what's not good in VR is not necessarily helpful right now. Hopefully there's just this fringe that continues to push things.
John Bucher:	What are your thoughts about the role of social VR in storytelling, and do you think that's going to be important?
Pete Billington:	I had this amazing experience watching the movie *Elf* in the theater. I watched it twice. The first time I saw it was a matinee, and there were very few people in there and it fell very flat for me. It wasn't funny. And then I saw it again on a Friday night, with a bunch of people, and it was hilarious. It was because there was a social component where that theater environment actually changed the way I experienced it. I think that's something theater owners figured out a long time ago. That crowd dynamic is important to the success of a piece in some ways. The ultimate holy grail, I think, is the co-op nature of being in the story together and partnering in a story together. You can imagine being in a story like *The Goonies* with your friends.

(Continued)

(Continued)

That's the evolution of the Dungeons & Dragons type of storytelling where you are with a group of friends, experiencing a story together, and each of you are playing a role. That's the *Ready Player One* concept.

John Bucher: Let's talk for a second about some of the ethical issues. In the HBO show *Westworld*, there's a line from the pilot where one of the characters asks another if they are real. And she responds, "Well, if you can't tell, does it make any difference?" And I think that is a question for our time.

Pete Billington: It's going to increasingly make a difference. I was actually reading a *Wired* article with the creators who commented that she could go play *Grand Theft Auto* and run down 30 pedestrians, then shut that game off and not really worry about that and move on with her day. But when you are no longer able to discern whether those were real people or not, is there a moral obligation to feel a certain way? Because if you're not sure, what does that mean?

We're a long way from that, and I think we all like the idea of creating something that is indiscernible from reality. But as a storyteller, it's not interesting to simply recreate reality. It's about asking an existential question. I think there is a moral question at some point. What are you trying to evoke in humanity with the things that you are saying? And are you bringing good to the world, or are you bringing negativity to the world?

John Bucher: Is there such thing as a responsibility of the storyteller, or is the storyteller's responsibility just to tell a good story and then let people interpret it?

(Continued)

(Continued)

Pete Billington:	That's a tough one. I think certain artists would say that they just are true to themselves and they want to create work for themselves and it's up to everyone else to interpret it. Some people define art that way. I think personally in the content that I create, I'm very conscious of how I want the audience to feel and think. It's very intentional. So I do feel responsible for the things that I put out in the world. I think that's a personal choice as an artist.
Jessica Shamash:	I'm in the same boat as Pete. I feel responsible for the content that I put out there, but there are artists that don't have that motive. For me, there is a responsibility there, especially as we are walking into this VR world.
John Bucher:	Most people who study scriptwriting and story take an Aristotelian approach. There is a basic three-act structure. Some people get more dogmatic about specific beats or sequence or having four acts. How do these approaches fit with VR?
Pete Billington:	Three acts are not out the window completely, in my view. Our stories are limited to a certain scale and size right now. There's not $200 million budgets for VR projects yet, which then implies that they're not going to be 2 hours long. It is a social experience at the moment. I think pacing figures greatly in to why things are currently often in a three-act structure. How long can someone sit in a coliseum on a stone bench before they have to get up and go to the bathroom?

In terms of storytelling and how we've been conditioned to hear stories, I think it's not something we throw out entirely. But what is interesting is to see how that needs to change when interactivity comes into play. Specific beat structures don't |

(Continued)

necessarily apply right now because we don't have productions long enough to support them. So you can try to shrink them and move them around, and that might be a good starting place. There are so many stories that have successfully leveraged that model that we should always be looking back. I subscribe to the Joseph Campbell idea that we're telling the same story over and over again. So I think it's a guide.

I would lean towards the mythological in storytelling. I think the (Plato's) cave metaphor is absolutely accurate. As we get into seeing avatars for the first time, we're talking about masks and the masks that we wear, how we represent ourselves to others, especially when we are now telling the stories socially. I also think being in a space is a universal human thing that we can relate to, much more than cultural-specific language of pacing or structure or composition. Because you put a human into a space, and for the most part they are interpreting that space in the same way.

John Bucher: Jessica, can you speak to the gender piece in VR? Is there a difference with perception in VR between men and women? Is it a good opportunity to try on someone else's skin?

Jessica Shamash: I think it's an amazing opportunity to try on someone else's skin. Not just as a woman, but what does it feel like to be a minority, or what does it feel like to be someone who's gay, walking their partner down the street, how do people react to you then? I think VR will continue to be amazing at creating empathy for all our differences. Because you get to see the world through someone else's eyes. So the more we can explore that and expose other people to that, the more empathy we can create in this world.

CONCEPTS TO CONSIDER FROM JESSICA SHAMASH AND PETE BILLINGTON

▶ We connect to stories through how we empathize with characters.

▶ VR storytelling connects to something primal within the viewer.

▶ The more layers included in an experience, the deeper the immersion in that experience.

▶ VR storytelling will continue to become more social in its opportunities.

▶ There are ethical considerations that should underpin the creation of Virtual Reality and its related technologies.

▶ Three-act structure should not be thrown out when creating VR stories.

▶ VR stories offer the opportunity to be immersed in the skin of someone of a different gender, ethnicity, culture, or class, thus creating a greater sense of empathy for humanity.

PUTTING IDEAS TOGETHER

While Shamash and Billington introduce a variety of different concepts around VR storytelling, we can boil their comments down to issues of immersion. We experience empathy through characters. The more realistic and human-like the characters are, the greater the immersive experience for the viewer. Narrative and descriptive layers are what make those characters realistic and relatable. The more we can share those characters with friends and family and, perhaps more importantly, the experience we have with those characters, the greater the potential will be for even greater immersion. Our minds and bodies are what create these experiences of empathy and emotion. Understanding how they respond to and craft narrative is essential for creators who wish to bring their stories into this emerging arena.

NOTES

1 Haven, Kendall. *Story Proof: The Science Behind the Startling Power of Story.* Westport, CT: Libraries Unlimited, 2007. Print.

2 Boyd, Brian. *On the Origin of Stories: Evolution, Cognition, and Fiction*. Cambridge, MA: Belknap of Harvard University Press, 2009. Print.

3 Mattson, Mark P. "Superior Pattern Processing Is the Essence of the Evolved Human Brain." *Frontiers in Neuroscience* 8 (2014): n. pag. Web.

4 Cohn, Neil, Martin Paczynski, Ray Jackendoff, Phillip J. Holcomb, and Gina R. Kuperberg. "(Pea)nuts and Bolts of Visual Narrative: Structure and Meaning in Sequential Image Comprehension." *Cognitive Psychology* 65.1 (2012): 1–38. Web.

5 Melia, Mike. "The Science of Storytelling: A conversation with Jonathan Gottschall." www.pbs.org/newshour/rundown/on-the-science-of-storytelling/

6 Baileya, Jakki O., Jeremy N. Bailensona, and Daniel Casasanto. "When Does Virtual Embodiment Change Our Minds?" https://vhil.stanford.edu/mm/2016/10/bailey-presence-change-our-minds.pdf

7 Ahn, Sun Joo (Grace), Joshua Bostick, Elise Ogle, Kristine L. Nowak, Kara T. McGillicuddy, and Jeremy N. Bailenson. "Experiencing Nature: Embodying Animals in Immersive Virtual Environments Increases Inclusion of Nature in Self and Involvement With Nature." https://vhil.stanford.edu/mm/2016/08/ahn-jcmc-experiencing-nature.pdf

8 Ahn, Sun Joo (Grace). "Embodying Animals in Immersive Virtual Environments." https://vhil.stanford.edu/mm/2016/02/ahn-experiencing-nature.pdf

9 Magliano, Joseph P., and Jeffrey M. Zacks. "The Impact of Continuity: Editing in Narrative Film on Event Segmentation." *Cognitive Science* 35.8 (2011): 1489–1517. Web.

10 Delafield-Butt, Jonathan T. and Colwyn Trevarthen. "The Ontogenesis of Narrative: From Moving to Meaning." *Frontiers in Psychology* 6 (2015): n. pag. Web.

11 Searles, Rebecca. "Virtual Reality Can Leave You With an Existential Hangover." www.theatlantic.com/technology/archive/2016/12/post-vr-sadness/511232/

12 McLean, Kate. "Late Adolescent Identity Development: Narrative Meaning Making and Memory Telling." *Developmental Psychology* 41.4 (2005): 683–691. Web.

13 Fireman, Gary and Ted McVay. *Narrative and Consciousness: Literature, Psychology, and the Brain*. New York: Oxford University Press, 2003. Print.

14 Fivush, Robyn and Tilmann Habermas, Theodore E.A. Waters, and Widaad Zaman. "The Making of Autobiographical Memory: Intersections of Culture, Narratives and Identity." *International Journal of Psychology* 46.5 (2011): 321–345. Web.

15 A definition given by Matthias Worch and Harvey Smith at GDC 2010, San Francisco, CA.

16 Jenkins, Henry. "Games and Narrative." http://web.mit.edu/21fms/People/henry3/games&narrative.html6

17 Shepard, Mike. "Interactive Storytelling—Narrative Techniques and Methods in Video Games." http://scalar.usc.edu/works/interactive-storytelling-narrative-techniques-and-methods-in-video-games/environmental-storytelling

4

Storytelling Principles for Immersive Space

A LOOK AT IMMERSIVE THEATER

Among the various fields that can teach us potential storytelling principles in VR, immersive theater ranks among the most helpful. The origins of immersive theater go back to the beginnings of modern theater in the 19th century. A great deal of experimental and interactive theater and their aesthetics in the modern setting is constructed around ideas that first came to prominence in the 1930s with John Dewey's book *Art as Experience*. Dewey teased out the significance of a piece of art from its "expressive object." He argued that it was the *experience* of that significance that stayed with the viewer and not the image of the object itself. Dewey built his work around the biological and psychological effects that art had on viewers around his own theories in functional psychology. His work moved many creators from thinking in terms of object-based meaning making to experiential forms, opening doors for immersive theater and eventually experiences such as VR. Even traditional theater has used some immersive or interactive elements from time to time. In 1985, the Tony Award-winning Best Musical, *The Mystery of Edwin Drood*, required that the audience vote on who killed one of the key characters, making seven different endings possible. Practices such as call and response and other interactive elements have fallen in and out of fashion throughout the decades, but there has long been a desire to more deeply immerse audiences in produced theatrical experiences.

Some date the explosion of the current immersive theater movement to the production of *Sleep No More*, a 1930s film noir adaptation of Shakespeare's *Macbeth*, based in New York. The defining characteristic of immersive theater is that it breaks the fourth wall, which has been discussed previously. As we recall, this wall is what traditionally separates the viewer from the audience both physically and verbally. Some of those working heavily in the practice have suggested that there are two major reasons the word "immersive" has risen in popularity. Mikhael Tara Garver has articulated these as such: "The first is that our audiences are in a cultural moment of two-dimensional overload and are craving experiences. The second is that from shopping to Twitter they are already participating in non-hierarchical interaction. When people say immersive the two things I believe they always mean are: multi-experiential and freedom to respond."[1]

One approach we can take to examine any immersive medium, including immersive theater, is to consider that it is a mediated attempt at creating a "real-life" experience. These experiences strive to replicate the sounds, images, and feelings we have become familiar with in given situations. For example, when sitting in a city park, we hear the sounds of the environment— the wind blowing around us, children playing nearby but slightly behind us, a fly that keeps buzzing by our ear, planes that fly by above us, and a variety of other even more subtle sounds that surround us in three-dimensional space. In mediated immersive experiences, this is accomplished through sound effects, performers' voices, and even recorded music that rouse our emotions to places that reality seems to offer so naturally.

THEATER OF THE OPPRESSED

In examining what can be gained by looking at immersive theater, we could likely find no better template than the Theater of the Oppressed. Created by Brazilian theater producer Augusto Boal in the 1950s, the Theatre of the Oppressed describes theatrical forms influenced by the work of Paulo Freire. Boal's techniques involved the audience in innovative ways, promoting social and political change. The audience becomes "spect-actors" in the Theater of the Oppressed. They explore, show, analyze, and transform their reality. The key characteristic that made this movement different was that it was based on the idea of dialogue and interaction between audience and performer.

The structure of productions in these experiences revolves around a neutral party to be at the center of the action. This performer is usually called the "facilitator." The facilitator takes responsibility for the logistics of the process and guides the experience but never comments on or intervenes in the performance itself. This is the domain of the "spect-actors," who are both spectators as well as actors in the experience. The philosophy behind this approach is that it eliminates the concept that the ruling class is forcing their ideals on the audience and thus making the audience victims of those ideals. In other words, the ideas and themes of the work are not given to the characters in the story, who end up becoming a substitute for the audience themselves, but instead directly to the audience, who are now free to think and act for themselves. The obvious applications and connections to VR, AR, and MR are endless. Most major cities now offer a number of immersive theatrical experiences. Creators of emerging immersive storytelling mediums would do well to investigate them.

EXPERIMENTAL ART INSTALLATIONS

The installation work of Janet Cardiff and George Bures Miller has offered concepts and ideas of interest to immersive creators. "The Dark Pool," shown in Vancouver in 1995, consisted of a dimly lit room as a highly designed set piece, complete with artifacts and props. As viewers moved through the installation, various sounds were triggered ranging from musical selections to snippets of conversations and narratives around objects. One of their most celebrated pieces, "The Paradise Institute," shown at the Venice Biennale in 2001, focused on the experience of cinema itself and consisted of a reproduced mini-movie theater. Viewers climbed a short stair case and entered a plush two-row theater. They could then peer over the balcony of a movie theater from the golden age of cinema. Headphones provided audio for the film once it began but also audience intrusions such as ringing from cell phones and whispers of conversation. The immersion was created for the viewer using a concept the creators termed hyper-perspective, in which a realistic experience is crafted through manipulating and mediating the viewer's point of view. Audio was also used as a major component in directing the user's attention in these installations. A viewer would tend to look in the direction of the source of an audio segment if they felt it was significant in some way and not just diegetic to the room, even if actors were engaged and visible in their direct line of sight. These techniques are now often used by VR creators to direct the audience's attention in 360-degree open worlds. As has been discussed in the work of Bolter and Grusin earlier, the installations gave users the immediacy they craved with the potential of transforming that experience into hypermediacy. The work of Cardiff and Miller provided early ideas about how audiences would respond in mediated immersive environments such as VR.

THEME PARK ATTRACTIONS

Another industry that has driven audience expectations for the immersive is that of the theme parks. Experiential attractions have offered visitors the opportunity to move from being simple spectators to active participants in adventure and relatively safe from risk—motion sickness notwithstanding. Of course, motion sickness has also been a risk and reality in VR experiences as well. Different than traditional theater or cinematic experiences that are presented to crowds, theme park attractions are experienced individually or in small groups. One other notable similarity is that the two experiences are relatively short compared with many other entertainment experiences. Theme parks have focused on giving audiences a number of short experiences, rather than, say, a two-hour roller coaster. Presently, VR experiences tend to be most effective when presented in experiences of similar lengths.

While we will likely one day see VR experiences that mirror that of feature-length films, it could be important to recognize that audiences have established paces, rhythms, and even tolerances for experiences that involve their physical immersion. Theme parks have built in passive attractions, such as shows and exhibits, that allow the visitor to escape the immersion the more active experiences offer. While there are significant differences between VR and theme park attractions, the similarities are important enough to mine for methods and principles we should at least experiment with as we move forward with our new technological possibilities.

NONLINEAR STORYTELLING

Nonlinear storytelling occurs when narrative events are portrayed out of chronological order or in ways such that the events don't follow a structure where effects are the direct result of causality. The structure and recall of human memory is often nonlinear, and this category of story is often meant to mimic that process. Some research suggests that even when stories are told in a nonlinear fashion, they still must adhere to *linear logic*.[2] Since audiences have gotten more familiar and comfortable with nonlinear narratives through the use of hyperlinked media on the internet, nonlinear storytelling in other mediums has become even more common. Many immersive theatrical experiences rely on a nonlinear storytelling approach while still adhering to other basic forms in storytelling, such as introducing a protagonist or empathetic character(s) for the audience to follow. A great number of the existing VR experiences and certainly many of those that will be to come will rely on the risks and rewards that are inherent to telling an audience a story in which chronology and causality take lesser roles. The key factor that will allow for their success will be continual reliance on linear logic—those inherent elements in our psychology that are needed to even engage an experience. As has been stated previously, the audience must be given *something* to orient *some* part of their experience.

SPOTLIGHT ON IMMERSIVE THEATER: Storytelling through Immersion
Noah Nelson, Creator and Host of the No Proscenium Podcast

Noah Nelson is the creator and host of the No Proscenium Podcast, a program that focuses on the world of interactive and immersive theatrical experiences.

John Bucher: Let's begin by talking about the idea of "experience" in this technological age. Whether it be experiential theater or experiential storytelling—why are people craving a deeper experience? Why is the word "experience" on everybody's tongue, from the people at Disney to the people in the technology world? What is it about "experience" that we need it right now?

Noah Nelson: I think we talk about it because we finally have the means by which to talk about it. We couldn't talk about it until we could see it, and we saw it once we

---

(Continued)

(Continued)

got the language. Now that we have the language, we are obsessed with it. It doesn't mean that there aren't other things that need to be considered, and it doesn't mean that it's the be-all and end-all, but it is a very potent tool. And these are the things that people have always done, but only now do we have the language to talk about them in these sorts of engineering ways. We talk about stories. We talk about memes. I happen to have a horrible allergic reaction when using the word "content." We started to view the world through the lens of engineers and their lens in terms of the experience of designers. The late Brian Clark gave some great speeches about phenomenology. That level of knowing that the final assemblage point for anything is in the brain of the audience member, of the participant, then you start to see that everything is conditional in the experience.

If you're keeping that in mind, you can either provide an optimal experience for someone to encounter the idea you're trying to engender on the set or you can manipulate it in such a way that it defies conventions. Or, in the world of immersive theater, we start bringing in more senses such as sound—which is also incredibly important in the world of VR—because sound is the main driver of attention. To get somebody to turn around, you're going to use that. Binaural audio has been around for a while now but is only going to grow in popularity with the emergence of these immersive experiences.

John Bucher: I want to expand and ask you even more about audio because I think there's something about audio where we are going back to an even earlier form of communication that's very telling, when memories and stories were passed down through word of mouth.

(Continued)

(Continued)

Before stories were ever acted out in a theatrical expansion, stories were *told*. Anybody that knows anything about modern story theory knows that we've pushed away the idea of *telling* people stories. Do you think we are returning back to some of those ancient telling of stories, or are we going to create stories in a different way altogether?

Noah Nelson: I don't think we are using story*telling*. TV didn't kill radio. Radio didn't kill books. VR is not killing film. If anything, there's a chance for a renaissance. There is a chance to rediscover some of the old tools. Podcast will start rediscovering radio tools again. Radio storytelling. The idea of an immersive audio landscape. Or even when you think about a piece of immersive theater like *Then She Fell* where storytelling is part of the game, there are parts where they are just telling you a bedtime story.

I think what's more interesting there is how interactive is a return to primordial storytelling. Whenever I would run into people in the transmedia world, people were like, "interactive storytelling this" or "interactive storytelling that." It was a brand new field for them, and I'm like, "when my mom told me a story, when I was a kid, it was interactive." Because I would be like, "what about this," or like, "what happened to the dog?" Then the parents are sitting there saying, "The dog did this." It calls upon that. So, there's that plasticity between the storyteller and the audience. You find that in role-playing games. You find it in improv. That strata is everywhere. But it's largely invisible, because you can't make money directly off that experience. You have to somehow invent the rule set that exists and sell that to people. That's how role-playing games do it. They invent a world and sell you all

(Continued)

(Continued)

the pieces of the world. Anyone who has Dungeons & Dragons explained to them could run off and make up their own Dungeons & Dragons rules in five seconds straight. You have to convince people to buy the paraphernalia in a different way. But that strata is there.

In VR what's interesting is every moment you're in the landscape, got the headset on, you're in that relationship with the story world that is unfolding. Whether or not the storyteller has accounted for that or has the tools to deal with that is what's an issue right now. I do know that there are people who are prepping a demo in about a month, some people will work on the problem of triggering events based on head turns, a bunch of people are working on that.

I know folks like Jessica Brillhart are working on editing and the idea of drawing attention and using that attention point to create a focus for an edit, and watching edits actually work in VR for the first time. Which, when the Ozo launched, I finally saw editing on the action and editing on points of focus. And some of what that is, is saying the point of an edit, or the thing that gives you the opportunity for an edit, is if you successfully capture the attention of the audience and now you've got them so you can move them into a new phase.

I think a couple people were at first obsessed with the idea that "they can look anywhere so I'm not going to restrict where they look," and I would respond, "yeah, but you can't tell a story if you don't have some of the tension captured." But even then, it'll have different end results from a very well-managed experience, in much the same way that there's a big difference between the immersive theatrical experiences *Sleep No More*, which is a sandbox experience where you

(Continued)

(Continued)

can go wherever the hell you want to go, and *Then She Fell*, which is guiding you from point to point. They know they have your attention, at least in terms of what room you're in, and so then they're playing with your attention other ways.

John Bucher: What can VR storytellers learn from immersive theater, which has been around much longer?

Noah Nelson: Let's just start by saying everything. It's funny because I've been saying this for a few years now. I know I'm not the only one saying it, but it's funny to watch everyone else catch up. I think the biggest thing, the absolute biggest thing, the fundamental, is space. The relationship of actors to physical space, of the audience to the physical space, and indeed the virtual physical space. When I see VR filmmakers fail, oftentimes the first thing they don't get right is camera placement or the distance between the subject and the camera. The next thing they screw up on often is constraints for the field of view.

Everything comes down to the bodies in space and reclaiming the z-axis. I like to talk about the reason why this generation of 3D films failed. Pretty much only James Cameron seemed to have an innate sense of what the z-axis does in a 3D film. That's not to say that filmmakers don't understand the z-axis, but they have a different relationship between the depth of field on a two-dimensional camera from the depth of field on a three-dimensional camera. It's a very, very different tool. One that I think you see is traditional filmmakers who haven't embraced 3D get arrogant about it because they think, "I know the way a z-axis works. I know what's going to happen if I do this." Not once you've kicked in the third dimension. Then you've got more stage direction.

(Continued)

(Continued)

This idea of design, of everything that's in that space is there for a reason. That's what creates that sense of heightened reality. It's the way that in *Star Wars*, that story world, everything's got a backstory. In VR, everything has to be there for a purpose. Figure it out, and if you can't figure it out, either take it out or create something. Because we will attach meaning to it. We want meaning. That's why we tell stories. Period. We want to make sense of the world.

John Bucher: Right now the majority of people that experience VR experience it through a headset. We'll obviously get away from that technology at some point—most likely. At what point do we stop calling it Virtual Reality and just call it reality?

Noah Nelson: For those that are looking far enough ahead, which I'm trying to do, there are great concerns about the ethics of this stuff. There are technologies that promise to eventually be indistinguishable from normal reality. At that point you don't, on some level, keep calling it Virtual Reality; it becomes a part of our world in much the same way that the internet increasingly has.

The AP Style Guide has now dropped the capital "I" from internet. I hate that because I like to think of it as a thing. But I'm from the nineties, and we like capitals on everything. Eventually, it will be just like water out of the tap. Of course, there's an automated data layer in this café. Of course, if I tap on my contact lenses and I look over there, I could wave my hand to the cash register and pay my tab. A lot of the game is going to be figuring out what the gestural and the nongestural language is for accessing the data layer in ways that don't feel stupid.

That's one of the things that's interesting about immersive theater and this move towards experience

(Continued)

(Continued)

	away from the digital tools. You can see it too in the slow food movement. You can see it in the resurgence of third-wave coffee shops. You can see this desire to get away from the screens. We used to go online to get away from reality, and now we go to reality to get away from online. The most valuable and dangerous thing in the world is going to be an off switch.
John Bucher:	At an immersive theatrical experience once, I had someone say to me, "This is salvation for the touch-starved and the lonely." Can you talk about the relationship between Virtual Reality and loneliness?
Noah Nelson:	The question is, how far does the tech go? How good do the haptics get? How long until I put a data glove on and when someone touches my hand in VR, it feels like someone's touching my hand? Because if I feel someone else's touch, then some of that existentialist loneliness might go away. But we are not necessarily functions of all the stimuli that are coming in to us in our minds. So, can it fake the smell? Can it fake the temperature of another person's hand? Can it do everything else? Until we're doing that, deep down inside, you know it's not real. I actually think we are aware now how disconnected we are from each other. We drive ourselves back to things that are. They talk about things not being authentic and then try to market "authenticity" to us and it's grotesque, but we are looking for that. We're looking for something that's real. Which is a luxury now. It's a very first-world problem. I just want an experience that's real.
John Bucher:	Is there a danger that we become Descartes's brains in vats just having a mad scientist send electrodes to us and thinking we're experiencing a reality that we're not?

(Continued)

> Noah Nelson: How do we know we're not already? It becomes harder and harder to avoid how good the tools are. At the same time, each successive generation becomes savvier and savvier. I read one of Ray Kurzweil's books in the late nineties—pre–9/11. I remember his metric was perfect transcription. We're not there yet. For that reason, I don't believe in perfect Virtual Reality because it always takes longer than we think it's going to.

CONCEPTS TO CONSIDER FROM NOAH NELSON

▶ Sound is the main driver of our attention and should be taken advantage of in VR stories.

▶ Immersive storytelling is a return to the form rather than an invention of it.

▶ An edit in VR should successfully capture the attention of the audience so that they might be brought into a new phase.

▶ The relationship of actors and the audience to space is key to creating immersion.

▶ Every element in a VR story experience should have a purpose.

PUTTING IDEAS TOGETHER

Noah Nelson rightly suggests that every narrative decision, from the color of a wall to the point of view of the audience, should be motivated. If not, the creator misses an opportunity to add a layer of depth to the story. Because of the level of detail that VR offers in narrative creation, it will be easy and often tempting to leave what may seem to be minor details to chance when creating a VR experience. Storytellers must avoid doing so. The ability to keep an audience immersed in a story is one held with a sense of great fragility.

Immersion can be broken at any moment. Having motivated reasons that serve the story for every creative decision within an experience provides one less opportunity for that immersion to be fractured. The narrative precision required for storytelling in VR may be higher than any other medium that has been available to creatives thus far. It should never be overlooked or taken lightly.

NOTES

1 Garver, Mikhael Tara. "Immersive Theater: The Senses to Take the Wall Down." http://howlround.com/on-immersive-theater-the-senses-to-take-the-wall-down
2 Martens, Chris, João F. Ferreira, Anne-Gwenn Bosser, Marc Cavazza. "'Linear Logic for Non-Linear Storytelling', ECAI 2010–19th European Conference on Artificial Intelligence," in Coelho, H., Studer, R. and Wooldridge, M. (eds.) *Frontiers in Artificial Intelligence and Applications*. Pittsburgh: IOS Press. pp. 1–7.

5

Designing an Immersive Narrative

There's an old adage in the advertising industry that the first two questions that should be asked at the beginning of any project are the following:

1. Who is my audience?

2. What is the *one thing* I want them to walk away with?

We will expand on these questions and add others to consider. However, these questions move us toward some basic considerations we must engage as we begin. They can act as filters to apply to the potential narratives we will consider.

VR experiences benefit greatly when these questions are addressed articulately in the earliest stages of the project. Answering these questions as specifically as possible can save a great deal of resources later in the process, as well. Many projects have been restarted or scrapped all together because these questions were not asked directly in the beginning. While you should have a general idea about the demographic you are trying to communicate with, developing specifics about the audience and their preferences can be helpful. Most creators have a plethora of ideas they want their audience to carry with them from a media experience. However, recognizing that we are fortunate if an audience member retains even a single idea is a realistic approach.

DETERMINING THE AUDIENCE

Most projects will have multiple audiences. However, it is important that we determine a primary audience for every project. Other viewers may be secondary audiences or even outlying audiences, but the demographic qualities of the primary audience should be as narrowed and specific as possible. The purpose of the project will likely be intertwined with the audience. For example, if the purpose of the project is commercial in nature, then the primary audience will be those in the demographic most statistically likely to buy it. The purpose of the project is discussed in more detail in what follows. We can further our focus into parsing out more narrow audiences within the general demographic as we proceed. A wide array of marketing books can provide demographic categories, which can be helpful in designing your narrative. However, a quantitative approach may be less helpful than a simple qualitative approach. Envision the person you assume most likely to buy or appreciate your project. Keeping the embodiment of that person in the forefront of your creation process will often be all that is needed in order to craft a successful narrative. Once you begin to design for this audience, the next step in the natural progression is to ask what you want them to feel or do.

DETERMINING THE PURPOSE

Like the audience, there may be multiple purposes to any given project. For example, the purpose of the project may be commercial as well as entertainment. Like with determining the audience, it is key that a primary purpose be determined. There can be secondary purposes and outlying purposes as well. However, there will be points in the project at which one purpose will need to trump another. These decisions can be agonizing without a primary purpose to act as a guide in decision making. If there are several key ideas that are important to communicate, prioritizing the ideas can at least give structure to the development of your story. However, it is not always the development phase of VR storytelling in which narratives get lost but often in the process itself. Though it may be tempting to do so, beginning the process of sketching out characters, environments, settings, and plot lines without first determining the purpose of the storytelling experience can lead to backtracking, wasted time, and errors in development. In determining the goal for a story, we must return to basic communication theory and rhetoric, which means returning to Aristotle. For the purposes of this text, we will simplify Aristotle's treatise on the subject and simply state that the purpose for your story should be either to entertain, persuade, or inform.

TO ENTERTAIN

A vast amount of the media produced today is for the sole purpose of entertaining the audience. This is perhaps especially significant for new mediums such as VR. If people don't enjoy and perceive some entertainment value with VR in the first few moments they experience it, it is less likely they will invest significant time with the technology in the future without greater influence from an outside source at a later time. Even uses for VR with a key purpose beyond entertainment will run into the barrier of this expectation until culture has normalized the technology, and in some cases beyond. Those migrating from other platforms in which entertainment is the chief function, such as video games, will likely have a higher expectation for entertainment.

TO PERSUADE

With all the content available to viewers at any given time, our tendency to be persuaded by what we see has become more refined and nuanced. However, audiences have become weary of content that begins to feel like propaganda. They know immediately when an attempt to persuade them is being made. This is not to say that immersive content should not be used for persuasion. Indeed, this is one of the things that VR does best. Creators should, however, be aware of the ethics involved with persuading the viewer by flooding the brain with immersive content. A more detailed discussion of the ethical issues in the field can be found later in this book. Because experience is one of the most significant factors in changing people's minds, persuasion can be a natural goal with VR experiences. Motivating or inspiring the audience, as well as moving them to action, are all activities that fall within the domain of persuasion.

TO INFORM

Of course, some content is simply constructed for the sake of informing the audience. VR has the potential to make stale data more interesting just through the fundamentals of the medium. However, even when the sole purpose of creating an experience is simply to inform, VR can open up an informative story in powerful ways. Journalism, training, and education are all fields in which informational storytelling can be used.

The sources for potential immersive stories can be just as vast as the purposes behind them. Just as many films originate from newspaper articles, myths and legends, and personal experiences, VR stories can come from any of the wells we draw from to create narratives for other mediums. Of course, as is popular with games, powerful stories often come right from the human imagination, having no identifiable inspiration. These ideas and concepts also can be fodder for the creation of narratives. The question that can act as a helpful guide will be: will this story be more impactful to my audience by further immersing them *in* the world where it occurs. The answer is usually yes.

ESTABLISHING YOUR STORY'S POINT OF VIEW (POV) AND UNDERSTANDING CHARACTERS

Once we have a concept to create a story from and have determined our audience and the purpose of the piece we are creating, we can begin to unpack other logistic concerns for crafting our actual story. The first concern we should address is the point of view or POV from which the story will be told. Herein lies the difference between story creating and storytelling. Here we again draw on the history of other mediums such as theater and the novel.

FIRST-PERSON POINT OF VIEW

This term refers to narratives in which the main character is telling the story. We only experience the story through this person's eyes, thus keeping us from any experiences or knowledge that this character has not personally experienced themselves. In immersive experiences, such as VR, this refers to the story playing out through the viewer's eyes. In other words, the viewer or experiencer is the main character and protagonist.

FIRST-PERSON PERIPHERAL

This term refers to stories in which the narrator or storyteller is a supporting character in the story but not the main character. What is key to remember with stories using this point of view is that there will be experiences and scenes that happen to the protagonist of the story that the narrator will not be privy to. This approach is different from the third-person point of view in which the viewer is a "ghost" in the scene. With first-person peripheral, the viewer should be acknowledged by other characters and have some role in the narrative, though not the driving role.

SECOND-PERSON POINT OF VIEW

This term is most often used in instructional experiences, where the "story" is told from the perspective of "you." This perspective is much less common in other narrative forms and will have limited use in narrative-based immersive experiences. However, a notable exception might be scenes in which instructions are provided in gaming or interactive narratives.

THIRD-PERSON POINT OF VIEW

This term refers to stories in which the narrator is not a character in the narrative but instead an observer. In immersive experiences using third-person point of view, the viewer is unnoticed by characters in the experience. They, in a sense, are a "ghost" in the scene, observing everything that happens but not making decisions that affect the narrative at all. This point of view is most closely related to the experience viewers encounter when going to the movies. Within third-person point of view, there are also several variations.

Third-Person Limited

This term refers to narratives in which the POV is limited to only one character. The narrator or viewer only knows what that character knows.

Third-Person Multiple

This term refers to narratives in which the narrator or viewer can follow multiple characters within the story. Caution must be used when moving from one character's POV to another, however, to avoid audience confusion.

Third-Person Omniscient

This term refers to narratives in which the narrator or viewer knows *everything* and is not limited only to what one character knows. This POV can be especially interesting in interactive and gaming experiences, as it allows the viewer a greater role as *supreme being* of the world they are immersed in.

THE SENSE OF "SELF" IN IMMERSIVE NARRATIVES

In realities in which we are literally redefining our self, it may be helpful to consider exactly what that self is, since the viewer will likely be working through this experience as well. Since the inception of consciousness, the self has been fairly binary. We experience our inner self, which ranges from our interior thought life to our virtual presence on the internet. We also experience our external self in the real world. This self interacts with and is partially defined by others. It gives us agency in the world around us. In Virtual Reality, we have been given, in effect, a second self. This self shares our internal experience but has been given a second external experience. In many cases, we have been given a second body in the form of an avatar. We have been given agency in a new and very realistic world. This new external virtual self is not yet made to live within the confines of natural or human-made laws, such as the law of gravity or the penal code. Yet we will continue to establish our presence in this new reality by what we know and have experienced in the world we originated in.

THE SHIP OF THESEUS

Returning to the philosophies of the ancients can help us further explore how the self orients and changes in immersive space. In the late first century, Plutarch authored a volume titled *Life of Theseus*. While recording the Greek legend, he asked whether a ship that had been restored by replacing every piece of wood on it remained the same ship. The question has become known as Theseus' Paradox and is applicable in immersive virtual spaces. Is a human being that has been completely replaced by digital and virtual "parts" still a human being? The question becomes more interesting when we consider the philosophy of Thomas Hobbes, who gave the question further nuance a few centuries later by asking if the original planks of the ship were gathered up after being replaced and used to build a second ship, which ship would be the original? Thinkers from Aristotle and Heraclitus to David Hume have attempted to provide answers and lenses with which to give insight to the question. The honest answer to these questions, as they apply to virtual immersive space, is that we don't know. There simply hasn't been enough time to research and study how these emerging technologies will change our perceptions of who we are and how we behave. Our best practice will be to consider these questions in crafting our narratives and to continue the conversation as more information becomes available and experiences become lessons.

SPOTLIGHT ON NEW FRONTIERS: A Master Storyteller
Chris Milk, Founder and CEO, Within

Chris Milk began his career in music videos and photography and has expanded beyond the traditional. His art straddles experimental genres and unfamiliar mediums, turning new technologies, web browsers, ephemeral events, and even physical gestures into newfound canvasses. He continues to test the frontiers of interactive technology and art as founder and CEO of Within (formally Vrse), a Virtual Reality media company, and founder and creative director of Here Be Dragons (formally Vrse.works), a Virtual Reality production company. Milk presented at TED in 2015 on the power of Virtual Reality as a medium to advance humanity.

Milk first gained recognition as a music video director, working with Kanye West, Arcade Fire, Beck, Jack White, U2, Johnny Cash, Gnarls Barkley, the Chemical Brothers, John Mellencamp, Courtney Love, and Modest Mouse. He has been honored with the top industry awards for his music video and commercial work, including the Grand Prix Cannes Lion, the D&AD Black Pencil, the Grand Clio, and SXSW's Best of Show, as well as multiple Grammy® nominations, MTV Moon Men, and the UK MVA Innovation Award.

In recent years, Milk has focused on using cross-media innovations to enhance emotional human storytelling, exposing the beauty in the things—physical, digital, intangible—that connect us all. He has built multiple projects with Virtual Reality as the canvas. His collaboration with Beck in January of 2013 called "Sound & Vision" represents the first live-action, fully spherical Virtual Reality film. It was exhibited in an Oculus Rift at the Future of Storytelling Summit, Sundance Film

---

(Continued)

(Continued)

Festival, SXSW, and Tribeca Film Festival. Milk and Within have since partnered with the United Nations, *The New York Times*, Nike, Vice News, NBC, Apple Music, and U2, among others, to tell extraordinary stories in Virtual Reality.

John Bucher: What phase would you say VR is in, from an artistic or storytelling perspective?

Chris Milk: You're sort of captured in a time capsule right now, that historically speaking, it's really interesting, but it's also a bit of an unknown. I think other new mediums have had to contend with it as well. The thing that I keep trying to explain is if you look at Virtual Reality and you think that it will evolve the same way that other mediums have in the past, then you're thinking about it the wrong way. There's a deeper reason for that, but fundamentally the language of cinema evolved out of a format that was birthed from a technology that was invented. The format and the technology were birthed at the same time, and the language grows out of that after many decades. In Virtual Reality, you have a technology, you have a format, and then you have a language. The language is unknown, but the format is also unknown. There's a deeper, more profound reason for that. What it means from a creative standpoint is you can't just build language, you have to build technology too. That's something that is a strange marriage because you're talking about Silicon Valley and Hollywood, and the cross-pollination is not always the easiest.

It's the reason that I'm now sitting here. Five years ago, I was just an artist and a director, and now I'm the CEO of a venture-backed technology company. There's no way that I could build the kind of language of storytelling that I wanted to without having a technology

(Continued)

(Continued)

company to also build the format because the two have to happen simultaneously. You have to be thinking about where does the evolution of storytelling go in this medium? How do we build the technology to suit that? Also, thinking about the reverse, which is what are the different technologies that will scale in the coming years and how can we combine them to make for new experiences?

The reason that this is different is that in cinema, you have a sequence of rectangles, in radio you have audio broadcast, in literature you have words on a page, and those formats all stay the same throughout the lifespan of the medium. The reason that Virtual Reality is different is because it's out of a completely fundamental technology. All the other previous mediums come out of inventions in the second half of the 1800s, of recording moving image and sound, except for literature. Out of those technologies come the telephone, radio, television, cinema, the internet even, and Virtual Reality is growing out of a new fundamental technology which is the tech—a computer system communicating with our human senses in the language that they experience in the world around us.

All other mediums, all other art forms are representations of human experience. From an abstract painting to an Oscar-winning film, it's an abstraction of human experience. Each one of those has a different language. A Picasso painting looks like a Picasso painting; Scorsese films look like Scorsese films, but it is an expression. They're the artist's expression. Their externalized human experience is compartmentalized and broadcast to me, the viewer, who witnesses it, interprets it, and internalizes it, but there's a transmission that has to happen. Why Virtual Reality and the fundamental

(Continued)

(Continued)

technology behind Virtual Reality is so unique is that it's actually capturing or constructing that human experience and broadcasting it to us as firsthand human experience.

A lot of the VR language that's evolving right now is evolving out of our understanding of cinema and how it works. As the technology evolves, it will allow us to do new things. You look at the work we've done, the cinematic VR work and it's essentially just you passing through the rectangle of the cinema screen and you're living inside of the film now, but it's a film that you're just living inside of. The only real interaction point is people in the film looking at the camera, and then it feels like they're looking at you, and that's really strong and you can feel the level of power that holds.

John Bucher: Can you drill down even deeper on this idea of representation and mediated experience? If we get away from the technology we're creating and the machine becomes invisible, I think we start looking for meaning in this virtual space, once the novelty wears off.

Chris Milk: I think that there's even a deeper level to that which is that right now we're telling stories that are still observational, and yes, you're inside of it, and can look in every direction, but in my vision for storytelling with what we currently call Virtual Reality, it is interactive, it is first person, it's experiential, and it is social. What does social experiential storytelling look like? It looks like our lives. What's the most incredible story that you experienced in your life? It was probably with another person that you cared about. In the same way that going to the movies with your best friend is better than going to a movie by yourself. There's a collective experience that we treasure. Even more so when we're having those experiences firsthand instead of

(Continued)

(Continued)

an externalized witnessing of that. I firmly believe in experiencing stories together, that are participatory, that are not observational. But telling those kinds of stories is both beyond most of our current storytelling model and our understanding of authorship, which is going to completely change.

The journey of the hero is that of a circle, as you know. He has a goal. He doesn't really achieve his goal, but he changes through the course of trying to achieve it—which is really like our lives as well—which is why it resonates with us. Nobody gets to do everything that they want to do, but they become the person that they are through that journey of trying to do those things. That's I think the fundamental core of good storytelling, and that comes out of your myths a long time ago. I don't think every VR experience will be the hero's journey, but it's a good place to start experimenting.

How do you tell a story that has essentially unlimited infinite branching points and characters that you're interacting with that are photo realistic? You're talking about technology that we don't yet have the ability to utilize yet. We have to start somewhere, so let's start trying to tell stories in the most infantile version of the technology—in the direction that we think it's going.

John Bucher: You have, in your music videos, masterfully used elements of storytelling without always telling a linear story or hero's journey-type story. You used what I call narrative shards of storytelling. Do you think that path is going to be, at least initially, the way to go with storytelling in immersive environments, or do you think we can figure out some sort of structural linear stories, or is looking to the format of movies too closely just a recipe for not moving forward?

(Continued)

(Continued)

Chris Milk:	It's tricky because we have to try to make the most compelling stories that we can with the tech that we have. We can't say we'll just wait. There's a lot of pressure from the community for good content. We need fuel to keep the medium going and get people to engage and buy headsets and keep watching things. The trick is you have to try to push the things that we're making to also push the tech so that we're able to do new things.
	I don't think we're always trying to tell concrete, distinct, linear narratives. I think there's also you as a character going through a narrative, and there will be a resting conclusion to it. Is that constructed by some guy with a typewriter writing out a script, or is it a more complicated digital system that is moving and adapting based on a set of storytelling parameters? Is there a narrative science that has to be developed rather than a language of storytelling? It's possible.
John Bucher:	There's this idea where Virtual Reality opens the door to having a full-body experience, where the internet pretty much only allows a mental experience. How do you think that's going to play into the storytelling as we are able to have a more embodied experience in this space?
Chris Milk:	In my experimentation, it makes everything more powerful. Feeling your physical presence in a space with another person connects you to that person on a deeper level, and it connects you to the place that you're in, and it connects you to the story that's happening. The story that happens will be a memory rather than just a piece of media that you consumed. When I'm making things for a screen, I'm constantly thinking about how can I make people connect on a deeper level to this character? How do I make this

(Continued)

(Continued)

character more relatable? How do I make their goal relatable so that people invest themselves in this character when that character runs then into obstacles? They are invested emotionally in the character, so then there is drama in the storytelling.

It's also experientially more complicated and difficult to tell that story. I think there's also an uncanny valley for branching narrative. Branching narrative is not a problem, the construction of a branching narrative is not a problem, it's just been a problem for us telling stories. Every single day of our life is a branching narrative, and you never stop and go, what the hell's going on? Now our level of sophistication has never been at that level. We're constantly running into doors that don't open, and the story is stopping and waiting for you to do something, and you know what you're supposed to do, and that doesn't happen in real life. Until we get to the level where it actually does feel completely natural, we'll constantly have skeptics saying we can't tell those kinds of stories—it's not natural. But it is the most natural story there is. It is the everyday story of your life. It has not been possible to tell those kinds of stories in the current technology of the other mediums that we tell stories in. A purist author would say there is no authorship. If I have not sat down and written with a pen on a page, then there's no author. If the viewer can decide what ending it is, then it can't be a great story. It can be a great story— it's tricky to tell—but if you're able to tell it, that story's going to be a better story than any story that you can tell through any rectangle.

Sometimes I get challenged on panels about this and I'll say to the challenger, "What's your favorite movie?" They'll say, *Shawshank Redemption*. I'll say, "Tell me

(Continued)

the story of *Shawshank Redemption.*" "It's a story of a guy wrongly accused, goes to jail, makes a best friend, escapes from prison." "Okay, sounds like a really good story. Tell me the best story that you've had in your life. What was the most amazing afternoon you had? Tell me that story." The guy might say, "I was in Mexico with my buddies and we were on a surf trip and we were surfing and this shark came and nipped the back of my friend's surfboard and cut his ankle just a little bit and we quickly all swam to shore and there was an Army base that was there, and we went into the Army base and they were able to patch up his ankle." "Okay, let's disconnect from the story. Which story on paper, as an authored story, is a better story?" "Clearly *Shawshank Redemption.*" "Which story meant more to you?" "Well the story that happened to me." Now, at any point in that day that you experienced that story, did you ever say to yourself, "This is amazing, but I wish there was a rectangular frame that showed me where to look at this moment in time"? But if you could experience that story with the level of drama and craftsmanship of a film, in the medium that you experienced the shark attack, how powerful could that story be? I think that's ultimately what we're talking about.

John Bucher: You said in a recent talk in Vancouver that consciousness is the new medium that we're working in. How does that relate to this point?

Chris Milk: Yes, there's the story on celluloid that runs through a rectangular frame and a motion picture projector, that is the medium. The story's been captured and represented and presented to you in that medium. The other story is consciousness. How do you tell a story for someone's consciousness? What does it look like

(Continued)

(Continued)

when you're running through the forest? Imagine a system where all of your senses are fully engaged at the full resolution that they are engaged in the real world. Potentially even at a higher resolution. There's a lot of science that you have to overcome before you get to that though.

Then we're going beyond just storytelling. We're talking about actual fundamental human communication and language. We communicate through these symbols, and these symbols are incredibly inefficient ways of communicating the things in my head to get them into your head, so there is so much miscommunication that goes on. But we're talking about a system that could allow us to interface the technological but communicate on a human level that is not possible with our current human hardware, you know?

John Bucher: Do you think what it means to be human will change as we enter these new emergent spaces?

Chris Milk: That's a great question. I feel like all we can do is the best that we can every day. Not just get caught up in what we can do but think about what we should do. Not just being about the power of technology but how we utilize it to its fullest extent. How do we take this technology and use it for the betterment of humanity? I think it takes a collective of thoughtful, concerned humans thinking in those terms for other humans.

John Bucher: You've said that *Citizen Kane* doesn't come in our second year of VR storytelling. What are the big barriers that we have to overcome in order for the storytelling that you're talking about to be unleashed?

Chris Milk: We need photo-realistic representations of environments and humans in a real-time interactive environment. That will sort itself out. There's that. There

(Continued)

(Continued)

is the ability to deal with branching narratives both in character development of external characters and for yourself, as well as communication with external characters and larger narrative structure. There's no way that one person and a typewriter can write every possible branching narrative in a first-person story. Nor can they write every line of dialogue for a character that you're speaking to. There's going to be AI involved. That quickly evolves to the place where you can puppeteer a photo-realistic digital human. This is probably the first step. Then the step beyond that is puppeteering the entire narrative. When AI actually writes the narrative from scratch, who knows? I preface this by saying that we can't get there without building the most amazing stories that we can build in every step of the technology.

CONCEPTS TO CONSIDER FROM CHRIS MILK

▶ The language and technology of cinema were birthed at the same time. However, with VR, the technology was birthed first. Now the language must be invented.

▶ Virtual Reality is growing out of a new fundamental technology, unlike mediums of the past.

▶ Virtual Reality captures, constructs, and broadcasts the human experience to us firsthand.

▶ Social experiential storytelling in virtual space will likely be significant in the future of VR.

▶ Not every VR experience will enforce Joseph Campbell's concept of the hero's journey, but it is a good place to begin experimenting.

▶ A gap exists between the branching narratives created in gaming or VR space and emotionally impactful branching narratives we experience in day-to-day life.

▶ There are technological barriers to overcome before VR storytelling can begin to explore its fullest potential.

PUTTING IDEAS TOGETHER

Chris Milk is emphatic that we not allow technological limitations to become barriers in our efforts to tell the best stories possible with the tools we presently have. While Milk likely has more resources at his disposal than the majority of creators reading this book, it should be comforting that he works within the same realms of possibility that all storytellers are currently experiencing. Telling good stories can never be about the technology available to us. It must always remain the tool with which we tell powerful stories. Experimentation and working with others both inside and outside of virtual space will be essential guidelines for moving VR storytelling into the future.

TRADITIONAL NARRATIVES

Taking the essential elements of story—characters, goals, conflicts, and resolutions—we can begin to explore how these elements fit together in narratives, keeping in mind we are looking for form and not formula. While entire volumes have been written on structure around visual stories, we will look at the basics used in three particular media: film, television, and webisodic storytelling. While there are vast numbers of exceptions, most films since the mediums' inception have been based around the three-act structure we received from Aristotle, having a beginning, a middle, and an end. Also, varying greatly, especially in the age of cable television, is the five-act approach used in the majority of produced television. The five-act approach evolved out of the need for commercial breaks in televised storytelling, a problem that has been eliminated with subscription-based cable, though much of the content produced for that platform still abides by this structure. Finally, web-based storytelling in the form of webisodes, online narrative gaming, and even Vines has not needed the rigidity of an act-based structure system and instead has opted for beat-based storytelling—an idea that is discussed in greater detail in what follows.

For some, the information that follows around historical media structure will be review. For those coming from technological fields, it may be new. Regardless of one's experience with narrative structure, reiterating the basic forms is essential due to variances in understanding around them as well as the nature of their deceptive simplicity. Master storytellers often return to the basic forms to reground their understanding and work.

THREE-ACT STRUCTURE

Traditional theater provides the basis for much of how cinematic storytelling would evolve. Stage plays had literally thousands of years of development before the first story would be projected on a screen. One act plays, stories told in three acts, and even multiact epics were not uncommon. However, it would be the Aristotelian suggestion of three acts that would resonate most significantly with cinematic storytelling. There are a wide variety of ideas around what precisely should be in each of the three acts. Traditionalists suggest that the first quarter of the story should occur in the first act, half of the story should take place in the second act, and the final act of storytelling comprises the third act. Some break the second act in half, adamantly affirming that there are actually four acts in cinema, making each act an even 25% of the narrative. Others take a minimalist approach, claiming that whatever happens near the beginning of a film is the first act, whatever happens near the end is the third act, and whatever happens between those two makes up the second act. Still others point to exact beats and moments that they believe should occur at fairly precise times within each act of the story. Believing that the wise approach is likely the middle road, we will look at each act in terms of what has been generally accepted and practiced within the industry.

Act I

Most theorists and practitioners agree that the characters and their general backstories should be revealed in the first act. Even if all the key characters are not yet seen by the audience, knowing who they are helps orient the viewer in the story world. In VR environments, the audience will naturally be curious to determine if they are watching the protagonist of the story or if they are the protagonist themselves. Depending on the scenario of the narrative, they will likely have equal curiosities about the antagonist and other side characters.

In Act I, it is important to establish the "before" world, so that by the end of the narrative, we have made clear the "after" world. Subtle cues as the norms in the culture of this world should be communicated. The importance of the first images and complete scene that the audience experiences cannot be overestimated. These initial impressions will orient the audience with psychology about what they are seeing that will be difficult if not impossible to alter later in the story. One of the easiest pitfalls one can fall into in the first act is creating confusion. While some confusion can be helpful in disorienting the viewer for a short time, at least a portion of the viewer's confusion should be alleviated quickly so that they have "handles" to proceed with as the narrative progresses.

Viewers will often subconsciously be asking the following questions because of training from established narrative techniques established in other mediums. Whose story is this? Which character do I find most interesting or appealing? Can I become invested in their journey? What are they trying to accomplish in this story? Who is opposing them or their goal? Other elements viewers often look for in the first act are hints at the themes that will be explored and reveals of the main character's weaknesses or flaws. It can be helpful in the first act to gently explore what lesson our main character needs to learn over the course of their journey.

One final element that can be crucial in the first act is the event that propels the story forward most dramatically. Some refer to this event as the catalyst moment, others call it the inciting incident, but the function of the element is the same. This event will be what shakes the normalcy of the "before" world. It will force the protagonist into a decision whether to go on their journey or not. It could be as simple as the moment when the boy meets the girl. However, it can be a tragic moment as well. Deaths, births, weddings, revelations of infidelity, escapes, and appearances of characters from the protagonist's past all can be events that alter life in unchangeable ways.

Act II

There is another dramatic event that subtly lets the audience know that we have entered into the main body of the story—the second act. This might be our protagonist choosing to go on the journey that the inciting incident provided. If the catalyst involved the death of a protagonist's father, this event might be the selling of the family home, which forces him or her into a new neighborhood or new schools. Most common is a scenario in which the main character makes a choice to enter the journey of the second act, as opposed to having a situation forced on them. An old film industry adage suggest that audiences resonate more deeply with characters that make decisions as opposed to simply reacting to events that happen to them and becoming victims of circumstance. This might be surprising to some storytellers who would feel that seeing a character have something beyond their control forced on them would create a deeper level of empathy. However, we must remember that narratives suggest a connection with who we want to be more so than who we actually are.

The second act can play out in a variety of ways. Sometimes, it features our main character trying desperately to get what they want, using a variety of means but always failing. Other times, the second act sets up the twists and turns that make the plot interesting to viewers trying to figure out where the story is going. Most commonly, a game of cat and mouse occurs between the protagonistic forces and the antagonistic forces. The protagonist(s) try to advance and do take two steps forward, only to be forced into taking one step back by the antagonist(s). In some narrative structures, we begin to explore the lives and journeys of more minor characters as well as smaller goals the protagonist may have, such as getting the girl in the process of getting the gold.

Usually in the middle of the second act, our protagonist is either in a significantly high moment or a significantly low moment. If they are in a significantly high moment, the floor is about to drop out from under them. If they are in a significantly low moment, there is an unexpected elevator about to rise for them. This moment is sometimes referred to as the turn, as in a turn of events is about to occur. Another event the audience may be unconsciously looking for is a moment in which it appears that the protagonist has lost everything they have gained, or what they now have seems insignificant. This event often leads to a moment of reflection, when another character must step in and remind the protagonist what they are fighting for, which inevitably gives them the strength they need to finish the journey.

Act III

The final act involves the most significant showdown between the protagonist forces and antagonistic forces. It is here that the audience has to see if the protagonist has learned the lesson or overcome the weakness they demonstrated in the first act. The theme that was hinted at in the beginning of the story returns with ringing clarity. Even within the third act, moments usually occur when we are unsure if the main character will prevail—and sometimes they don't. In traditional Hollywood films, the main character often gets what they want as well as what they need. However, sometimes this character does not get what they want and instead gets what they need. In fewer cases, the character gets what they want but not what they need. And rarely, outside of Greek tragedies, does a character get neither what they want or what they need.

Whether the main character emerges victorious or is left licking their wounds, it is important to demonstrate what life is like in the "after" world. There are various techniques for bookending a story with visual metaphors and echoes of what the audience initially saw and experiences in the story. All these techniques, however, are about accomplishing one thing—resolution in the mind of the audience. The viewer wants to feel that the story has truly ended. When things feel completely unresolved at the end of the story, viewers feel a sense of frustration. This doesn't mean that every narrative story line and character arc must be wrapped up with a bow on top. However, feeling some sense of resolution in each character's story helps the audience complete the narrative in their mind and create some sort of meaning out of what they have seen. Often, there is a final moment referred to as the dénouement that shows us how life goes on after the story has resolved. This tag or button at the end of the story serves as a cherry on top of our narrative sundae.

FIVE-ACT STRUCTURE

The basic arc of five-act television structure is not unlike the three-act structure we see in film, with a few key differences. The origin of using five acts to convey a narrative is almost as old as the idea of using three. The Roman poet Horace understood Aristotle's three-act model and advocated it be expanded to five for playwrights. Hundreds of years later, German playwright Gustav Freytag modified Horace's model to analyze Shakespearean dramas in five acts. The first act was known as the exposition, when the audiences were introduced to the setup of characters, backstories, and settings. The second act was called the rising action. In this act, action leads to the most intent moment of the story. The third act was the climax, which was the turning point of the play. The fourth act was referred to as the falling action and contained plot twists and reveals. Finally, the fifth act was termed the dénouement or resolution.

With television, these five acts took on additional modifications to situate a narrative around commercial breaks but also to provide intrigue that would bring the audience back to the story after the break. There are a number of formats used in television. There are one-hour dramas or serials, one-hour procedurals, half-hour procedurals, and half-hour sitcoms, as well as the limited series and the mini-series. Here is a breakdown of the structure used in many traditional episodic television series.

Teaser

Most TV shows begin with an element called the teaser. Even in a one-hour drama, the teaser is usually five minutes or less. The teaser, in a sense, calls the story to action. It opens the story world and reminds us who the characters we are following are but often has little to do with the conflict that will be explored in the episode of the show, though on some shows it sets this up as well.

Act I

This act introduces the story at hand. It gives enough backstory for the impending conflict that we are not confused when it arrives. Unless we are watching the pilot episode of the show, the creators assume we are familiar with the characters, their backstories, their weaknesses, and the locations in which the story will take place. The first act concludes with a moment that sometimes feels like a cliffhanger but at least in some ways resembles the inciting incident discussed in the section on three-act structure. This moment should present the central conflict in the episode.

Act II

The second act begins to unpack the central conflict. Viewers become privy to how the characters are going to deal with the problem. By the conclusion of the second act, audiences usually feel hopeful that the characters are going to be able to resolve the central conflict—until the final moments of this act—when the floor drops out from under them. This moment again sets up another cliffhanger or catalyst that reverses the fortunes of the central characters.

Act III

This segment of the story resembles the end of the second act in three-act structure, when the central characters often feel like the antagonists will win—all hope is lost. The hope we had earlier that they will succeed in their goals is proven false in Act III. The end of this act resolves by creating a situation that makes the viewer curious about how the characters will be able to succeed in the end.

Act IV

At this point in the story, the central characters begin to gain ground again. The viewer has a sense that they have learned from the mistakes they have made in the past. The audience feels a payoff watching the characters not repeat the same mistakes but instead approach the problem from a different angle. At the end of this act, the story usually resolves. We see the central characters succeed (or fail) at their goal.

Act V

Act V is about wrapping up the story and bringing closure. The audience is given a feeling of resolution. Depending on the nature of the show, sometimes this act provides a tease for viewers to tune in for the next show—a dénouement of sorts.

Webisodic Structure

In our modern digital age of storytelling, we are beginning to see shifts in structure to accommodate new mediums as well as the elimination of elements that are no longer needed in emerging formats. It is important to remember that this is not a sign that all structural narrative design is being abandoned. Instead, it simply points to the latest evolutions in structure as creators find new ways to bring resonating stories to their audiences. Programming streamed on services that no longer require commercial breaks continue to use structure that holds to that format for two reasons. The first is that in this transmedia world, a creator can never be sure of all the eventual distribution platforms for his or her work. For this reason, many hold to the traditional structure in case the program eventually does become available on a commercial-based platform. The second is that traditional structures are based around how human beings solve problems, as stated earlier. Many of these structures are used because they work, not because that's how it has always been done. We can recall the examples of architecture and musical structure.

Beat-Based Structure

Webisodes and other digitally based programming will often embrace beat-based structure. This is a format in which the audience is guided from one narrative beat to the next. This can be particularly helpful in stories that fall under the "slice of life" genre. In these stories, we get a glimpse into who a character is by watching them live out their days. There is not necessarily an external goal trying to be achieved, and if there is, it may seem insignificant. A character arc might not be occurring, but certainly significant moments or beats in the character's journey are.

Two cautions should be mentioned when working with beat-based structure. The first is that many storytellers hide behind such structure because they are unable to execute a traditional structure. Obviously, few would readily admit such. However, vast amounts of evidence can be found in the stories they execute. This flavor of structure should not be used simply because one wants to avoid using a traditional structure. Instead, it should be used if this format best fits the story a creator is trying to tell. The second caution that creators should be aware of is the lack of commercial potential for content structured in such a way. Films with alternative structures or beat-based structure rarely perform well at the box office. Television programming with such structures has been virtually nonexistent. And while digital content and webisodic programming have had a few success stories, there are very few creators currently able to sustain careers solely in this format. This is not to say that these types of content are not important, however. Such experimental programming and structure pushes the envelope of the medium of visual storytelling. We learn through such work. Those lessons learned can be brought into traditional formats in order to bring fresh and creative approaches. It should also be stated that many of these formats are quite young compared to more established mediums such as film or certainly theater. We may very well see such formats find commercial success in the future.

Interactive and Immersive Structure
Applications for VR Experiences

As has been discussed earlier with remediation, VR has recrafted, modified, and redefined many of these structures and concepts. However, it is also important to recognize that some of these concepts, such as three-act structure, have worked well within VR contexts without modification. Matt Thompson's VR experience, *Lucy*, available as a case study in this text, would be an example of this. Using traditional concepts and structures as a jumping-off point, the following section offers suggestions for methods and techniques in crafting VR narratives using the elements of traditional structures and combining or configuring them in new ways.

Interactive Three-Act Structure

With this technique, the basic elements of three-act structure are maintained as discussed earlier. However, it includes an interactive element through which the user experiences agency and is given some degree of choice at the beginning of the narrative, between each act, and in the conclusion of the piece. The interactive elements should further the user's immersion in the piece but not allow the user to change the overarching narrative. The basic story should remain the same. This technique can be useful when introducing new users to VR and in cases in which agency and immersion might be overwhelming to a user. It may also be helpful when creators wish to show the potential of an experience without the time or resources to craft a more in-depth immersive experience with complete agency.

Interactive Five-Act Structure

With this technique, there is greater room for the user to actually drive and recraft the story with their decisions and agency. Interactive elements are introduced more often, though still between act breaks, creating greater senses of possibility for outcomes. This structure works with narratives that function like television procedurals such as *Law and Order* or *NCIS*. Those familiar with the board game or film *Clue* may also see connective possibilities. Agency beyond interactive decisions at act breaks can provide for further viewer immersion. Options common to many video games, such as choice of weapon, character-related abilities or powers, and maps are examples of possibilities. Obviously, the greater the agency, interactivity, and immersion, the greater the amount of time and resources a story needs to be properly executed.

Interactive Beat-Based Structure

Many if not most current VR narratives echo the beat-based structure found in webisodes, many online, and some video game experiences. This is partially due to technological constraints, audience attention spans, and the industry desire to produce as much content as possible so that a wider adoption of the technology can be achieved. It can also be attributed to the fact that a beat-based structure simply works better for many VR experiences. Many immersive experiences are not intended to tell a story in the way that a film, television program, or video game is intended to. They do, however, need and use the narrative shards that have been discussed in order to draw the audience into and further engage them in the experience. Any number of methods or techniques may be applicable and appropriate. Slices of life, simple game-like challenges, or even just narrative characters all may be brought from the wider storytelling world into beat-based structure. Any of the beats mentioned in the previous section on beat-based structure may be helpful. While three-act and five-act structures are linear in nature, interactive beat-based structures may be circular in nature. A viewer or player may not need to complete the entire narrative circle in order to return to the beginning of (or any point in, for that matter) the experience.

BACKSTORY STRUCTURE

VR experiences may not only be about the journey of a character but also or instead about the preparation of a character for that journey. In narrative discussions, this is called the backstory. While the backstory can involve an entire narrative itself, much in the way that *Rogue One* provides a backstory for *Star Wars: A New Hope*, this is not always the case, nor need it be. Sometimes, in gaming or VR narratives, the backstory may be simple preparatory experiences a user is offered to help familiarize them with the controllers or gear used in the experience, either outside the virtual world or within it. While this experience may not follow anything as elaborate as the three structures just mentioned, it may follow a simple structure with three elements or acts, such as the one that follows:

▶ *Explanation*: This element or act will explain to the user, through either words, text, graphics, icons, or other intuitive suggestion, how to navigate in the virtual world they are about to enter, the agency offered to them, and the interactive choices they will be allowed to make. These explanations may be spelled out explicitly or instead implicitly implied through a variety of means. In many ways, this act mirrors the first act or set-up in dramatic structure.

▶ *Offering of Options*: This element or act will allow the user to make the choices mentioned in the explanation. In this phase, the user may want to compare options and change their mind several times before committing to a choice. This element is similar to the transition scene between the first and second acts in dramatic structure.

▶ *Practice*: This element or act will allow the user to experience the choices they made before engaging in the experience itself. An important element of this phase is to allow the user to return to the offering of options in order to select another choice should they be unhappy with theirs in the practice phase. The practice phase loosely mirrors the second act in dramatic structure. The game or experience itself mirrors the third act.

ETHICAL CONSIDERATIONS FOR VIRTUAL REALITY

The trend is toward human beings' ability to turn more and more of their world into game space and narrative space—you've got peak TV, you have VR. We're starting to ask, why are all these narratives so similar? Why are many of these narratives so violent? And the series very much asks the question: What the _____ is wrong with us?

—Jonathan Nolan, cocreator of *Westworld*
WIRED Magazine, October 2016

The HBO series *Westworld* has opened a wider conversation about the potentials and dangers of immersive environments like VR. The series, based on a book and film by Michael Crichton, features a futuristic theme park in which robotic *hosts* allow visitors to live out their fantasies through artificial consciousness. Part of the fun in the series is being unsure who is human and who is AI. In an early episode, a character we have learned to be human asks another character, "Are you real?" She responds, "If you can't tell, does it matter?" Cocreator of the show Lisa Joy has asked, "Now as technology develops, you start to wonder: Where is that line where it becomes immoral not to have empathy, even if you know these creatures are artificial?"[1] This seems to be not only the driving thematic question of the show but also a driving thematic question being asked in global culture. The age-old question—*What does it mean to be human?*—seems more relevant than ever before.

Too often, ethical considerations regarding emerging mediums are not considered until deep in the development process. The potential ramifications of VR, specifically as it intersects with AI technology, have driven some, including Elon Musk, Bill Gates, and Stephen Hawking, to voice concerns about exactly what technology we allow to be developed and what might be better left in Pandora's box. Certainly, all concerned voices are protechnology and are realistic about stopping or slowing *any* type of technological advancement. However, their concerns are well founded and should encourage dialogue about how immersive technologies should be consumed and developed.

The potential ethical issues of immersion are not a new idea. The power of immersive narratives made Plato distrust the poets as a threat to the Republic. In *Don Quixote*, Miguel de Cervantes writes, "In short, he so immersed himself in those romances that he spent whole days and nights over his books; and thus with little sleeping and much reading, his brain dried up to such a degree that he lost the use of his reason."[2] Huxley warns in *Brave New World* against the dangers of letting multisensory art diminish reason and eventually imagination. Losing oneself in another world has long been a goal of immersive entertainment experiences. However, technologies including VR seem to offer a more intense level of immersion with fewer guardrails to protect those who might be more vulnerable to its dangers from flying off the tracks.

The ethical concerns in VR range from the minor nausea akin to that experienced on theme park rides to the more serious, AWS (alternate world syndrome) and even virtual sexual assault. Technologies continue to develop more rapidly than social science can study phenomena, and little money is available for the research that is conducted. The bottom line is that we simply don't know what dangers may be lying in the virtual worlds and will not likely have much indication until it is upon us. We do, however, have research that indicates that in order for an experience to remain pleasurable, it must be temporary and remain distinct from addiction.

CONSIDERATIONS FOR IMMERSIVE EXPERIENCES

For a number of years, there have been ongoing discussions in other immersive fields, including theme parks and immersive theater, as to where ethical boundaries lie. While not necessarily outlining firm rules, there are certain questions and conversations that often happen around these experiences. These discussions can be helpful in some VR experiences as well. The first issue is that of permission. It can be argued that when a viewer puts on an HMD, they are "going through the turnstile" or *opting in* to the experience. However, the question must be asked if they have granted permission for *any* virtual experience just by entering VR. There is currently no set of standards or code, either voluntary or enforced. At a minimum, viewers should be made aware of any potential extremes in the experience. This protects not only the viewer but the creator as well. While this might seem like common sense to some, the power of and temptation for surprise in a VR experience can be difficult to resist, as it demonstrates the great power the immersion holds. Because the immersion in VR is unlike any that previous entertainment or educational mediums have previously offered, it becomes imperative that creators lean in to negotiating the experience before the viewer enters, as it is a *mediated* experience. Consequences of experiences must be considered in advance.

RISKS IN VIRTUAL SPACE

In late 2016, a woman named Jordan Belamire was shooting zombies along-side strangers in QuiVr when another player virtually rubbed her chest and shoved his "hand" toward her virtual crotch. The incident was reported internationally and gave voice to emerging risks when entering virtual space. While there are laws that would protect Belamire and punish the offender in the real world, no such laws exist in the virtual arena. When QuiVr developer Aaron Stanton learned that a woman had been groped while playing the game, he stated, "Our first response was, 'Let's make sure this never happens again.' It's up to developers to create controls to make players feel safe inside the world that they've brought to life. We need to offer tools that give players better controls, not simply better ways to hide."[3] Altspace VR, a virtual chatroom, offers users a virtual bubble that can be enabled. QuiVr offers this option as well, but its developers feel it should be a standardized control across VR. Stanton has suggested that developers unite to create a universal "power gesture" to combat harassment in VR. This would essentially be a "safe word" in the form of a motion that would give the player the power to protect themselves.

PRIVACY IN VIRTUAL SPACE

There is an ongoing discussion in the VR creator and storytelling community about whether VR is a public or private space. Should a user be assured some level of privacy when they put on an HMD? There will likely be a great deal of discussion and trial and error before any standards are eventually developed. However, recognizing the importance privacy has played in real life as well as in online space, the significance of the issue for VR cannot be underestimated. Creators would do well to be forward thinking in their development of new games and experiences if they anticipate a long shelf life for the products that they create.

SPOTLIGHT ON ETHICS: Considerations for VR Storytelling
Steve Peters, Experience Designer, Host of StoryForward Podcast and CCO of Mo Mimes Media

An Emmy®-winning experience designer, Steve Peters began his career as a roller coaster operator. A pioneering force in alternate reality games and transmedia entertainment, he has worked on some of the largest and most significant interactive experiences to date. In addition to founding Mo Mimes Media, he was VP of experience design at Fourth Wall Studios, where he worked on projects such as the interactive web series *Dirty Work* and *6 Minutes to Midnight* (for the Warner Bros/DC Comics film *Watchmen*). Prior to that, he served as Experience Designer at 42 Entertainment for projects including *Why So Serious?* (for the feature film *The Dark Knight*). Steve founded the Alternate Reality Gaming Network in 2002, has guest lectured at schools including USC, Georgia Tech, and Cal Arts, and has spoken at media conferences around the world. Aside from continuing to design experience both in the real world and in virtual space, Peters hosts the StoryForward Podcast, which explores the future of storytelling.

John Bucher: When you are creating an experience, what are some of the ethical issues you consider?

Steve Peters: The biggest thing I think that is always at the top of my list is that I'm a very strong proponent of being upfront about where that line between fiction and reality is. The biggest red flag for me is whenever somebody says, "We'll do this thing and people will think it's real, and then they'll go along thinking it's real for a certain amount of time, days, weeks, months, and then we'll reveal that it's part of this cool thing. They'll think that's amazing!" My reaction is, "No, they'll feel betrayed. Some of them will think it's amazing, but most of them will feel betrayed and feel like they got hoaxed and feel dumb, or feel resentful, and you're going to get a backlash."

(Continued)

(Continued)

I was playing an ARG once where I had this envelope with the guy's name on the envelope and I was supposed to go his apartment in Berlin. I show up at his apartment and it's a secure apartment. I can't even get in the lobby. I ring upstairs to his apartment and nobody's home. It's four or five in the afternoon. I figure I'm just going to wait. I wait around for a couple hours. He never shows up, so I think, "I'm going to take a break. I'm going to get some dinner and get warm because it's raining." I'm walking back toward the station, and it couldn't have been better. There's one lone streetlight and this figure comes walking toward me, and as he gets closer I realize this is the guy that I'm supposed to deliver this to. I think, "This is perfect." I wait and, as we pass, we meet eyes for a second and we go on. I was sure it was him and I stopped and I turned and I said, "Patrick." He stops and he turns around. He says, "Yes?" I said, "This is for you," and I reach in. I was wearing a black trench coat of all things. I didn't plan this. I reach out and I hand him this big manila envelope and it's got his name written on it. It's like a magic trick. He's like, "What is this?" I said, "Just open it and all will be revealed." I turned and stepped and started walking away. Inside I'm going, "This happened! He's walking along and I made him feel like he was in a spy movie." Now, the end of the story is I get about 12 paces away and I hear, "Steve Peters, is that you?" He finally put it together. Because he blogged about Alternate Reality Games, he knew who I was, but he had that great moment. He wasn't put in jeopardy. He wasn't being pulled out of his house. He wasn't being asked to get into a car. He wasn't being asked to do anything out of his comfort zone other than to reach out and take something that was being given to him. That's about as far as I ever

(Continued)

(Continued)

want it to go, because if you start taking things farther, it sounds cool but then you start getting into weird problems.

Even in the community, if there's a forum where I don't know who is a player and who is a character, then you become very paranoid for good reason and it becomes not fun anymore. Everybody looks at the movie *The Game* and says, "Wouldn't that be so cool?" In reality it's fraught with a lot of peril. Legally, too, you run great risks. For me, the safety of your audience is the biggest priority for these immersive experiences. You need the equivalent of a safe word. You've got to have a way that they can very quickly and easily either stop it or find out for sure if it's fake or real. We talk about fictional websites that are put up for campaigns from the future and talk about this cancer cure, but then cancer patients stumble onto it out of context, and they're applying for clinical trials for this new miracle drug and it's giving them hope and it's all fiction. There's ethical questions that need to be addressed.

An audience has to opt in. Even if it's a soft opt-in. There were times during *Dark Detour* where people had given us their phone numbers and later on we texted them in character, and if there was any indication that they were confused and didn't know if this was real or not, we would just back out because of that. You always have to be stopping to put yourself in the shoes of somebody who is stumbling on it and thinking, "What's the worst that can happen? What's the worst-use case?" and try and design against that.

John Bucher: Some conversations around VR ethics have turned to assurances that we don't eventually eliminate ourselves as a species off this planet. Any wisdom you would offer?

(Continued)

(Continued)

> Steve Peters: There's a design responsibility that I think game pub-
> lishers and developers need to embrace that basically
> says they will design responsibly and for good and not
> take advantage of people's lives and not take advan-
> tage of people's vulnerability. I think that's the respon-
> sibility of the developers. I would say just create an
> experience that in and of itself is a good experience,
> but not just a means to an end to generate income or
> to generate addiction that generates income. For the
> future, I would love to see a manifesto, the equivalent
> of the Hippocratic Oath, but for creators and design-
> ers, that says I will do no harm. Because while VR has
> the capability to do great good, it also has the capabil-
> ity to be very irresponsible.

CONCEPTS TO CONSIDER FROM STEVE PETERS

▶ Experiences should allow users to "opt in," making the line
between fiction and reality clear to any user that desires to be
aware of it.

▶ Creators should consider the variety of reactions that an audience
may have in a given experience. Feeling betrayed, hoaxed, or
unintelligent usually provides for an unpleasant experience for
many users.

▶ Audiences who engage an HMD are vulnerable and should be
treated with respect by responsible creators.

PUTTING IDEAS TOGETHER

Anyone who's watched another person experience VR for the first time
can appreciate Steve Peters's caution about the vulnerability of audiences.
A greater amount of trust is required of the audience than in perhaps
any previous medium of storytelling. These immediate concerns about

immersive narratives must be addressed in every new experience brought to market. However, the long-term ethical issues surrounding VR are greatly unknown. It is likely that we will see individuals become addicted to their virtual life and experiences, as has been the case with the internet. It is also likely that tremendous ethical challenges and questions await us that we have no way of determining. Creators and storytellers would do well to continually be asking questions of ethics in each phase of development with their experiences. Even if answers to these questions aren't readily available, keeping potential issues as part of the conversation will benefit users and creators alike.

EXERCISES

The following exercises may be helpful in creating a narrative for VR, AR, MR, and other immersive spaces.

EXERCISE 1

THE SEED IDEA

OBJECTIVE: 1.   To focus views of storytelling by identifying the two most important elements in a narrative you are familiar with—the **PROTAGONIST/MAIN CHARACTER** and the **EXTERNAL GOAL**.

2.   To capture ideas for potential narratives.

ASSIGNMENT

PART 1

▶   List your TOP 10 favorite films, games, television shows, plays, or novels of all time.

▶   Choose three stories from your list.

▶   Take each story and tell it in one sentence. The sentence should at a minimum have who the protagonist or main character is and the external goal—the one thing they are trying to accomplish in the narrative. Refer to the section on external goals if you have difficulty remembering what distinguishes the external from the internal goal.

PART 2

▶   Remove all character names from each sentence and replace them with a description of that character instead. For example, if you used Indiana Jones, replace him with a phrase such as "an adventure-seeking archeologist."

(Continued)

(Continued)

> ▶ Remove any specifics from the external goal and make it as general as possible. For example, if you said the character's external goal was "to find her kidnapped son," replace this with a phrase such as "to get back that which she values most."
>
> **PART 3**
>
> ▶ Take the character descriptions from each sentence and mix and match them with the external goals from other sentences. See if any new story ideas arise.
>
> **NOTE**
>
> ▶ Not all combinations will produce a logical narrative. However, some may spark an idea for a story that captures your interest.
>
> ▶ Consider the ramifications of each narrative in immersive space. Identify the advantages and disadvantages.

EXERCISE 2

DEVELOPING A MAIN CHARACTER

OBJECTIVE: 1.   To craft a character (protagonist/hero) with
enough substance to carry the narrative.

2.   To capture ideas for potential characters for future
narratives.

ASSIGNMENT

**Develop the MOST INTERESTING character that you can possibly
think of.** Use the checklist below to construct various areas of the character's life and personality.

Define each of the following characteristics:

▶   **Name:**

▶   **Gender:**

▶   **Age:**

▶   **Ethnicity:**

▶   **Socioeconomic Status:**

▶   **Occupation:**

▶   **Relationships Status:**

▶   **INTERNAL conflict** (Your protagonist's GHOST—What
haunts them?):

▶   **INTERNAL goal** (The thing they internally long for):

(Continued)

(Continued)

> ▶ **EXTERNAL goal** (HINT: The achievement of your protagonist's EXTERNAL goal should be visual. In other words, you should be able to take a picture of it.)
>
> ▶ **EXTERNAL conflict** (Antagonistic force):
>
> ▶ **Write a paragraph or two describing your protagonist in detail. Consider the role of immersive space in the ways the audience will encounter the character.**

EXERCISE 3

DEVELOPING A SIMPLE NARRATIVE

OBJECTIVE: 1. To craft a narrative with solid logic and structure.

2. To practice working with the narrative elements in constructing the overall narrative.

ASSIGNMENT

Develop the MOST INTERESTING narrative that you can possibly think of. Create *a two-paragraph pitch* of this narrative, but before you do, provide the following:

ONE-SENTENCE PITCH/LOGLINE: Tell your story in one sentence. The sentence should at a minimum have who the protagonist or main character is and the external goal—the one thing they are trying to accomplish in the narrative. Refer to the section on external goals if you have difficulty remembering what distinguishes the external from the internal goal.

WHO IS THE MAIN CHARACTER OR PROTAGONIST IN THE STORY? GIVE A BRIEF DESCRIPTION OF HIM OR HER. (See the *Developing a Main Character Exercise* if you have difficulty.)

WHAT IS THE ONE MEASURABLE, VISUAL "THING" YOUR MAIN CHARACTER IS TRYING TO ACCOMPLISH OR OVERCOME? (See the section on the *external goal* if you have difficulty.)

WHAT VISUAL CHOICE WILL YOUR CHARACTER MAKE AT THE END OF THE STORY SO THAT WE KNOW THEY HAVE ACCOMPLISHED THE EXTERNAL GOAL? (Remember, we cannot SEE a character "come to realize" or "learn" something. We have to SEE them perform an action that demonstrates they've learned or realized something.)

(Continued)

(Continued)

WHO OR WHAT IS THE ANTAGONIST OR ANTAGONISTIC FORCE
IN YOUR STORY? (See the section on the *antagonistic force* if
you have difficulty.)

COULD THE NARRATIVE WORK IN IMMERSIVE SPACE? Will there
be elements that lend themselves to the medium? Will other
elements work against the medium?

NOTES

1 Interview with *Wired* Magazine, October 2016.
2 De Cervantes Saavedra, Miguel and Edith Grossman. *Don Quixote*. New York: Ecco, 2003. Print.
3 O'Brien, Sara Ashley. "Developer on VR sexual assault: 'My heart sank.'" http:// money.cnn.com/2016/10/25/technology/developer-sexual-assault-virtual-reality/

6

Characters in VR

SOLVING FOR X

As has been mentioned earlier, formulas rarely remain consistent in the world of art making. Too often, storytelling is considered basic addition. While it would be tempting to try to establish a simplistic approach to storytelling within immersive space, something that resembled $(a + b = c)$, experience tells us that the reality is closer to $(a + x = c)$. We are then tasked to solve for x. In essence, storytelling more closely resembles algebra than addition. Our x factor can sometimes be a moving target with a number of variables that affect its form, shifting with genre, audience, and creation purpose. This is, of course, not to say that there are not standard principles that guide the use of algebra. There certainly are. In the same way that mathematicians use truths about the use of numbers in order to consider incredibly complex equations, we can take a similar approach with crafting narratives.

NARRATIVE SHARDS

Certain narrative elements are used in anything culture terms a story. We will refer to these elements as *narrative shards*. Imagine the larger world of story as a massive sheet of glass, containing every element that could be found in any flavor of narrative. If we broke that glass apart and examined the many pieces, we would have the shards that made up the larger whole. The concept of shards is perhaps more helpful as opposed to thinking of the larger whole of a story as a puzzle, with machine-cut pieces. The inexact nature and abstract shape of shards of glass serves as a better metaphor for how these elements are actually used. Certain Shards are quite general, such as characters. It is difficult to imagine anything that someone would refer to as a story without at least one character in the narrative. Other Shards, such as *contagonists*, might be less familiar to those outside the world of narrative studies. In many situations, Shards are the x factor in our story equation. We will often be unconsciously, but eventually consciously, asking what Shards can be most useful in a given narrative situation.

Narrative Shards are often found in experimental work and stories that don't always fit our traditional definitions of what a story is. For example, some of the work by filmmaker Terrence Malick more resembles visual poetry as opposed to classic storytelling. However, Malick always uses Narrative Shards combined with symbolic imagery in his work to craft thought-provoking explorations of themes. His work may or may not fit neatly within a three-act structure. However, we can easily identify Narrative Shards in every one of his films. The way that Shards will be used and arranged will depend on the artist. A similar metaphor would be to think of these Narrative Shards as colors on a painter's palette. The colors may be used individually to create a straightforward still-life image. However, the colors may also be mixed and combined to create an abstract concept that takes on different meanings with different viewers. If we consider the immersive piece we are designing as the canvas we will work with, we can play with mixing various Narrative Shards in order to craft our VR film, game, or experience. An entire text could be devoted to defining and exploring these Narrative Shards. However, here are a few Shards that will be helpful in the immersive realm. The definitions of some terms come from one of my previous books, *Master of the Cinematic Universe: The Secret Code to Writing in the New World of Media*, coauthored with Jeremy Casper.[1]

CHARACTERS

A character is generally a person, animal, or inanimate object. If the character is inanimate, the object usually takes on human characteristics. Characters, of course, are *who* the story is about. While some stories are crafted around *concepts*, we miss a compelling opportunity if we do not take advantage of the natural connection audiences have with characters. In immersive media such as VR, the character may very well be the viewer themselves.

PROTAGONIST

The protagonist is the main character of the story—sometimes called the hero or heroine. This is the character or characters through who the entire story unfolds. In some cases, several characters or a group of people will serve as the *protagonistic* force. In well-developed stories, the protagonist should have a very specific external goal he or she must pursue over the course of the story as well as an internal conflict that needs to be resolved. The protagonist must be a person capable of making a believable, proactive choice at the end of the story in order to reveal to the audience that they've completed their character arc. This holds true even if the viewer is the protagonist.

ANTAGONIST

The antagonist or antagonistic force is the opponent to the protagonist. It is a common misconception in storytelling that the antagonist's goal will be the exact opposite of the protagonist's. This method, however, would not maximize conflict in a narrative, as both characters could potentially accomplish their goals without ever confronting each other or even being in the same space. In well-crafted narratives, the protagonist and antagonist will want the *same thing*. Both football teams will want to win the big game. Both adventurers will want to find the ultimate treasure. Both the superhero and the supervillain will want control of the streets of the city. Both boys will want the same girl, and the list goes on.

CONFLICT

Conflict is the engine of story. It's what makes things move. Protagonists have little reason to go on any journey until conflict comes into their lives. Conflict may come in the form of another character (such as an antagonist), a ticking time bomb, a natural disaster, an inner demon, or any other force that presents a problem for the protagonist or the achieving of their goal.

EXTERNAL GOAL

The external goal is what the protagonist spends most of their time trying to achieve. Regardless of whether the protagonist likes the goal, the goal should be imperative. It should be the thing that drives them. In well-crafted stories, the ending will reveal whether the protagonist achieved their goal, and sometimes, it's more effective when the protagonist does *not* get what they *want* but instead gets what they *need*.

INTERNAL GOAL

The internal goal refers to what the protagonist wants most deeply—even more so than achieving their external goal. Many times, this will be to find love, to gain acceptance, or some other universal human need. Sometimes the internal goal is extremely obvious, but sometimes it's so nebulous it can't be articulated. Internal goals may or may not be necessary in some immersive experiences.

RESOLUTION

The resolution is the revelation of the answer to the problem the protagonist has been trying to solve—did they or did they not achieve their external goal? A good resolution also addresses the world in which the story took place—is the world now a better place after the protagonist has completed their journey?

EXTERNAL STORY

The external story refers to the external journey of a story's protagonist— what the protagonist *wants*. A good external story should have a clear external goal—something that, when achieved, can be seen or visually represented. This Shard is nearly essential for most immersive experiences.

INTERNAL STORY

The internal story refers to the internal journey of a story's protagonist— what the protagonist *needs*. The internal story requires that your main character have an internal weakness or flaw that needs to be fixed. While on their internal journey, the protagonist must discover and confront this weakness. In the end, the internal story reveals whether the protagonist's internal problem was resolved. While its use can be powerful, the internal story may or may not be seen in VR gaming experiences.

INTERNAL FLAW

The internal flaw is the inner weakness that the protagonist must overcome. The internal flaw often stems from lies the protagonist has come to believe about him- or herself. At the beginning of a well-constructed story, the protagonist is unaware of their internal flaw, but as the story progresses, they discover it and contend with it, and by the end, they have to choose whether or not to overcome it.

INCITING INCIDENT

Story gurus have called the inciting incident by many names over the years, but regardless of what they call it, they all agree you need one. The inciting incident is the moment that starts the story. It's the moment when the protagonist becomes aware of their external goal. After the inciting incident, nothing should remain the same for the protagonist. The inciting incident forces the protagonist to make a decision about whether to go on the journey.

REVERSAL

A Reversal occurs when something unexpected occurs in a story. This Shard can be especially effective if the audience is expecting a character to make one decision and they make the opposite choice. This idea can also refer to the changes of fortune that occur between the protagonist and antagonist as the story progresses.

CHARACTER ARC

Character arc refers to how the protagonist changes over the course of a story. In well-crafted stories, a character grows, develops, learns something, or realizes some truth by the end of the narrative. However, it's important to remember that these elements are part of a character's internal journey and not something the audience can experience directly like the external journey, unless they are the protagonist in the experience.

RESOLUTION

The resolution of the story is the revelation of the answer to the problem the protagonist has been trying to solve—did they or did they not achieve their external goal? A good resolution also addresses the world in which the story took place—is the world now a better place after the protagonist has completed their journey?

THE ROLE OF THE BODY IN IMMERSIVE STORIES

Many of the Narrative Shards are likely familiar to you, though you may have referred to them by different names. These story concepts are ancient and originated long before concepts such as VR had ever been conceived. To fully understand and embrace the usefulness of these ideas, however, it may be helpful to look at one philosophy in particular that helped us to arrive at our current understanding of users in immersive space, especially in interactive and embodied storytelling experiences such as video games.

While we could easily go back farther, a natural beginning place for any discussion on the ideas surrounding storytelling, bodies, and machines is René Descartes (1596–1650). Descartes formulated the modern version of the mind–body problem. Many scholars believe that, for Descartes, consciousness is the defining property of mind.[2] While the mind is fully present in VR space, the body, of course, is not. It is only represented with varying degrees of interactivity and agency. In the *Discourse*, Descartes presented the following argument to establish that mind and body are distinct substances:

> Next I examined attentively what I was. I saw that while I could pretend that I had no body and that there was no world and no place for me to be in, I could not for all that pretend that I did not exist. I saw on the contrary that from the mere fact that I thought of doubting

the truth of other things, it followed quite evidently and certainly that I existed; whereas if I had merely ceased thinking, even if everything else I had ever imagined had been true, I should have had no reason to believe that I existed. From this I knew I was a substance whose whole essence or nature is simply to think, and which does not require any place, or depend on any material thing, in order to exist.[3]

Later, in his work *Meditations*,[4] Descartes changed the structure of the argument. In the Second Meditation, he established that he could not doubt the existence of himself as a thinking thing but that he could doubt the existence of matter. However, he explicitly refused to use this situation to conclude that his mind was distinct from his body, on the grounds that he was still ignorant of his nature.[5] This mind–body debate has continued to rage throughout the present age. In VR, there is still a divide between the mind and the body, though most would agree that it is only a matter of time before mediated representations of the body will mirror our actual organic beings to such a degree that they may be indistinguishable. The distinctions and nuances surrounding the discussion of the mind and the body are significant for creating a new language to explore immersive environments and stories. We must be realistic about where we are with the technology that drives the distinctions. However, we should also be aware of where the technology will likely go and try not to be limited in what we imagine to be possible. In part five of his work titled *Discourse on Method*, Descartes examines the nature of animals and how they are to be distinguished from human beings. Here Descartes argues that if a machine were made with the outward appearance of some animal lacking reason, like a monkey, it would be indistinguishable from a real specimen of that animal found in nature. But if such a machine of a human being were made, it would be readily distinguishable from a real human being due to its inability to use language. Descartes' point is that the use of language is a sign of rationality, and only things endowed with minds or souls are rational.[6] Of course, he never lived to see the computer age or modern AI technology that would seriously call his assumptions into questions.

While Descartes' ideas have been vastly updated through philosophical history, Cartesian dualism and thinking brings up important matters to question and consider as we design experiences for viewers in immersive space. As human beings enter virtual space, especially in environments as immersive as VR, do the human principles that have upheld our philosophical approaches to life and thus informed our stories still apply, or do we begin to develop new ideas and philosophies that consider the mechanical forms we have assumed in this new space? Do all humans experience their bodies the same way? What are the challenges and perhaps ethical dilemmas of creating experiences that further blur the lines between the mind and the body? Historian Michael Saler has argued that "realized worlds" of role-playing games (and perhaps video games in general) go beyond the restraints of Cartesian dualism. However, the concept remains important to the full understanding of embodied interactive and gaming experiences and serves as a grounding for the future potential of the relationship between the mind and the body.

THE ROLE OF AVATARS IN VIRTUAL IMMERSIVE SPACE

Our current technology allows one a completely different external self, apart from his or her body, in the form of an avatar. We can assume the complexity and realism associated with avatars will only continue to develop and gain traction. The term *avatar* refers to a Hindu concept that literally means "descent." It refers to the incarnation or appearance of the divine on earth. Gods such as Vishnu or Ganesha could take a physical form and appear to and interact with humans on earth. The forms or avatars that the God could take were many and varied. This mythological origin gives us our modern understanding of avatars. In virtual spaces, avatars refer to our embodiment in a virtual space. Gaming has long used the concept of avatars to invite players into more immersive experiences. Social media and similar experiences on the internet have furthered the concept of what an avatar in virtual space could be.

VR, AR, and MR, however, offer us an experience in using avatars that we have never seen before. Now we are not only afforded an external presence or body in virtual space, but that body can be completely designed around our preferences. We can now *be* whoever we want to be with greater realism than we have ever known. In considering the role of avatars in narrative environments, we should remember that avatars have always been and still present themselves as *characters* in a story. Avatars that will bring a viewer or player further into an experience will be those who have been brought through the same rigorous character development that those who develop film, television, and gaming content employ. Well-developed characters or avatars will give those who embody them the experience of actually *being* the figure they inhabit.

SPOTLIGHT ON ACTING: Storytelling through Drama
in Immersive Experiences
Keight Leighn, Actress

Keight Leighn is a Los Angeles–based actress with a background in Chicago theater. She has played lead roles in a number of immersive theatrical experiences. Her work has been recognized by the Hollywood Fringe Festival for her role in *(A)partment 8,* a production that was lauded by *LA Weekly* in 2016 as Most Extreme Audience Immersion in a theatrical production.

John Bucher:	Did you go to school for theater? Did you have an epiphany moment where you became interested?
Keight Leighn:	I studied theater at DePaul University but started doing summer stock when I was eight, thanks to my grandmother. I also have two sisters, and they're both actors. There was no epiphany moment, but this is what I love, and this is what I'm going to do. With theater, you have a family backstage, and when you learn that young, you don't let go of it easily. I went into experimental theater when I was in high school. The drama teacher there liked to be controversial, let the students write their own stuff that was about incest or whatever topics, because that sort of honesty makes good theater. That introduced me to experimental theater. Then I went to the Ontological-Hysteric Theater in New York and asked if I could sweep their floors one summer, because I couldn't fathom a summer without doing theater. They said, "Well, we do have an internship, but it's usually for people in college." They interviewed me. I got the internship and slept on a yoga mat in a closet in Brooklyn for the summer. I learned New York experimental theater and the intensity that comes with artists that are in that world.

(Continued)

(Continued)

	I started performing with this punk rock band, a self-described cabaret punk rock band. The singer and I just really hit it off on a performance level, so I would start creating performances. I did that for a while, and that really shaped a lot of my walking past this threshold of fear.
John Bucher:	Let's talk a little bit about the first time you were approached with a piece that was an immersive experience. How did the director describe it to you? How did she paint this picture? I'm sure she didn't just say, "It's a play."
Keight Leighn:	I think she literally said, "You'll be interacting with the audience. It's going to be like speed dating, and you're going to have these character arcs, and then the audience members are going to change seats and you're going to continue your story as this character. You're allowed to respond to them if they ask you questions and engage with you, but I'm going to be writing this character through the rehearsal process that is developed for you."
John Bucher:	How did you go about preparing for the character that you had in that first piece? What did that look like?
Keight Leighn:	The director developed the script and the characters by asking us questions. Then she would give us this piece of the story and direct us to answer questions a certain way. Then she started writing based off of our characters and the story lines coming from the answers to our questions. Finally, she would send the actual script. By that point, we had gotten there in this organic way, so it wasn't that much of a hop at all, because we weren't starting with a script.
John Bucher:	Did you have exact lines you had to say?

(Continued)

(Continued)

Keight Leighn:	Yes. There were these certain beats we had to hit in order for the story to be created in the piece. You'd find out these character stories were weaved in as you heard other characters' stories.
John Bucher:	What did you learn through that first experience?
Keight Leighn:	You always have a way out. Even with the craziest people that could be throwing you totally side balls, just because they want to see if they can knock you off. That's what they're there for. Just sit and connect. That's all you've got to do. You'll figure it out, and you'll figure out how to make your story work. You've just got to learn to work on a live wire. In summer stock, when I was a kid, a bat once flew out, because it was in a barn. That's the magic of theater. You have to work within the moment, and it's alive.
John Bucher:	With immersive experiences, there's already a heightened level of trust between actor and audience. Were you thinking about that? Did you decide if somebody does something weird, I'll respond to it? How did you approach that?
Keight Leighn:	By default, I trusted people. I had to.
John Bucher:	Did you find men and women responded differently? Was it just all individual responses?
Keight Leighn:	It's interesting because they did respond differently. I think men were a little more difficult, but it's not necessarily what you think. It's more that there's this alpha presence verses another alpha presence—so who's controlling the situation? Some people are really hard. They're just not going to let you in.
John Bucher:	Sometimes it becomes about an energy and communication beyond what the language area of the brain can process?

(Continued)

(Continued)

Keight Leighn:	Heidegger would call it the clearing. It's the poetry. It's where new language has to be created because it's just this clearing to something else.
John Bucher:	Is there a Meisner equivalent in interactive theater?
Keight Leighn:	You can do anything, that's the point of immersive theater to me.
John Bucher:	The energy that's going back and forth rather than a technique?
Keight Leighn:	That was so essential, just being on your toes with their every microexpression.
John Bucher:	What would you say to an actor who has never done any sort of immersive theater before and who has been hired now to be a part of an immersive experience? How should they prepare for this experience?
Keight Leighn:	It depends on who it is that's acting—their personality. How that needs to be, how they need to shape that to interactive theater. You're going to be probably working a really different muscle than you have before. Not hugely different, but still. You want the audience to go through an experience, that's the goal. Ask yourself, what's that goal in the experience? That comes first. Then if you're an actor who has trouble letting go or get upset when anybody does anything wrong, I think all of those things need to 100% go out the window, because you just have to come into it with this mentality that you're riding a wild horse. The goal is to get it to bring you home. You have to either trick it, or you have to feed it, or you have to beat it. Use what you know about yourself.

CONCEPTS TO CONSIDER FROM KEIGHT LEIGHN

▶   Performing in immersive space requires a certain fearlessness on the part of the actor.

▶ There is a heightened level of trust between actor and audience in immersive environments.

▶ A deep understanding of oneself is helpful when performing in an immersive experience.

PUTTING IDEAS TOGETHER

Animation and digitally crafted characters allow creators to tell stories in ways never possible before. There is a certain comfort in knowing that a fellow human being is responsible for communicating the nuances of a story to you. The term *uncanny valley* has been used to describe the gap that still exists between the believability of our most lifelike digital creations and actual human beings. There's something within us, which is difficult to articulate, that knows when we encounter a being that looks like us, talks like us, and acts like us but somehow just isn't one of us. Advances in AI will continue to move forward, and we may very well one day create machines that achieve human-like consciousness. The more significant issue will be whether we can endow those beings with a conscience. Until that time, human beings, with all their flaws, nuances, and idiosyncrasies, will be what makes immersive experiences *fully* immersive.

THE VR PROTAGONIST

The most significant character or avatar that will be developed for an immersive experience will be that of the protagonist. Creators have used a number of methods to identify their protagonist to their audience, depending on the medium. In novels, many times the protagonist is actually the character *telling* the audience the story. In theater, supporting characters often discuss or refer to the protagonist in scenes before they actually appear on stage. In film, a combination of techniques including lighting, lens focus, and positioning the protagonist in prominent times and places in the story have been used. However, VR is a new canvas. We must take elements from other disciplines to establish our protagonist, as well as establishing new ones.

Establishing a Protagonist with Position, Light, and Dialogue

The visual language associated with film has become familiar to many audiences. Movie attendance is at an all-time high, and several generations have now grown up speaking "the language of cinema." Historically, several tropes were used in filmmaking that indicated to the audience that the person they were seeing was the protagonist of the story. Some of these tropes can still be helpful to us today. As we have stated throughout the text, these are *forms* that can be used not *rules* that must be followed. A method Hollywood used for many years to indicate the protagonist was to make that character the first to appear on screen. Because our brains tend to make meaning by ordering things and placing structure around what we see, the first character on screen gave the audience a starting place. It placed the character at the top of the dramatic pyramid they would see unfold. It was important that the audience be able to see the character's face and, even more importantly, the *eyes* of the character. The first character we saw was usually also the first to speak. We quickly became familiar with what this character looked like, how they sounded, and their mannerisms before introducing any other characters in to the narrative. As viewers need some time to orient when placing an HMD on their heads, using this technique to establish the protagonist can be helpful.

Some stories open with two or more characters speaking or interacting, so using the technique described here can be difficult. In cases such as these, the protagonist can still be positioned either in the center of the frame or toward the right axis in order to establish dominance. Sometimes it can be helpful to place the protagonist slightly forward of any other character. This can be especially helpful when working with the z-axis in immersive environments. Lighting remains a field experiencing the growing pains of a new technology in immersive narratives. Many creators work with animated content in VR specifically to avoid the challenges it creates. Still, there are a number of ways to use lighting as a practical element in immersive environments. There are also a number of production techniques that allow for shooting with staged lighting, eliminating the equipment in postproduction at a later time, so we should not discount this element as a tool for helping to establish the protagonist. Protagonists are usually shown in the most established lighting available. Some scenes allow the protagonist to begin in a poorly lit area and then step in to established lighting, giving the viewer a visual cue that this character is now stepping into prominence in the story.

As mentioned earlier, early Hollywood techniques had the protagonist speaking first in the story, a technique that can still be useful. However, even if another character opens a scene by speaking first, the protagonist should be the *driving force* in the dialogue of most scenes. This indicates to the viewer that the protagonist is not a victim, which audiences have historically had less empathy for. Instead, when the protagonist drives the conversation, they are positioned to make the difficult decisions in the narrative, causing the audience to relate to their plight in more invested ways. This, of course, does not mean that the protagonist never displays weakness. Skilled writers will learn how to allow the protagonist to forward the character and his or her story through vulnerability as well. This vulnerability can be established in dialogue. More than a century of cinematic stories have taught viewers to look for the protagonist to be the character *most capable of change*—the character we are most likely to see *arc*. If your narrative does not give space for the character to make a difficult decision or learn something near the end of their journey, there is a greater risk for the viewer to have less investment in the story.

Establishing a Protagonist for First-Person-Viewer Narratives

Of course, in VR, the viewer is often the protagonist in the narrative. This will eliminate some techniques from potential use and greatly expand others. While lighting and dialogue become less significant, position remains important. A balance must be struck between the interesting places the viewer can be positioned in VR and establishing the viewer's role as the protagonist. Granted, because human beings generally feel like the protagonists in their own life stories, first-person experiences tend to allow the viewer to feel as though they are the protagonist by default. However, just because an experience allows the viewer the first-person point of view (POV) does not necessarily mean they are the protagonist in the experience. Not only does where we position the viewer in the space become important but where we position them in the narrative as well.

As mentioned in the previous section, viewers are entering VR experiences with many established ideas about the ways that visual narratives work. If a viewer is to feel as though they are the protagonist in the experience, they must feel as though they are the driving force. This is true in both gaming and cinematic experiences. Viewers will feel as though they are driving the narrative if they recognize they are capable of change, are able to make decisions, or can learn something throughout the course of the journey. We often refer to these elements as the viewer's *agency* in the experience. The degree and varied ways that viewers will experience change in a narrative can depend on a number of factors. Whether the experience is interactive or cinematic, the purpose of the experience, and length of time spent in the immersive space all affect the viewer's ability to experience change. How the viewer changes will depend on a wide field of factors as well. For example, in a VR gaming experience, the viewer may change by simply acquiring more weapons or powers than they began with. Knowing that these changes are possible at the beginning of the narrative is an important part of the viewer's psychological experience if they are to feel some degree of reward or satisfaction with the narrative.

Change only occurs when the protagonist, in this case the viewer, is allowed to make decisions or at least feels as though they have made decisions. A viewer in a cinematic experience feels as though they too have made a decision when the character on screen makes a decision the viewer feels *they would have made as well.* Some genres generate success by allowing the viewer to feel the *opposite* of this. In the horror genre, the viewer may feel a sense of exhilaration when the protagonist chooses to open a door they would not have opened in real life. This experience can work even when the viewer is in a cinematic narrative, where they technically did not make the decision. Viewers feel they have *learned* something when they have experienced the *theme* of the narrative. In this case, the term "learn" refers to the neurological reward a viewer feels when they resonate strongly with an idea or feel they are slightly different in some way than when they began the experience. In the case of the horror experience mentioned earlier, the theme might be as simple as not opening doors when we don't know what is behind them. In that particular experience, the viewer would *experience* this theme by opening the door and contending with whatever horror lay before them. Because of the emotional needs viewers tend to express when in an experience, either interactive or cinematic, discussions on theme should be prioritized in the development process.

ESTABLISHING THE EXTERNAL GOAL OF THE VR PROTAGONIST

Once we have established who the protagonist is in the experience, there are several other factors that should quickly be determined. First among these is the external goal of the protagonist. The external goal will be what we *see* the character accomplish on screen, as opposed to some sort of change or accomplishment that occurs *within* him or her. The external goal should be made clear early in the experience, unless the entire purpose is allowing the viewer to explore and wander. It should be recognized that many viewers will quickly tire of these sorts of experiences, however, unless a goal or narrative is introduced. The quicker the viewer knows what they are supposed to be doing in the experience, the quicker they can become engaged.

Many creators struggle with the external goal, often confusing it with internal processes. For example, finding love is not an effective external goal, as this happens within a character's psyche. Technically, we cannot *see* someone find love. We cannot take a picture of it. We can only see moments that would seem to indicate this has taken place. The viewer has no way of actually knowing if this has really occurred. Thus, we can never truly know if the goal has been accomplished or not. On the other hand, finding a date to the prom is an effective external goal. We can *see* that this goal has been accomplished. We can take a picture of it. The "picture test" is a good way to determine if you have established an effective external goal.

ESTABLISHING THE INTERNAL GOAL OF THE VR PROTAGONIST

Internal goals can be difficult to execute in narrative experiences, especially when the experience revolves around something very external, like, say, killing zombies. Even if the external goal is simply inferred, the audience psychologically seeks *why* we want to kill these zombies. If there are reasons beyond zombies simply being *bad* or *disgusting*, the audience will have deeper investment in the experience. Simple narrative motivations such as establishing that zombies killed the protagonist's father can provide enough impetus for a believable internal goal—which in this case might be to avenge the character's father's death. The simpler the immersive experience, the simpler the internal goal is likely to be. However, internal goals that reinforce the theme of an experience are often *why* people return to certain narratives even after they know how the plot points will play out.

The internal goal is oftentimes something the protagonist is completely unaware of in third-person experiences. Other characters may reference it at the beginning of the story, but the protagonist learns what this internal goal is over the course of the narrative. It is the lesson the character learns. In first-person narratives, the internal goal may never be directly stated. It may be inferred as a motivation for the character the viewer is stepping in to. Because viewers bring such varied experiences with them into immersive space, the internal goal should always be universal and archetypal when possible, ensuring that the largest percentage of the audience will resonate with it. Knowing what the theme of the experience you're designing is helps you craft the internal goal of the protagonist. If you can identify that the experience you are creating explores the theme of forgiveness or overcoming fear or confronting loneliness, the execution of the internal goal within your protagonist is much easier, as these elements should be connected. Because present VR technology lends itself to singular experiences for an audience of one, the internal goal may be more focused or nuanced or potentially personal if you are aware of the specifics of the demographic that will be engaging the experience.

THE VR ANTAGONIST

After the protagonist has been created in your experience, attention should be given to crafting the second most significant character—that of the antagonist. In some narratives, there is an antagonist force as opposed to having the opposition situated solely in one character. This force might be an institution such as the government, a force of nature such as a tornado, or a supernatural force such as zombies. Regardless of whether the force is centralized in a single character or represented by a group or concept, there should be *something* opposing the protagonist's accomplishment of his or her goal. For the sake of simplicity here, we will simply refer to any and all these possibilities as the antagonist. The antagonist should be just as motivated as the protagonist to accomplish their goal. The stakes they face should be just as high. In other words, the protagonist and the antagonist should be equally matched.

One of the ways to ensure that the protagonist and antagonist are equally matched is to make sure that the antagonist has a strong argument for accomplishing their goal. It should only be their motivation or method that is flawed. Luke Skywalker and Darth Vader both want control of the galaxy. They have different *reasons* why they fight for this goal, however. They have different ways of going about accomplishing their goal. Vader has a strong argument for the success of the Empire. He wants to bring order to chaos. His order comes with an iron fist, however, where Skywalker's is laced with freedom. In *Star Wars*, we see two competing philosophies fighting for the hearts of the audience. Evenly matched antagonists with strong arguments will keep the audience engaged in the narrative as the conflict unfolds.

Establishing an Antagonist with Position, Light, and Dialogue

Once a protagonist has been visually established in a narrative, the antagonist will be easier to identify, as much from their actions as from anything else. However, there are several techniques that can be helpful in visually establishing some antagonists. Where the antagonist is positioned on screen will likely be established by where the protagonist is situated. However, positioning the antagonist in shadows, corners, and off-axis does give the viewer the cue that there is something to be investigated further with the character. Creating shadows on the antagonist's face with lighting can also indicate the *shadowed nature* of the character visually. Bringing the antagonist closer to the protagonist or the viewer can be effective but does tend to raise tension in a scene and can make the viewer feel threatened, which may be exactly what the creator is attempting to accomplish.

There is often a temptation with creators to most fully execute antagonists through dialogue. While some dialogue is usually necessary in establishing the motivations and methods of the character, this can easily create uninteresting situations for the viewer in which the antagonist explains the plot of the narrative to another character. What we *see* the antagonist do is more important than what we hear them *say* in any visual narrative. Oftentimes, having the antagonist say one thing but do another can increase their villainous and hypocritical nature, making the audience more actively root against them and their goals. Dialogue is important to crafting a successful antagonist, but relying too heavily on it will cause greater narrative problems for the creator.

Establishing an Antagonist for First-Person-Viewer Narratives

Some experiences may allow the viewer to actually *be* the antagonist in the story. In this case, we will want to take most of the elements we use to craft the protagonist mentioned earlier and apply them to the antagonist. The fun for the viewer in these experiences will be knowing just how flawed their moral argument is but still getting to pursue it anyway—a psychological fantasy many human beings enjoy and that can be healthy in certain situations. Even when the viewer is not directly the antagonist in the narrative, they very well might fit the definition of an antihero, to whom many of the same principles would apply.

ADDITIONAL CHARACTERS

Most narratives will expand beyond the journeys of the protagonist and the antagonist. Additional characters can be some of the most memorable and fun for the viewer. It is important, however, that additional characters have a narrative purpose. This purpose is usually related to either the protagonist or the antagonist and their respective goals. These characters, in some sense, should either be helping the protagonist move toward their goal or actively pushing the character away from their goal. These characters come in many forms and represent a great many archetypes. The best friend, the sidekick, the wise old sage, the minion, the bitter coworker, and the annoying boss all have their place in the narrative world.

EXERCISE 4

DEVELOPING A MORE ADVANCED NARRATIVE

OBJECTIVE: 1. To craft a more advanced narrative with solid logic and structure.

2. To practice working with the narrative elements in constructing the overall narrative.

ASSIGNMENT

Use the instructions for the previous exercise to create *a two-page pitch* of a new narrative, but this time, do not allow yourself to use any of the techniques below, as they can *sometimes* be crutches in crafting narratives:

▶ No voiceovers

▶ No flashbacks, flashforwards, or adjusting real time

▶ No dream sequences

▶ No stories that take place inside people's heads

▶ No inanimate objects as main characters

▶ No demon possession/schizophrenia in main characters*

▶ No mentally disabled main characters*

▶ No main characters who are homeless*

▶ No main characters who struggle with OCD*

▶ No main characters who struggle with addiction*

▶ No characters incapable of change

(Continued)

(Continued)

* While these struggles can make a character seemingly more interesting, they also saddle the character with issues they are usually incapable of changing in a believable amount of time. If you choose to work with a character that struggles with one of these issues, the narrative should *not* be about the character trying to overcome the issue.

EXERCISE 5

RECOGNIZING AN ANTAGONISTIC FORCE

OBJECTIVE: 1. To demonstrate the ability to identify the characteristics of a strong antagonistic force in a story.

IDENTIFY 20 STRONG ANTAGONISTS OR ANTAGONISTIC FORCES from stories that you enjoy. Name the character, the story they are identified with, and the character's external goal. (Remember that a strong antagonist will have the same goal as the protagonist. See the section on *Antagonistic Forces* if you have difficulty.)

ANTAGONIST/ANTAGONISTIC FORCE:

STORY:

EXTERNAL GOAL:

EXERCISE 6

IDENTIFYING THE INTERNAL JOURNEY

OBJECTIVE: 1.   To demonstrate the ability to identify the internal
journey in a story and utilize it to strengthen the
external journey.

**IDENTIFY 5 STORIES IN WHICH THE PROTAGONIST GOES ON
A SIGNIFICANT INTERNAL JOURNEY.**

Write two pages about how this internal journey enhances and affects
the external journey that we see carried out. Identify the internal goal
and conflict of the character as well. Also, discuss how the storyteller
gave external cues as to what was happening with the character's internal journey.

STORY:

PROTAGONIST:

INTERNAL JOURNEY/GOAL/CONFLICT:

VISUAL CUES ABOUT INTERNAL JOURNEY:

NOTES

1 Bucher, John and Jeremy Casper. *Master of the Cinematic Universe: The Secret Code to Writing in the New World of Media.* Los Angeles: Michael Weise Productions, 2016. Print.
2 Rozemond, Marleen. *Descartes's Dualism.* Cambridge: Harvard University Press, 1998.
3 Descartes, René. Discourse on Method. 6:32–33. N.p. Broadview, 2017. Print.
4 Descartes, René. Laurence J. Lafleur. Meditations on First Philosophy. 7:27. Indianapolis: Bobbs-Merrill, 1951. Print.
5 Ibid.
6 Stanford Encyclopedia of Philosophy Online. www.iep.utm.edu/descarte/#SH8d

7

Creating Narrative Structures

There has been disagreement about the role of structure when writing stories for visual mediums. Writers of film, television, games, and even comic books have often bristled at the idea of needing dramatic structure in their medium. This problem is somewhat unique to the art form of writing. Few musicians bristle at the idea of using notes, measures, keys, and chords. Few painters refuse to use shades of blue because other painters have done so in the past. Few architects try to avoid including windows, doors, floors, and ceilings in a home only because every other livable home has included these same elements. Yes, many writers spend a great deal of time trying to avoid any familiar trope that an audience might recognize. There is certainly something to be said for creativity. However, many creators fail to recognize that basic narrative structure is actually based on the way human brains solve problems. Structure provides a natural chemical reward to the brain when a viewer sees patterns in the narrative they are watching. These patterns allow the viewer to create meaning from the experience. This was stated at the beginning of this book but bears repeating in this discussion:

Structure is about form, not formula.

As a matter of review, basic three-act structure was first articulated by Aristotle in his *Poetics*. Essentially, Aristotle states that stories should have a beginning, middle, and end. He is more elusive about exactly what should be included in each of these three sections. Many instructors have outlined possibilities for what works best when detailing beats and moments throughout each act. For those interested in greater detail, the work of Syd Field and Chris Vogler is essential. Rather than outline the precise beats that could structure a narrative within each act, we will instead examine a broader perspective. Refer to Chapter 5 for a more detailed look at each act in three-act structure. Before examining structure further, it should be stated that three-act structure is not the only possible way of approaching narrative. Other structures certainly exist. There are also narratives that completely ignore three-act structure and take a more abstract approach that have been successful. However, these stories have been executed by artistic masters, the ranks of which are much slimmer than we would care to admit. In a sense, three-act structure takes advantage of the constructs that already exist in the mind of the audience. Efficiency can be an essential tool in efforts to engage viewers with modern attention spans.

METAPHOR, SYMBOLISM, AND IRONY

While structure is the skeleton that must be present to create a living, breathing narrative, it is the flesh, hair, and features that truly make a creation unique. Clever uses of metaphor, symbolism, and irony can compose those features. Finding ways to incorporate these elements seamlessly into your narrative will create a greater sense of audience engagement and enjoyment.

METAPHOR

As fundamental review, metaphor means for us to compare two ideas by presenting one idea *directly* as the other idea. Imagine a scene in a narrative where two partners decide to end their marriage. We could have these two characters discuss the reasons why the relationship must end. This is using dialogue to explain the plot to the viewer. We should remember, however, that we are working within a visual medium. A more powerful scene would simply have one partner taking a key off their key ring and sliding it across the table to the other. This scene would then be incorporating visual metaphor in order to demonstrate the end of the relationship. This image is more powerful than any piece of dialogue could be.

SYMBOLISM

In the visual scenario, the key becomes a symbol for the relationship. Rather than only having it present in one scene, we would do well to find other ways to incorporate this symbol into various scenes throughout the narrative. It is notable that the key itself doesn't directly have innate qualities that link it to a relationship. This keeps the symbol from being pandering to the audience. The risk in symbolism is walking the line between allowing the audience to comprehend the symbol and making it so obvious they feel it is insulting.

IRONY

While potentially having a variety of meanings in a narrative, for our purposes, irony refers to the ending of a story and the relationship between the external narrative (wants/desires) and the internal narrative (needs). As briefly mentioned in Chapter 6, there are four types of endings in narratives structured around a hero and his or her journey:

1. Positive—the protagonist gets both what they want and what they need.

2. Positive irony—the protagonist gets what they need but not what they want.

3. Negative irony—the protagonist gets what they want but not what they need.

4. Negative—the protagonist gets neither what they want nor what they need.

CREATING AN INCITING INCIDENT OR CATALYST IN VR

Every story needs a moment that accelerates the narrative action. Something should happen early in the experience that gives the protagonist a reason he or she must go on their journey. It might be a phone call informing them of a death in the family, the reappearance of an old lover, or the purchase of a house that some claim to be haunted. All these scenarios provide us the opportunity to establish each character's goals, motivations, and plans for success. With VR, this incident might actually be the viewer finding themselves in immersed virtual space, especially in a first-person experience. This may provide all the momentum we need for the viewer to begin their journey. However, many times, this incident will be more dramatically significant. It will quickly move the characters into pursuit of their goals. Even in first-person experiences, the viewer can be further engaged in the narrative after finding themselves in the virtual space, with an event that acts as a "starting clock" for them to accomplish their task. While the first few moments of any narrative often give the participants orientation, it is this inciting incident that accelerates the conflict for all involved—protagonist, antagonist, and supporting characters.

TYPES OF INCITING INCIDENTS

Propelling the protagonist into the narrative action can be achieved through a variety of approaches. While no inclusive list exists, following are a few approaches that may be helpful when creating inciting incidents for immersive experiences.

The Magical Opportunity

An unexpected magical opportunity or gifting is most effective when the narrative has already established that a protagonist's life is either monotonous or difficult. However, in gaming and interactive experiences, the magical opportunity is inherent upon entering the virtual space. In more developed narratives, a strict theme emerges from stories that offer their protagonist such opportunities—you cannot use magic to solve your problems. Near the end of the narrative, the protagonist is usually required to reject or dispose of the magic. This will often be the lesson the protagonist must learn over the course of the story. Again, gaming and interactive experiences with less complicated levels of narrative may be the exception.

The Test

A major challenge is forced on the protagonist in order to have the life he or she wants in narratives in which the inciting incident introduces a test. The test often comes just after some major component of the protagonist's identity has been taken away or threatened. The test may be multilayered and involve levels of riddles, endurance, and conflict. If a test is presented as the inciting incident of the story, there should be either an implicit or explicit moment in the narrative, in which the protagonist accepts the challenge. Audiences tend to root for active protagonists *who make choices* as opposed to victims who simply are *thrown from scenario to scenario*.

An Enemy Arises

When the life of the protagonist is thrown into chaos by the arrival of an unexpected force, he or she must choose to confront the emerging enemy or lose what is important to them. As discussed earlier in the section on the antagonist, this force may or may not be concentrated in a central character. It is worth noting, however, that audiences often more quickly relate to the struggle of the protagonist when their opposition has a *face*. Usually defeating the enemy that has arisen, the protagonist must sacrifice something important to them or overcome a flaw within their own life.

The Missing Piece

Inciting incidents in which a missing piece of the protagonist's life is introduced usually present this piece in the form of another person. It becomes clear to the protagonist that if they could only win this person over, life would be better. Unfortunately, the "missing piece" is reluctant to fill that hole initially and must be persuaded or won over. Again, this inciting incident is often connected to a theme. In these narratives, the protagonist must usually come to recognize that "missing pieces" are not possessions to be had but instead actual people that must be engaged with and sacrificed for. The protagonist only becomes complete when they realize that this *person* is not the missing piece, but that thing inside them that they had refused to face completes their psyche and makes the healthy relationship with someone else possible. Of course, this lesson may involve losing the "missing piece" altogether. While many VR narratives have been focused on very external experiences, the future of immersive experiences will no doubt involve more nuanced internal journeys in which viewers are thrust into worlds where they will confront their most basic desires and struggles.

SPOTLIGHT ON VISUALIZATION: Cinematic Storytelling in VR
Chris Edwards, Founder, Chief Production Officer, and CEO, The Third Floor

Chris Edwards is the founder and CEO of The Third Floor, the world's leading previsualization studio, which services up to 40 major studio

---

(Continued)

(Continued)

feature films each year. Recent credits include Marvel franchises like Avengers and X-Men, the new *Godzilla*, *Gravity*, and many more. He began his career in digital cinematography at Disney before working for George Lucas at Skywalker Ranch.

John Bucher: You're someone who's had quite an accomplished history in storytelling, before we even get to VR. Can we talk about that first moment when you experienced VR? What were your thoughts?

Chris Edwards: Well, for me, VR reminded me instantly of two other big experiences I had in my life, long before VR even existed. That is the theater and theatrical events and, secondly, going to the theme park. I feel like the theater is a lot like VR because, of course, you as the director of the theatrical experience have the ability to place all of these people and objects and set pieces, and rearrange them, and do these transitions, and yet, you know that even sometimes, the actors can break the fourth wall, they can go down the aisle, they can go past the proscenium. If you go to a Cirque du Soleil show, there are people dangling from bungee cords sometimes. If you go to Pink Floyd's *The Wall*, you see tons of things that involve the audience, involving multiple forms of media and physical objects all around you.

When I first saw VR, I wasn't too impressed with what was actually happening, because I knew that it had been done before, in reality. Along the lines of the theme park, it was very similar. The whole point of it is to go beyond the movie or the franchise or the character and actually step into that character's world. Even in the original Disneyland, you could go in and be part of Sleeping Beauty's story, or one of the Disney classics, yet it's all a bunch of mechanical gags and different pieces of

(Continued)

(Continued)

artwork that pop up at the right time. That's still very effective.

Fast-forward to all these panels that are talking about the film language of VR. Scientists are getting up on those panels and saying, "Well, this is so new, we will not know the full language of this for many generations, and it's a long process, and we really don't have many conclusions yet." I say, "Well, no, we actually do have a lot of conclusions. There are certain things about VR that are custom to this new medium, for sure. Still, the large majority of it is based on traditional directing in film, before film even existed. Film was just the medium that had to put it in a rectangle. Now we're going beyond the rectangle.

One of my soapboxes is that a lot of people still think that VR is a binary decision, it's an on or off switch. You have to use full 360, or nothing. You're back to the traditional medium. I think you can play with how much of the environment you show. Sometimes, 180 degrees works just fine. You can put floating windows out there, of different media. The impact of that switch from the choices of individual little shots collaged to one big image is undeniable.

I think that the language of VR is actually quite sophisticated and will increasingly create new subgenres of media within VR. There's a lot of people impressed by certain introductory forms of VR, where you are in a place, and it's a slice of life of that place, and that works well for news, it works well for documentaries, but from the moment that someone steps into that type of VR experience, it starts feeling quite realistic to them and they want

(Continued)

to move forward. But they can't. They can't even lean from side to side. There's no parallax. It's still just a prescribed image that's the same for everyone. You get to see a different swath of it than what someone else would have chosen to see.

I think that that form of VR, the 360 video VR, is going to look very simple, and perhaps not of interest to many consumers, unless it reaches a certain level of artistry, crafted by the best Hollywood filmmakers that use it in such an innovative way, where you're actually entertained, looking around the 360 or different aspects of that for a sustained amount of time. I think the vast majority of the audience out there is going to, in short order, get addicted to, or become enamored with an ability to at least have more sense of presence in VR, and by that, they need to at least have some area that they can at least lean, if not move, into the space, and probably do some limited form of interaction.

John Bucher: Let's build on that for a moment, because I think it's important. I was talking to Jessica Brillhart over at Google, and we were speaking about the nature of experience and the need for experiences in our current culture. Can you connect what you're talking about to that, philosophically? Why is sometimes the 180 or the 270 experience enough?

Chris Edwards: I think fundamentally, what's cool about VR is that you can experience something that someone else experienced, and you can add those experiences to your own collection, that enriches your life. I think it's the same way that people tend to download iTunes music that they identify with, that has been authored by other people but remains a unique sound that you admire, and that gives you a certain

(Continued)

emotional feeling. Whether or not you actually listen to the whole album, it feels good, it's a human response to want to collect it, and to say that you own it, so that it's just there, just in case you need it.

I think that's what's going to happen with VR. I think people are going to choose the types of experiences that they identify with. They're also going to follow creators that have a certain style or certain thing that they like about how they use the medium of VR. It's going to be from the gambit of people just collecting VR versions of sports events that happened in real time, that are recorded for posterity, all the way through super-interactive, build-your-own, choose-your-own-adventure worlds, like a *Minecraft*-like application for VR. There's really no right answer. It's whatever you want.

There's something very visceral about it. Right now, it's scratching the surface of what it's going to be, but for me, it's exciting that for the first time in history, I don't think there has been such a rapid shift of focus by so many industries and so many large tech companies that all have shifted some division or created something new to be able to contribute to the VR critical mass. In fact, one of the reasons why we got into the content creation business, or VR in general, is that we saw that there was a gap. There was a large amount of hardware that's being created. The problem is, there's not nearly enough software or experiential entertainment to actually put on that. That's why you see many companies crop up, and they've created a camera. Well, they get instant funding from somebody, and then they can create their library of stuff. We did the same thing, as partners with VRC, the Virtual Reality

(Continued)

(Continued)

Company, knowing that The Third Floor is a company that can create all this content. In fact, we're the largest visualization company in the world, for real-time visualization, for storytellers working on many big Hollywood movies—so why not?

We also work in video game cinematics, and we design theme park attractions for Universal and beyond. I felt an obligation, a calling that we needed to do something to help Hollywood understand the full capabilities, the full potential of this. Certainly, the folks in the gaming world, many of the game developers and publishers totally got it from the get-go. There are harder specs to keep the frame rate up on. A bigger challenge, but they're willing to step up, and they're actually tooled up to do that for games, but my assumption is that with gaming on one end of the spectrum and passive film media on the other end of the spectrum, the real holy grail will be to do a little bit of both. In the middle, VR and soon to be AR, should be the nexus of great storytelling, directed by excellent storytellers, and involving some form of appropriate interactivity and therefore, presence.

That is the key to the vast majority of the revenue, I think, for this, because this is beyond the scope of what the gaming industry itself is currently profiting from. I think that a lot of times, people really underestimate this because they're looking too short term, they're looking too much at the projections from some analytics company, which is all very important, but look at what's happening in terms of the internet, the future internet's capability. Look at what's happening in terms of devices and how the devices are becoming smaller

(Continued)

(Continued)

	and even going away, and leading towards this AR future. Because as soon as we have Magic Leap, as soon as we have a widespread adoption of Hollow Lens-like devices, or other dark horses that haven't been announced yet, all browsing of the internet will feel a lot more *Minority Report*. You can see the signs everywhere that everyone wants this. If everything outside of entertainment is doing this type of sophisticated navigation in an increasingly 3D world of interactivity, to take a break from all of that, humanity is going to want to turn on something that's art-directed, turn on something that takes them to another place, or informs them in an entertaining way. Our medium is going to have to match that.
John Bucher:	What do you feel like were the story elements that you took from what you have done, historically, with The Third Floor and LucasFilm? What were the story elements that you feel have been the most beneficial to bring into the VR world? What sort of story principles or story elements didn't play in this new environment?
Chris Edwards:	It's been interesting, because there's been a mash-up of philosophies here within The Third Floor about how to tackle this type of new media. If you ask the game engine guys, they say, "Well, we need to know what kind of world we're building, first, and then we need to work on the core technology that makes that possible, so that we have the means to tell the story. Then, out of that, we add the art to that, and technology, well-established, plus art to make it prettier equals product." It's completely opposite to the way that you think about the film development world, where you don't really want to

(Continued)

(Continued)

limit your imagination up front. I wouldn't want to look at Alfonso Cuarón or James Cameron or Steven Spielberg and say, "Well, we only have so much money, so you better just keep it reined in, guys."

That's the whole purpose of Third Floor is to say, "Look, don't worry about it. I know this is a big scary script with lots of big things in it, but let's take it and let's visualize it as if it is the best version of the movie you could ever imagine." Then, over time, as we begin to home in on the core emotional underpinnings of the story, and the beats that take us from a moment to moment, in an innovative, almost hypnotic way, it will be very clear, at some point, what needs to go and what needs to stay in, and what needs to go beyond that, or be enhanced.

Then, once you have built your perfect baby, and usually you do that sequence by sequence, you check it versus the "Is this doable?" test, the litmus test, and that's a combination of time, money, schedules, and a bunch of other people's opinions. We make adjustments to make sure that's all going to work. Sometimes, those adjustments that we make are actually even more elegant and effective than the original pie-in-the-sky version of it, if that makes any sense.

I guess what I'm saying is that what we're trying to do right now is to have a phase where we can brainstorm as if there are no limitations for a VR project like we do in linear media, but then we will then put pencils down with that and hand it over to the tech team. If you don't give the tech team a chance to validate it and to maybe even get a running head start, building that functionality that you seem to

(Continued)

(Continued)

be calling out in your crazy idea, it's going to be a train wreck at the end.

We do that. We take a pause. We do some core tech, and then we end up going back into it together, but in lock step, knowing the mold that we have to fit it into, then we take all those great creative ideas and start adorning the tree with all of that magic. The last lesson in VR is that you cannot publish it like you normally do with linear media, which is color-balanced, with good audio, and the right compression—sent over the internet to the person that needs to receive it. Then it goes to consumers. As you know, and as the gaming world knows, if there's any form of interactivity, it's got to be supported like a game, so that means it needs to be tested. There are a number of systems that the piece must be qualified for and meet the minimum spec for the hardware capabilities.

You have, of course, not only the PC market, but if you're publishing on PlayStation, you've got to make sure it works on that. Every single platform has its own parameters that you must meet and procedures for publishing that are all different. Not only is it a bureaucratic challenge to meet or exceed those expectations, but it's a support challenge long into the future, because if someone in Boise, Idaho, tries it on their 486 at home, and it's not working, well, you want to try your best to consider a change to the core technology, the core build of that software, to make sure that it actually will play better on their underpowered system.

That's something that's really awakened us to the realities of game design. It's exciting to see the mad scientists come together with the mad creators,

(Continued)

(Continued)

and the artists, and that side of the fence, and a mash-up of their ideas. I think even after several projects, we are coming out of the woods with a much more sophisticated understanding of how to do this. I guess our advantage as The Third Floor is that we've always prided ourselves on being nimble, whereas most of Hollywood went towards final visual effects, and was working on pushing the quality of that last pixel, and making it as realistic as possible, we decided, "No. We're going to temper our expectations for quality, and make sure that the quality we provide is not just superficial quality, it's the quality of the storytelling. It's the quality of the pipeline that allows us to be fast and responsive to the creator's vision, and the entire creative entourage that comes with them, making sure that we become a binding force, a hub of everyone's ideas."

John Bucher: As your team looks at game theory and entertainment design, you're putting all these decisions in the hands of a user. Gamers are certainly used to having a level of decision making, but people that go to the movies are used to sitting there and zoning out. You have a wide variety of people you're entertaining, from people that have a middle-school education, or children, all the way up to people that have Ph.Ds. Where do you find the sweet spot of decision making to keep an audience engaged on a general market level?

Chris Edwards: I think most of the people that are fans of movies and television shows are almost the same demographic as the people that go to family theme parks. Maybe not Six Flags, which is more based on roller coasters and thrill rides, but certainly Disneyland, Disney World, and Universal Adventure Parks.

(Continued)

(Continued)

I think it's the same general family audience, and so knowing what we know about that audience, and what works in cinema, and what works in themed entertainment, I think that the solution is just to make sure that it is something that they can sit down and enjoy, with some level of interactivity, but that doesn't require them to do anything too sophisticated. That way you get the parents, the grandparents, and their uncle, who may come from a lot of different walks of life and training in terms of technology.

I like the idea of having experiences created with multiple modes, so that if you are more ambitious, you can get up and walk around, or if you're the type of person that wants to be more entrepreneurial and creative, then you can have a function, in certain types of apps, that will allow you to create your own adventure, or do something a bit more. It takes more initiative. It's a very broad answer, but I think that what audiences want right now are things that they recognize, because in any new medium, it's kind of scary. Something proven, a franchise that's recognizable that will draw a larger audience. It still has to be good, because I think as many spin-offs from major motion pictures that were, in themselves, good, but the actual spin-off, ancillary product of the game version of it turned out to be very disappointing to hard-core gamers, because they saw it as a reskinned version of some other old, tired game that didn't really even work that well, and was frustrating. Clearly, the developers tried very hard, but they were just given a certain mandate with a day and date time that they needed to deliver by, and it wasn't their best

(Continued)

(Continued)

efforts. They probably weren't integrated into the main thread of the creativity of the whole project—meaning that the film director had no idea that there was even a game being made—or if they did, they didn't know where it was happening and no one consulted them.

We get visits from a lot of studios, from major IP holders, all asking, "Will you align forces with us to help mandate, and encourage a standard to happen whereby we can all be working together as one, because we only have more to gain through synergies, through a reduction of redundancy and all that." These discussions are blowing wide open as a result of the VR. I would call it a second revolution of VR that we're experiencing right now. It's an exciting time, for both the technical people and for the creative people. We see ourselves as that bridge in the middle that's saying, "Hey, you guys need to talk to each other. We'll build a bridge for you."

CONCEPTS TO CONSIDER FROM CHRIS EDWARDS

▶ VR shares connections with elements of theater and theme parks.

▶ There are various situations in which the 180-degree field of view is preferred to the 360-degree field.

▶ VR experiences allow for a simultaneous individual and collective experience.

▶ Technical limitations should not be considered in the earliest stages of immersive designs, as they can inhibit imagination.

▶ The technological and entertainment/artistic industries need each other's expertise in order to take VR storytelling into the future.

PUTTING IDEAS TOGETHER

Chris Edwards managed to turn his creative process into a large-scale company. His grounding philosophy was to let imagination trump limitation. Fields like VR can quickly become consumed by concerns about technology, an important partner in the storytelling process. However, the technology should serve the stories we dream and allow us more efficient and powerful ways to tell them. This approach in prioritization has served many other industries, such as animation, gaming, and even traditional theater, as well as historically. There is little reason to believe that the storytellers in disciplines creating immersive media will be any exception.

CONNECTING CLASSICAL STORYTELLING AND PHILOSOPHY WITH IMMERSIVE MEDIA

Exploring classical narrative techniques and figures alongside how these concepts might fit into emerging platforms is relatively uncharted territory. Some new technologies develop quickly and become embraced at such paces that reflective studies and spectrums of effect, which take time to develop and test, can risk becoming obsolete or irrelevant. Fortunately, there is a significant body of work around storytelling in classic literature, which we can build a base from in attempting to connect it with emerging media.

PLATO, SOCRATES, AND VR

Most scholars have conventionally held the position that Plato saw *logos* and *muthos* as fundamentally opposite ideas. *Logos* being the medium of philosophy and *muthos* that of poetry. This idea originates in the *Protagoras*, with Socrates' criticism of poetry in the *Republic*, where *muthos* appears to refer to a story and *logos* to an argument.[1] Socrates continues to make his case for this in *Theaetetus* and the *Sophist*. However, if we expand the definition of *muthos* to encompass storytelling beyond poetry to our wider understandings of narrative, the opposition becomes less stated. In *Plato the Myth Maker*, Luc Brisson argues that *logos* is an argument that follows a logical order and aims at demonstrating a conclusion for Plato. *Muthos* is an "unfalsifiable discourse that can be characterized as a story because it relates events whose sequence does not respect a rational order"

(100, 110).[2] Even if Plato was not a proponent of *muthos* and storytelling, there are still some significant thoughts we take from his work for VR and immersive experiences, most notably in his allegory of the cave and discussions of *digesis* and *mimesis*.

PLATO'S ALLEGORY OF THE CAVE

Originally written as a dialogue between Plato's brother Glaucon and his mentor Socrates about the effect of education and the lack of it on our nature, this narrative stands as one of the most memorable ideas in the *Republic* and has been used as a metaphor for a great number of postmodern ideas. The allegory describes a group of people who have lived chained to the wall of a cave their entire lives. They face the wall. All they can see is the wall. All they know is the wall. There is a fire behind them causing any person, animal, or object that passes between them and the fire to cast a shadow on the wall. The chained people begin to name the shadows, which become their concept of reality, unaware of a more vivid reality that exists right behind them. In the narrative, philosophers are prisoners who have been freed from not only the wall but the entire cave. These freed people are able to observe the actual world, including the sources of the shadows on the wall they have long watched. However, the blinding sun in the real world temporarily makes them unable to see when returning to the dark cave to tell the other prisoners about what they have witnessed. When the prisoners see their blind friend, they refuse to undertake freedom, willing to kill anyone who might try to drag them out of the cave.

There is a sharp division between those who would consider the blank wall that the prisoners stare at to be the "old world" we have known and those who consider it to be the "new world of media." Is Virtual Reality a new reality that some have emerged from darkness to find new freedom in? Or is it the shadows being projected on the wall that only point to a faint image of actual reality? What are the implications of each philosophy? Does the allegory fall flat if the prisoners *know* that they are simply seeing shadows and that they are free to exit the cave any time they like? As with any cultural change or emerging technology, there are issues to be mindful about and consider. We will discuss further implications of Plato's allegory in the section on ethics. However, for now, let us incorporate Aristotle's ideas about narratives with Platonic approaches.

DIEGETIC AND MIMETIC APPROACHES IN ARISTOTELIAN NARRATIVES

Aristotelian narratives are those that follow the simplest structural three-act form. Simply stated, they have a beginning, a middle, and an end. Within Aristotelian narratives, scholars have differentiated between those that take a diegetic approach, in which a narrator *tells* the story, and a mimetic approach, in which there is a visual representation or direct embodiment of things that play out or *show* us the story. Narratologists such as Gerard Genette have further defined and divided the diegetic into levels such as the intradiegetic, the extradiegetic, and the metadiegetic.[3] With the intradiegetic, a narrator exists within the fictional story world. With the extradiegetic, the narrator exists outside the fictional story world. In a metadiegetic narrative, the narrator exists within the story world, participates as a central character, and conveys a story of his or her own to other characters within the central narrative—essentially *a* story within *the* story. While some narratives stay strictly within the bounds of one approach, others have thrived through the combining of these approaches. The combining of these forms may be not only compelling but necessary in cinematic and VR storytelling.

THE DIEGETIC AND MIMETIC IN CINEMATIC STORYTELLING

Plato differentiated in the *Republic* between the *epos* (or epic) and the drama. Epic narratives *told* their stories through narration. Dramas *showed* their stories by having players enact the narrative. Cinema employs the epic through its use of dramatic tropes and technology. The camera has *told* us where to look in cinema. Lighting and lenses have further provided avenues for a diegetic approach. Editing brings us from one story point to the other by shifting time and space as the cinematic creator narrates our journey through the story. It might be easy to assume that films that employ a narrator or voice-over to tell us what characters are thinking and fill in gaps for us, much like the Greek chorus, which will be discussed later, also should be considered diegetic. However, voice-over, titles, and subtitles are usually considered nondiegetic elements in cinematic storytelling. The potential elimination of the edges of the frame in VR, AR, and MR should cause us to consider how these traditional terms might apply to storytelling in immersive media. Some VR is edited cinematically and some is not. This can further complicate our view of these concepts and use of these terms.

It is important to remember that the key behind the classification of these ideas is *intent*. Is the storyteller *trying* to narrate the story for us through the use of these elements?

Aristotle suggested that humans are inherently mimetic beings, with a drive to imitate and capture reality through art. Cinema has always been a *captured* or represented experience—a mimetic experience. When inside an immersive experience, it is difficult not to consider the experience in real time. As immersed as we become in a movie, it would be rare that an audience member forgets that what is happening before them isn't actually real as it might be in a play. This distinction becomes less clear once an HMD is put on, which is certainly the point. It may be important for storytellers to remember that diegetic storytelling usually proceeds the mimetic within an art form, or at least our observation of it does. VR experiences that employ a diegetic experience will likely be an easier transition for those still becoming used to the technology. The potential with intradiegetic, extradiegetic, and metadiegetic stories offers a wide variety of ways to tell a viewer a story in a VR experience. Their impact should not be underestimated. However, mimetic experiences will likely have even greater emotional impact. As with cinema, the most effective VR experiences will likely take advantage of both approaches. For those with greater interest in the diegetic and mimetic approaches in Virtual Reality, the work of Sandy Louchart and Ruth Aylett should be considered.[4]

AESCHYLUS, SOPHOCLES, EURIPIDES, AND VR

While we only have a fraction of what was likely written, the work of Greek tragedians has played a highly significant role in the way the average viewer experiences a visual story. While we know that many more existed, only the tragedies of Aeschylus, Sophocles, and Euripides remain. Here is a brief list of the comparative points among the three.

Aeschylus (525–455 BCE)

▶   Expanded from a single actor on stage to two

▶   Used the Chorus front and center as the protagonists of the story

▶   Themes of his work were the most theological and traditional of the tragedians

Sophocles (497-406 BCE)

▶ Expanded from two actors to three and sometimes four

▶ Expanded the role of the Chorus but removed them as the protagonist

▶ Added painted scenery to settings

▶ Themes of his work included political ideas and strong women (*Antigone*)

Euripides (480-406 BCE)

▶ Expanded the cast to multiple actors

▶ Limited and sometimes eliminated the Chorus

▶ Themes also focused on strong women (*Medea*) and satirizing traditional Greek heroes

It is helpful to look back at the history and development of how our modern storytelling evolved, as we have been conditioned by these changes throughout the centuries to arrive at the place we are currently. No one would argue that immersive technologies such as VR, AR, and MR are in their earliest stages. Is it possible that we are in our own VR age of Aeschylus, still transitioning from a single viewer experience to a more social experience? Have early VR storytellers used a digital chorus that may be eliminated at some point? Theorists such as Schlegel have famously interpreted the role of the chorus as that of *an ideal spectator*.[5] This would, of course, have significance in immersive experiences for a long time to come. The work of Euripides most closely resembles the types of dramas we most frequently see today. However, we must remember that it would not have been possible without the preceding work of Aeschylus and Sophocles. Euripides was able to see what had worked and what could be transcended in the work of his predecessors. VR storytellers must study the work of earlier creators in order to learn what can now be transcended in VR in order to fully envision the potentials of this new medium as distinct from other art forms such as cinema and gaming.

BALANCING THE APOLLONIAN AND DIONYSIAN APPROACHES IN THE IMMERSIVE

There has not yet been a great deal of discussion on the role of mythology in the discipline. However, because mythological concepts and structures are largely connected to the development of storytelling in both literal and unconscious senses, it is worth our time to consider some of the principles from this discipline. Let us begin by considering the Apollonian and Dionysian philosophies and literary concepts from Greek mythology. Famously linked to Nietzsche's *The Birth of Tragedy* in our modern era as artistic impulses, the concepts originate with Apollo and Dionysus, both sons of Zeus. Though the Greeks did not consider the duo to be rivals or opposites, the nature of each did sometimes cause conflict in various myths. For our purposes, we will look at striving to find a balance between the approaches that creates the most effective immersive experience. First, let us give greater detail on each approach.

The Apollonian Approach

Apollo and thus the Apollonian approach is based on logic and reason. Apollo was referred to as the god of the sun, giving him a natural connection to truth and light. Apollonian approaches value restraint, cultural good, harmony, and discipline. They prioritize order, control, moderation, clarity, and rules. From a technological perspective, experiences and games with an Apollonian approach will be those that clearly spell out to the player how to successfully complete the experience. They will err on the side of guiding the player through the experience and minimize confusion or wandering.

The Dionysian Approach

Dionysus and thus the Dionysian approach is based on instinct, emotion, unbridled passion, and, in extreme situations, chaos and irrationality. Dionysus was the god of the earth, spring and renewal. He was known to be the god of wine, madness, tragedy, and the theater. His approach often arises in discussions of expression and the body. Dionysian approaches value spontaneity, intuition, feelings, and imagination. From a technological perspective, experiences and games with a Dionysian approach will allow the player to explore the world put before them. They will err on the side of allowing players to get lost and even frustrated with the experience. It is also worth noting that theorists such as Brenda Laurel have compared the experience of Virtual Reality to the Dionysian cultic experience in which a shaman led initiates into a cave for a mediated experience of ritualistic significance.[6]

FINDING BALANCE

While we will consider interactivity in storytelling later, it is worth noting that much of the philosophies behind the different approaches to telling stories in immersive space tends to lean toward one of these approaches. How far an experience should lean into one approach or the other will vary depending on the experience being created. However, throughout the history of other art forms that have relied on the tension between these approaches, common practice has led creators to look for a position somewhere between the two. Balance tends to create the most successful experiences. Early *Flash Gordon* serials set in space relied completely on the emotional storytelling so common to the Dionysian approach. Often, the technology and science surrounding space travel and living was either glossed over or completely ignored. Later, *Star Trek* would set stories in space with a distinctly Apollonian approach, basing the crew's success greatly on logic and reason. It was not until *Star Wars* that a successful balance of Dionysian and Apollonian approaches brought both camps together, which made for successful storytelling that eclipsed all space stories that came before it.

THE ROLE OF RITUAL

It is difficult to bring up the topic of the Dionysian without giving some voice to ritual. "Ritual" might be another term surprising to find in a discussion of storytelling in immersive space. However, repetition and ritual are key components of the logic in immersive experiences both inside and outside of interactive stories and video games. Both Aristotle, who pointed to the dithyramb (sung and improvised poetry performed by the cult of Dionysus), and Nietzsche, who used Aristotle's work as the basis of *The Birth of Tragedy*, have contended that ancient Greek tragedy, and thus most of modern storytelling, derives from ritual. Religious historian and cultural critic Mircea Eliade argued that ritual is the reenactment of the foundational events that are commemorated in myth.[7] In other words, we repeat what the "gods" did in the beginning—we repeat the creative act. The recreation of events, time, and space that becomes a new reality mirrors the act of transubstantiation found in religious rituals such as the Eucharist. The fact that we must currently either blind our vision of actual reality with the use of an HMD or enter a CAVE (cave automatic virtual environment) to experience Virtual Reality further links it to our concept of ritual activities. Even Augmented and Mixed Realities require some sort of mediated experience that again provides the link. The discussion of ritual in immersive experiences, to which entire volumes have been devoted, reminds us that we are indeed creating *mediated* experiences. These experiences come with their own sets of ethics and techniques in making them successful.

> The old gods are dead or dying and people everywhere are search-ing, asking: What is the new mythology to be, the mythology of this unified earth as of one harmonious being? One cannot predict the next mythology any more than one can predict tonight's dream: for mythology is not an ideology . . . Indeed, the first and most essential service of a mythology is this one, of opening the mind and heart to the utter wonder of all being.
>
> —Joseph Campbell
> Introduction to *The Inner Reaches of*
> *Outer Space: Metaphor as Myth and Religion*[8]

MYTHOLOGICAL APPROACHES TO THE IMMERSIVE

While this topic likely deserves its own lengthy exploration, we will attempt to give a brief overview of relevant mythological approaches significant to the discussion of VR, AR, and MR. There are a number of mythological theorists whose work figures in to thinking about the immersive. However, none more so than that of Joseph Campbell. Campbell wrote a great deal about mythic dimensions and journeys that one can become immersed in by entering certain spaces and engaging with specific practices. In one par-ticular discussion about the metaphoric journey of engaging a Navajo sand painting, Campbell discusses the archetypal adventure of physically enter-ing the painting, which is the way the art form is meant to be experienced. He goes on to suggest that we actually become mythic figures through the experience, and therefore our experience becomes mythologized.[9] It does not require a great leap to assume that Campbell would have had a similar perspective about immersive experiences like VR. He furthers his expla-nation of immersive art and mythological art comparing the sand art to a rainbow, which is composed of both matter and light, formed by reflection and refraction. It is both material and immaterial in the same way that VR is both material and immaterial.

Another area of Campbell's work of particular interest to creators of immersive experiences involves the interpretation of symbolic forms. Using symbolic forms cuts through the rigorous task of explaining to a viewer the meaning behind objects, landscapes, and even certain characters when constructing a narrative. For example, if we see a character wandering through the desert, no one must explain to us the hardships of the desert that the character will encounter, even if we ourselves have never experienced the trials one faces in such terrain. This is because the desert serves as a symbol. Because of the initial shock a viewer can experience while orienting to a new immersed space, relying on symbolic form, at least initially, can be helpful in achieving a successful narrative. Campbell grounds his thoughts on symbolic form in Jung's four basic psychological functions of virtue, of which we apprehend and evaluate all experience. These are sensation and intuition, which are apprehending functions, and thinking and feeling, which are those of judgment and evaluation.[10] Campbell explains that Jung suggested we tend to shape our lives by combining one function from each pair. For example, one might embrace sensation and thinking, leaving intuition and feeling undeveloped. Understanding the potential for the psychological perspective one could hold when entering immersive space can be helpful in considering how the viewer may conceive narrative. A great deal more could be considered of Campbell's work, including how his monomyth in the now-classic *The Hero With a Thousand Faces* might function in virtual immersive space. However, those thoughts must be left for a later volume. For now, we can simply ponder the connection between the opening of the mind and heart to wonder, which Campbell claimed was the service of mythology, and the immersive experiences we are creating.

SPOTLIGHT ON NARRATIVE: Fiction Versus Nonfiction Storytelling
Steve Peters, Experience Designer, Host of StoryForward Podcast and CCO of Mo Mimes Media

This interview is a continuation of the discussion with Emmy®-winning experience designer Steve Peters in Chapter 5, now focused on issues and nuances surrounding fiction and nonfiction storytelling in immersive spaces.

John Bucher: Tell me about how you became interested in storytelling, especially in the digital space.

(Continued)

(Continued)

Steve Peters:	For me it all began in 2001 with the AI alternate reality game *The Beast* that was built by Elan Lee and the guys at Microsoft. I was a music producer in Seattle in the summer of 2001, and I was playing along with this online murder mystery that was tied in with a movie. I thought, "This is really interesting how it's done." I was leaving my office for lunch one afternoon and my phone rang. It was a character from the AI game calling me. I forgot all about lunch. I ran back into my office and got online again because I knew something happened in the story. I knew something happened in the game. Afterwards, that night I remember thinking, "That was crazy because literally this game just reached out and grabbed me and pulled me back in when I wasn't even thinking about it." I thought, "That is a game changer." For 2001, this was before social media and push notifications and all that stuff. It's the first time a game actually called me.
	That piqued my interest. That was a crossroads for me. It was the point where I started thinking, "This is an interesting, very cutting-edge way to entertain people," and I got really into it. I built communities, then ultimately built my own grassroots alternate reality with some friends. Over the years, I became friends with Elan Lee and Shawn Stewart, who went on to found 42 Entertainment. Then they hired me for my audio production knowledge, but because of my experience as a player of these things, it became obvious that I could help a lot with the design as well, and so I immediately started helping them—learning from the best, the pioneers.
John Bucher:	Tell me a little bit about your first experience with VR.
Steve Peters:	I didn't try an Oculus Rift until a couple years ago. It was my first VR experience. It was very low resolution,

(Continued)

(Continued)

but very effective. I was struck by how I felt I was in a physical environment even though it was pixelated. That immediately piqued my interest. From a design standpoint, I've been holding back before diving into a lot of VR projects because the vocabulary of storytelling for VR is not quite there yet, so I'm in a wait-and-see attitude with VR narratives. With gaming, I'm totally on board. I totally get it, and doing narrative storytelling in Virtual Reality requires a lot of game mechanics that should be considered.

John Bucher: Let's go back to the vocabulary of storytelling, especially as it relates to these new canvases. Can you talk about what you see as necessary elements to build a vocabulary for storytelling in VR?

Steve Peters: There's a lot that VR can learn from gaming. I think back to my days playing *Half-Life 2*, and there was a version of it where you could actually play along with a developer's commentary. They explained something that they did as far as creating vistas or creating ways to draw the player's attention to look in a specific direction, even though it didn't feel like they were doing it. They would build scenarios where the player would turn a corner and then they would come across this huge vista, and it was an establishing shot for whatever was going to happen. Or a little sound would then grab your attention and you'd look up there in time to see something that was happening, or a light was subtly shining on something.

They had so many ways to subliminally direct your attention. It's tough with audio because true binaural audio isn't responsive, so it's tough to pinpoint a location for somebody and direct them by sound. My frustration is invariably that I'll be watching or doing something in VR and something's happening behind

(Continued)

(Continued)

me. I don't like having to get up out of my chair and turn around. For me, when I'm immersed in true VR as opposed to 360 video, I want to be able to interact with things around me. It's the game of *Myst*. It's a 3D environment. Whereas filmed narrative, which is basically 360 video, where you're an observer, it creates a lot of the dilemma of where do I look and also who am I on the stage, and where is that proscenium? If I'm in the scene surrounded by the scene, who am I?

There's the issues of the third person or first person and understanding that it's a weird thing to be somewhere and feel like you're really there but nobody's paying any attention to you and you have no agency. It's things like how do you effectively do an edit in 360 video that's not really jarring? A lot of people are experimenting with stuff like that. It's an education because just like film audiences didn't know how to respond the first time they saw camera movies and edits. It took a while to establish that filmmaking vocabulary. I think we're still in those early stages. We've got that film camera and we're putting it on a tripod and we're just shooting a stage play because we haven't developed these other ways to tell stories based on the technology. I think it's a process and I think we're still in the very beginning stages of that.

John Bucher: Let's talk about this idea of an immersive experience. Obviously, immersive experiences go back as far as human beings have been on this planet. Especially in the last 100 years we've seen a rise in really manufactured immersive experiences. We've also seen the rise of things like immersive theater, trying to create a sense of immersion in theatrical experiences. What is your theory on why we continually crave a greater and greater immersive experience?

(Continued)

(Continued)

Steve Peters:	The pendulum is swinging back from, "Look at this digital stuff that's so amazing and so shiny." I think that's losing its luster a bit. In a day where we can watch 4K movies with surround sound in our living rooms, when we go out, there's got to be a reason, and the one thing that you can't get in your living room is an actual experience. Disney is struggling with trying to find ways to limit the attendance because they're overrun with more and more people wanting their experience. Real life has the best immersion because you still cannot beat it.

It's ironic when at Universal Studios, with a lot of their big attractions, you have to put 3D glasses on to experience them. I'm thinking, "They're missing the point of a real location with things that I can touch and things that I can't get digitally." They're doing other stuff. They've got *Harry Potter* World. Huge immersion there. Building it in a way that you can dress up and feel like you're actually there near Hogwarts. They opened up a *Walking Dead* attraction where, it's all real people. There's no 3D projections. That's the same thing with escape rooms. I think people are now starting to crave the organic. They're starting to crave the analog again. With our little black screens, we've seen it all and done it, and now it's like, "I want something I can touch and hold." I think that's a challenge for VR because it's yet another way that I can immerse myself.

As far as entertainment, I don't know that people are going to continue wanting to take a step deeper into digital unless it's giving them something that is impossible for them to experience physically. Going to the bottom of the sea or going to Mars, I can totally see the value of that. As far as watching a movie and feeling like you're there, it's going to be a challenge. We're

(Continued)

(Continued)

	going to have to see where that goes. The pendulum's swinging back to the real world, and I think that's a good thing.

John Bucher: You brought up agency, which is a big topic of discussion in this world. It seems in digital environments, whenever we bring up the topic of agency, we immediately go to game theory. Can you talk about agency outside of the world of gaming?

Steve Peters: I think a lot of people, when they talk about interactive anything, especially interactive storytelling, they immediately go to the *Choose Your Own Adventure* books. That's the agency. Let them choose the ending. As my friend Shawn Stewart always said, "How many *Choose Your Own Adventure* books do we have on our shelves?" Ultimately, that's not a satisfying story because you feel like it's video games with alternate endings. When you finish one ending, what's the first thing you want to do? You want to go back to a save point and now see the stuff you missed. Whereas if it feels like somebody has crafted a story and I can have an unexpected result at the end, I think that's better.

I think there are ways to give people the illusion of agency. In alternate reality games, we've done this a lot over the years—giving people the illusion of impacting the story. Even though we know and they know in the back of their minds that it's on rails. But we are able to give them the illusion so that they can suspend their disbelief and feel like they have made this happen. A simple example is *The Dark Knight* project that I worked on. We had players register to vote and become part of Gotham and they would get voter registration cards. Then there was the actual election. We had an election that voted Harvey Dent into office as district attorney. Now, everybody knew that he was

(Continued)

(Continued)

going to get elected. At the same time, I was amazed at how much they just loved that. They loved the voter registration cards and they gathered in their districts and even made websites for their districts.

We knew they were going to vote that way. We set things up so that even if they didn't somehow vote that way, they would have no way of knowing because they weren't actually shifting the story. Now you can build things where maybe something will happen and you can have a branch for sure, but it ultimately comes back to the same major story arc. I found that to be a lot more satisfying for people. They don't want to ask, "If we had done this thing, would we have been able to save this person's life?" Maybe you could've ultimately, but would that have changed the main story? No, not really. At the same time, we're able to give them agency in feeling like this is a living, breathing place and I helped elect Harvey Dent into office.

There's an interesting approach with Alternate Reality games where my goal is to try to make it feel like the story, and I guess that is the ultimate agency— that what we're telling is actually taking place right now in the same world that we live in. There's all sorts of little tricks we can do to make that feel real. Obviously, phone calls do that because somebody's calling me, or I call a phone number, or I email and I get a message back. That feels very real. You surround the people with the story in whatever ways you can and in whatever ways that would make sense to the story.

John Bucher: Steve, in your work, you encounter the cutting edge of narrative design and storytelling, and these new forms seem to rise all the time. Can you talk about what disciplines VR can learn from?

(Continued)

(Continued)

Steve Peters: Specifically, to me, experience design is not so much creating rules to follow but being able to develop a sense after working with people of anticipating unanticipated consequences of audience actions or inactions and creating a more and more finely tuned sense of empathy over time with your audience. In whatever project I'm doing, I find myself asking why are they going to do this? What's going to be their motivation to do this thing you're asking them to do? In VR, that's the main question. What is going to be your audience's motivation for even looking in a certain direction? Or, from a bigger standpoint, what's going to be their motivation to put on that headset as opposed to just watching the content on a screen?

It's like with the balancing of game design; you got the ask versus the payoff. More and more, once the novelty of VR wears off, then your payoff has to be even better. I'm asking you to put on this headset and turn it on and be uncomfortable. The payoff better be great. From a storytelling standpoint, I always like to think of, in the case of novels, what is the biggest ask a book requires of you? To turn the page. To get you to turn the page, they have to make sure the story is compelling enough to make you want to do that. What's the digital equivalent? I think with digital stuff, with VR, it's even more important than that because you're asking a lot more of an audience than just flipping the page. You're saying, "Now go do this thing." Whatever the interaction is, there's a balance between interaction that makes sense to move the story forward and interaction that then just becomes busywork or homework or gimmicky to move the story forward.

I think geolocation games have that challenge now, too. *Pokémon Go* touched on actually getting people

(Continued)

up out of their chairs and out into the streets. That's going to wear off. The thing that VR creators can learn from gaming is there has to be a constant balance of difficulty versus reward in order to keep them as a player. Because if all of a sudden the game gets too hard, they're going to get frustrated and they're going to turn it off. If all of a sudden they get confused and they don't know where to go or what to look for, or they lost track of the story, then you're going to lose them. The statistic that's the most well-kept secret in the games industry I heard was only 17% of gamers make it to the end of the games they purchase. I don't know if it's 17%, but it's very low. It's 17% to 20%. One in five people actually finish a game.

CONCEPTS TO CONSIDER FROM STEVE PETERS

▶ VR requires game mechanics that must be considered when developing an experience.

▶ Gaming has established a vocabulary effective at getting users to look in directions that creators desire.

▶ True VR should allow the user agency and the ability to interact with the environment.

▶ Cultural cravings for the organic and tactile will be a challenge for VR.

▶ Agency can include the illusion of impacting the story.

PUTTING IDEAS TOGETHER

Steve Peters mentions what could be one of the biggest obstacles to success in VR storytelling, the potential of digital exhaustion with users. This factor could greatly impact the length of time that an audience is willing to be immersed in VR, especially if that immersion involves wearing an HMD. Stories must be crafted at a pace that honors the audience's tolerance for the experience. Technological advancements that allow tactile responses with objects and other users will certainly have impact on this tolerance. However, the ability of the story to engage the viewer will likely always be the determining factor in the success of the experience with the user. The immersive experience will always be a dance between the creator and the audience. Recognizing the subtleties of the dance will come with time and experience on the part of both parties. It will be the role of the creators, however, to lead the dance and not to step on the toes of their partners.

EXERCISE 7

DEVELOPING MORE ADVANCED CHARACTERS

OBJECTIVE: 1.   To demonstrate the methods for creating strong, advanced, well-developed characters.

ASSIGNMENT

1.   Create a character using the Developing a Main Character exercise.

2.   Create a five-page backstory for the character that includes physical and internal attributes and how those attributes came to be. Use one of the following attributes in your description: a scar, nontalkative, talks too much, a limp, hair that covers their eyes. (*Remember, you are creating a backstory and describing detail about the character NOT telling the story of the character. Any mentions of stories or scenarios should be brief and only relate to something we know about the character's present state.*)

3.   Create a one-page description of things we could *only* learn about the character in 360-degree immersive space.

EXERCISE 8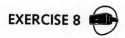

DEVELOPING A SIMPLE IMMERSIVE NARRATIVE

OBJECTIVE: 1. To develop the thought process necessary for thinking through immersive space that would support strong narratives.

ASSIGNMENT

1. Create a narrative using the Developing a Simple Narrative exercise.

2. Create three different scenes for the narrative that take advantage of different settings or environments.

3. Create a two-page description of each scene and environment it takes place in. Describe what can be seen when a viewer looks north, south, east, west, up, and down. Also, describe any other characters, animals, or objects that enter the space while the protagonist is there.

4. Create a one-page description of what the protagonist is meant to feel and experience in this narrative if it is designed as a first-person experience.

EXERCISE 9

DEVELOPING A MORE ADVANCED IMMERSIVE NARRATIVE

OBJECTIVE: 1.   To develop a more advanced thought process necessary for thinking through immersive space that would support strong narratives.

ASSIGNMENT

1.   Create a narrative using the Developing a Simple Narrative exercise.

2.   Create 10 to 12 different scenes for the narrative that take advantage of different settings or environments.

3.   Create a two-page description of each scene and environment it takes place in. Describe the role that the environment will play in the storytelling. Also, describe any other characters, animals, or objects that enter the space while the protagonist is there.

4.   Create a one-page description of how the protagonist will move through or be transported through space. Discuss how transitions between scenes will occur if they do.

5.   Create a one-page description, for each scene, of what the protagonist is meant to feel and experience in this narrative if it is designed as a first-person experience.

6.   If the narrative experience you have created is interactive, create a one-page description describing the agency the viewer will experience while immersed.

NOTES

1 Stanford Encyclopedia of Philosophy Online. http://plato.stanford.edu/entries/plato-myths/
2 Brisson, Luc and Gerard Naddaf (trans.). *Plato the Myth Maker*. Chicago: University of Chicago Press, 1998. Print.
3 Gennette, Gerard. *Narrative Discourse: An Essay in Method*. Ithaca, NY: Cornell University Press, 1980. Print.
4 Louchart, Sandy and Ruth Aylett. *Towards a Narrative Theory of Virtual Reality*. Salford, UK: The Centre for Virtual Environments, University of Salford. Digital.
5 Foley, Helene. "Choral Identity in Greek Tragedy." *Classical Philology* 98.1 (January 2003): 1–30. Digital.
6 Laurel, Brenda. *Computers as Theatre*. Menlo Park, CA: Addison Wesley, 1991. Digital.
7 Ryam, Marie-Laure. *Narrative as Virtual Reality*. Baltimore: The Johns Hopkins University Press, 2001. Print.
8 Campbell, Joseph. *The Inner Reaches of Outer Space: Metaphor as Myth and as Religion*. New York: Harper Perennial, 1995. Print.
9 Campbell, Joseph. *The Inner Reaches of Outer Space*. Novato: New World Library, 1986. Print.
10 Campbell, Joseph. *The Mythic Dimension*. San Francisco: Harper, 1993. Print.

8

Theory in Practice

Interviews and Case Studies

Since our earliest days, humans have sought new ways to express ourselves. Like language itself, our stories are one expression that have become more rich as time moved forward. Finding new ways to tell those stories has also been part of our journey of expression. Discovering new mediums, pushing them to their limits, and eventually transcending though not completely disposing of them has been the pattern that we've repeated over and over again with our storytelling efforts. Virtual Reality may hold the most potential of any medium that has come before it. However, it will still be subject to all the trial, error, experimentation, and eventual transcendence that its predecessors were. The speed at which this process occurs is largely dependent on us. The number of adherents and the volume of stories they choose to tell will determine the speed with which VR reaches its fullest potential as a storytelling medium, as well as the speed with which the next potentially related medium begins to show promise.

This examination of VR purposefully ends with a lengthy look at more storytellers. The most evident path for the emergence of a storytelling language in Virtual Reality will be found on the trail blazed by the early creators in the field—those doing the largest volume of and most imaginative work. Hearing what has worked and what has failed in their efforts saves us valuable time in our own experimentation. Listening to their processes, backgrounds in, and journeys toward effective and articulate communication with this medium will sharpen our own tools for creating within it. The insights of creators working within, and perhaps more importantly *outside*, the corners of the VR industry that we find ourselves in can expand our work in ways that don't seem readily applicable at first glance.

Perhaps the single characteristic that unites every creator featured in these pages, besides the obvious connection to some area of VR, is the humility with which they approach the field. In nearly every interview conducted for this book, the creator was quick to state that no one has completely figured out this new language of storytelling, that all efforts thus far are simply the earliest efforts, and that the most important issue was to be aware of and learn from the efforts of everyone else creating work in this space. Holding VR storytelling somewhat loosely with an open hand was a practice this author frequently encountered. It is easy to become dogmatic about theories involving art forms. That dogma usually falls apart when the discipline of practice enters the picture. Recognizing that every story and experience in Virtual Reality should be to the benefit of the user is an ideal that should be fundamental but can easily become lost.

STYLE OVER SUBSTANCE

One of the disadvantages of our rapidly advancing technological progress has been that the ability to look professional and engaging without having any real content to back up such characteristics has been put in the hands of all users, regardless of their level of expertise. This can lead to implementations of style over substance. Trailers for upcoming films promise stories packed with action, plot twists, and surprises. However, once audiences have paid for the product, they quickly discover that all that the trailer promised was actually *in the trailer*. The final product offered nothing more. While the novelty of VR is still fresh to many, we won't be able to rely on the "shiny" factor for much longer. Audiences will demand more from every VR experience they engage with. If they fail to find it over a lengthy enough period, they will eventually reject the medium entirely—even if it offers an experience the user has never had before. Readers old enough to remember superior technologies such as the Betamax and DAT machine can testify to the graveyard of discarded technological mediums that has grown larger with each generation. Good stories are the best method to avoid such a fate for VR. If storytellers and VR creators are willing to invest the time in learning and executing the timeless arts of narrative, the technology stands a chance. It will be tempting to believe we already know all we need to know about story to create successful experiences. However, even the savviest of storytellers are constantly studying and developing new ways to express their characters and their journeys. In the quick progression of technology, it can be easy for well-developed and layered stories to get lost in the mix. If we believe in the power of this medium, we can't allow this to happen.

While there are ancient elements and principles of narrative that coincide with the human psyche and will likely not change, there are other elements and principles that are constantly evolving. The ways that audiences change as they engage new media are countless. The most intuitive creators will find the ability to hold the never-changing principles of story in one hand while holding the ever-changing principles in the other. This has long been a path forward for creators in emerging media fields. Perhaps surprisingly, there is little argument about the importance of the timeless elements. There are few, if any, creators suggesting we attempt to tell stories without charac-ters, for example. This seems to be one element, that when removed, takes away the "story-ness" from stories. The length and even structure of stories, however, has been and will be up for debate. Certain practices work in cer-tain mediums and other practices work in others. As has been repeated, the experience of the end user and what they walk away with should drive such decisions.

ENTERING A FOREST OF DIGITAL TREES

This examination began with the metaphor of a stone bridge covered in microchips. There is a final image and metaphor that may be helpful to con-sider as you move forward into telling your own stories in immersive space. Imagine a forest of digital trees. While their leaves appear to be real, they are synthetic. The green pulsing of their glow provided by the smallest of LED lights. Their stems are connected to branches of silicon. The branches are connected to trunks of reinforced steel. Beneath the surface, root-like wires wildly spread in all directions, tangling with each other and the wires of other nearby trees. There is a low hum caused by the electric soil that pow-ers the roots and thus the trees themselves. The forest looks alive. In some ways, it even feels alive. But the life is manufactured, in a sense. Inexplicably, one day, a piece of fruit appears on a branch amid the synthetic leaves. The fruit is not digital. The fruit is organic. It is real. It is sweet and it is delicious.

Day after day, more fruit appears on the trees in the forest. Some fruit rots and dies, as is the nature of living things. Other fruit remains and is enjoyed by all who enter the forest.

This, in some ways, is a picture of the field of Virtual Reality. The experiences created by storytellers in this space evoke real emotions in users. The journeys they make while immersed create feelings that are just as real as any they experience outside of the space. Amid all the technology and digital complexity, something real, organic, and meaningful emerges. Something that sparks a user's imagination and sense of wonder. That which was never before possible suddenly appears before them in a quite realistic fashion. Opportunities arise that never existed before. Out of lifeless wires, silicon, plastic, and steel, a new reality is breathed into existence.

INTERVIEWS AND CASE STUDIES

THE STORYTELLERS

VR in a Galaxy Far, Far Away
An Interview with
Rob Bredow, Chief Technology Officer, LucasFilm

As the chief technology officer of LucasFilm, Rob Bredow oversees all technology operations for LucasFilm and Industrial Light & Magic. Bredow joined Industrial Light & Magic, a division of LucasFilm, in 2014 as a visual effects supervisor. In December 2014, he was named vice president of new media and head of LucasFilm's Advanced Development Group. Bredow was instrumental in launching ILMxLAB in 2015, a new division that combines the talents of LucasFilm, ILM, and Skywalker Sound to develop, create, and release story-based immersive entertainment. Previously, Bredow was the CTO and visual effects supervisor at Sony Pictures Imageworks. He has worked on films such as *Independence Day, Godzilla, Stuart Little, Castaway, Surf's Up,* and *Cloudy with a Chance of Meatballs,* as well as the *Star Wars* VR experience, *Trials on Tatooine.*

John Bucher: I'm one of a billion people on the earth who have been a lifelong *Star Wars* fan. What sort of philosophical mindset does it require to take these characters that are such a core part of the culture into a new digital space with the work ILMxLAB is doing?

Rob Bredow: That is one of the most fun things in my mind about getting to work at LucasFilm. If you look at the way George Lucas created and developed the world, he was embracing technology and new forms of storytelling all the time. That spirit of innovation has really just stayed alive in the studio, which has been one of the most fun things to discover as I joined—how innovative the thinking is, how fearless the crew is about trying new things, and experimenting with new forms of storytelling and technology—just to tell stories. That's really been a part of the DNA of LucasFilm since the beginning and really holds true today.

John Bucher: Can you talk about the *Star Wars* VR experience, *Trials of Tatooine*? How did the game come to be? As massive as the *Star Wars* universe is, how was it decided to set the game on Tatooine?

Rob Bredow: Our initial creation of *Trials on Tatooine* was an ILMxLAB experiment. It was based on trying to get our heads around the question, "What does it feel like to be immersed in a simple story in Virtual Reality?" In our case, of course, a *Star Wars* story. We then would ask, "Is it fun to interact with that story when you have a first-person role in the experience?" There's been a lot of VR done where you get to witness the story happening around you, but there's been less VR done where you are present as a first person—present in the narrative. So what we wanted to do was find a simple, and hopefully satisfying, story that would let us experiment with what it feels like to be in Virtual Reality, and experience the story where you're actually playing a simple role in it.

We had the asset, the ability to use the *Millennium Falcon*, because we just finished getting that working from *Episode VII*. We thought what would be more fun than to have the *Millennium Falcon* come and land right on you? Some of us have gotten to stand under the real *Millennium Falcon* that we built in the studio, but not many people have gotten to experience that, and no one has gotten to experience what it's like to stand under the *Millennium Falcon* when it's landing practically on your head. So that was the very beginning of the experiment. We met with Kathy Kennedy and showed her that. Skywalker Sound came in and rigged up this really amazing sound system that was probably the kind of system that you'd usually use to fill an auditorium that holds 2,000 people, and it was just all pointed at Kathy as she was experiencing the *Falcon* landing on Tatooine right above her. It was one of her early VR experiences, too. She took off the headset, and of course everyone is looking at her to see what she thinks, and she was like, "That's what I'm talking about! That's a new kind of entertainment right there!" So we had the start of something that was going to be interesting to experiment with.

John Bucher: Historically, with LucasFilm people have enjoyed the stories of *Star Wars* in a collective fashion—with community. We go into a movie theater and sit with a group of strangers and experience it as a group. We've sat in front of our televisions and watched the cartoons or the films with other people, as well. With these new experiences, we are on our own. We're watching them in a headset where we are there with the characters by ourselves. Can you talk about the different approach of bringing someone into this more immersive environment?

Rob Bredow: The kind of experiences you will see in Virtual Reality aren't going to be solo experiences for very long. In fact, you're already seeing a lot of work being done with multiplayer games. VR experiences will have multiple users at the same time very soon—which is going to really change the game. For this particular experiment that we did, it is a single person at a time, so we wanted to make sure the whole story was told around you so you felt like you still had social connection. You were listening to Han Solo give you instructions from the cockpit or interact with you from the *Millennium Falcon*, and you have other characters in the environment that you have to interact with to keep it alive and to make it as immersive as possible.

John Bucher: LucasFilm is partnering with directors like Alejandro Iñárritu on new projects. Can you talk about what you're hoping these masters of the cinematic realm are going to bring into VR space now that this new medium has started to arrive as a canvas they can work on?

Rob Bredow: We're really fortunate to get to work with people like David Goyer on the VR experience that we're creating in xLab that will have Darth Vader in it. As you mentioned, we're working with Alejandro on an upcoming project, as well. Our goal there is to work with some of the best creative minds in the world who are interested in building experiences in these spaces. There's certain spaces that we can explore that happen to be the kind of projects these folks are interested in making, and we think there's a really nice match there. So that's really what we're about, finding folks who have very ambitious and creative projects and experiments that need to be made and are best made in this format. These are people who can make movies or TV shows if they'd like, but there's certain stories that may be best told in Virtual Reality or immersive experiences.

John Bucher: Even though George Lucas was not the sole creator of *Star Wars* experiences, it seemed as though this mythological sensibility remained with LucasFilm and the projects that have been created, after he left. LucasFilm has obviously been masters at being the bridge between these universal mythological feelings we experience as human beings and the latest cutting-edge technology. How do you stay focused on being the bridge between the ancient and the cutting edge?

Rob Bredow: That's a really interesting question. There's a huge opportunity there with Virtual Reality or Augmented Reality. For example, we're doing a lot of work with Magic Leap right now. We know that we as people need something familiar to tie things back to—to relate the experience to. So we have those mythologies that people understand that are universal storytelling tools, and we also have this world of *Star Wars* that a large percentage of the world can relate to. When we put a *Millennium Falcon* or a droid in with you, that can be an immediate resonance that gives us a leg up when introducing someone to a new experience. You get something familiar in a way you've never seen it before.

John Bucher: What opportunities does Augmented Reality present? What people are at that table in those creative meetings in order to come up with these ideas and execute them?

Rob Bredow: It's really a fantastic table to get to sit around and to be a small part of, because we do get to work with the best of the best. At LucasFilm, there's this team called The Story Group that is responsible for the continuity of the *Star Wars* universe. We are really fortunate at xLab to have a close connection to The Story Group. They're in all of our meetings. They help drive us creatively, which is really fantastic. All of us started at LucasFilm because we love the projects. We love this universe, so a lot of it is brainstorming the kind of stuff that we would want. We'd want these droids to be in our living room with us. We'd like to see what that's like. What does that feel like? What can they do? What would those interaction models look like? Really it comes from a whole team of people who are *Star Wars* fans that want to invent these things that we want to experience ourselves.

John Bucher: Is there any intentionality to connect the worlds that you're building in the VR space at ILMxLAB and the future cinematic projects that are coming out? Will we see connections between those worlds, or will they remain different canvases that we see different stories separated on?

Rob Bredow: Some of that I can't speak to yet. The thing that I can say that's specific to that is that we're really fortunate to get to work really closely with the LucasFilm story groups, and they are the team that is responsible for the overall storytelling universe that we get to play in. I can't say what specific experiences might relate to specific things in the canon, but it's really great to have that close interaction with the team.

John Bucher: Let's talk about the idea of audiences experiencing empathy in these environments. Obviously, people have a great emotional connection to the *Star Wars* characters and the *Star Wars* universe. VR has been called the ultimate empathy machine. Do you have consultants in the science community that talk about empathy and how that's achieved with the digital technologies, or is it more of an organic process of intuitively knowing how people will emotionally respond to this sort of content?

Rob Bredow: I think our main focus is really about what a good story is in this world. The thing we're looking for more than explicitly empathy per se is emotional resonance, which I think is slightly broader than just empathy. Empathy is great, but we're looking for a story that has emotional resonance with the audience. And that's often our threshold. Is this something that people would want to experience, and worth our time to build? We only get to build a tiny fraction of the total ideas we have, so we want to make sure when we're building something, it's going to be one of the best ideas we have. Really that vision comes from Kathy Kennedy. That's been her mantra for the kind of projects that she expects to be made in LucasFilm.

John Bucher: What makes a good *Star Wars* story?

Rob Bredow: One of the biggest components *is* emotional resonance. Is there something that we universally can relate to as people?

John Bucher: In *Trials on Tatooine*, players get an opportunity to hold a light saber and have that experience. As you mentioned, these are first-person experiences, as opposed to third-person experiences where we're just a ghost observing these things in front of us. Can you talk about the differences in approach between something that we just observe and a story where we are the protagonist?

Rob Bredow: There are quite a few differences, actually. I think the biggest one is the state that it puts the participant in. If you are just observing the things around you, you can tell very powerful stories that way, and there's lots of stories that can be explored that way for sure. The moment you have agency in the story and you can interact with it, it really changes your overall perspective and what that story means to you, and the kind of emotions, and the impact you can have on people as they get to experience it that way. One of the experiments we did with *Trials on Tatooine* is to take it to a *Star Wars* celebration in London. That's where a lot of fans go to get to meet the people involved in making the projects and hear about what's coming up next. It's a fantastic opportunity to interact with the fans firsthand. That audience was pretty excited to get to be in this world and experience what it's like to stand under the *Millennium Falcon*, or to interact with R2, and of course hold a light saber. We had a lot of really positive responses and people who were very emotionally engaged in the experience.

John Bucher: What would you say, on a big picture scale, would be the ideal opportunity that Virtual Reality will provide for Lucas-Film? What is your ultimate hope in using these new technologies to continue to tell *Star Wars* stories?

Rob Bredow: I think the big opportunity with Virtual Reality, or Augmented Reality, is being able to tell stories that are really well suited for this medium—that can only be told in this medium. We think there's actually quite a few stories that are best, or perhaps *only* able to be told, with this sort of format.

John Bucher: Will LucasFilm and ILM look through the VR lens beyond the *Star Wars* universe?

Rob Bredow: I definitely wouldn't rule anything out. ILMxLAB is work-
                ing on projects that are outside of the *Star Wars* universe
                already because we think the *Star Wars* universe is a great
                place to tell these stories, but it's certainly not the only one.

John Bucher: You are someone who is a master storyteller that has worked
                for many years in these cutting-edge environments of tech-
                nology. What are some of the key things that you have been
                able to bring from your background from working in film
                and special effects to the world of VR storytelling? What
                have been some of the key tools that you've continued to use
                with this new experience?

Rob Bredow: Well, the same core emotional storytelling tools, I think, are
                completely applicable for cinema and Virtual Reality. I think
                the biggest differences are the things that have been the
                most interesting. I can give you a story from the making of
                Trials on Tatooine.

                We had it pretty far along, and the experience was quite a
                lot like what you see today, but it had some extra dialogue
                in it. We put Kiri Hart (SVP of development at LucasFilm)
                through the experience, and after she came out, she said,
                "Give me the script, I want to make a couple suggestions."
                And she did an edit on the script where she tried taking out
                all the dialogue that wasn't directed right at you the user—
                the player. The dialogue that was happening between Han
                and Chewy, in the cockpit, she tried striking it out. She tried
                striking out pretty much anything that wasn't happening to
                you directly in first person in the story. She said, "Try it with-
                out these lines and see how it feels." Ironically, some of those
                lines were some of my favorite lines that Pablo (Hidalgo) and
                I had written, so I was like, "Oh man! That's a super-fun line.
                I don't want to cut that." But you have to try it and see what
                it's going to be like.

                The next day we had that version up, without those lines
                in it, and it was the first time that our brains completely
                relaxed playing *Trials in Tatooine*. What we learned, at least
                in that moment and in this phase of Virtual Reality, is if you
                want somebody to believe that it's a first-person story, you
                can do it. But you want to continually remind them that

the story is directed at them. If you are in a virtual environment where you're already imagining you're standing and moving in the *Millennium Falcon* and then the storyteller asks you to imagine that in another room, let's say the cockpit of the *Millennium Falcon*, there's another conversation going on between Han and Chewy, that's not directed at you but instead just overhearing—it's pretty complicated to ask somebody to pick up on it and not get distracted by it. The moment we simplified it down to be all about you, the story got that much clearer and better as a first-person experience. That's just an example of the kind of learning and experimentation that's happening right now at Lucas-Film and ILMxLAB with our storytelling process in Virtual Reality. We're getting surprising results.

Acting and Directing in VR Stories
An Interview with
Tye Sheridan, Actor and Star of *Ready Player One*
and Cocreator of Aether Inc.
Nikola Todorovic, Director and Cocreator of Aether Inc.

Tye Sheridan has been named one of *Variety*'s 10 Actors to Watch. Seen recently as Cyclops in *X-Men: Apocalypse*, Sheridan has played leading roles alongside Brad Pitt in Terrence Malick's *The Tree of Life*, alongside Matthew McConaughey in *Mud*, and portrays Wade Owen Watts/Parzival in Steven Spielberg's *Ready Player One*. Nikola Todorovic is an emerging director in the world of VR with a background in visual effects. Together, Sheridan and Todorovic created Aether Inc., a VR production and development company.

John Bucher:	Let's start by talking about why VR has become so important. What is it about right now that, for whatever reason, makes this the right season for its large-scale adoption?
Tye Sheridan:	That's a good question. I actually had a director show me a short that he did in 1998 or '99, and it revolved around Virtual Reality where a guy had a virtual girlfriend.
Nikola Todorovic:	Millennials are so open to technology. When I was a kid, if you were doing something on the computer, your dad told you that you were wasting your time. Now everything is about technology. I think another reason VR is succeeding now is because the internet is faster. If you wanted to stream VR four years ago, you would have trouble. I think that's a big issue. You have to have broadband that's really fast to be able to do it, because everything is streaming now. People are also way more open to wearing an HMD now than they used to be. I think Google Glass was a good introduction to that, although it failed. People are still more open to wearable technology. The "Wow" factor in VR just completes that circle.
Tye Sheridan:	Especially for people who haven't seen it before. I showed it to my 73-year-old grandpa and he takes the headset off, and looks at me and I said, "Well, Papa,

what did you think?" He just can't wrap his head around it and goes, "It's different." He just couldn't comprehend what it actually was. It was funny to watch him inside the virtual world. I said, "Papa, you know you can look left and right and it will track wherever you look." He starts to hesitantly turn his head left and then he realizes the frame is moving, and he can look anywhere, and it's going to be filled by frame in a 360 environment. It was a great experience.

Nikola Todorovic: I don't like the idea that people have compared VR to 3D and its failure to be adopted en mass. 3D has existed for so long and does not really add *that* much to the average user's experience. I think it's quite different. It can't be compared. This transforms you. It puts you in a world. It really does. We're in such an early stage right now. This is early filmmaking.

John Bucher: Chris Milk famously called VR *the ultimate empathy machine*. What do you think the relationship is between immersive environments and empathy? What's the connection?

Tye Sheridan: It really is a different plane of entertainment—a different experience. I remember being at Sundance 2014 and Oculus had a booth and I walked in and saw all these people trying Virtual Reality for the first time. They'd completely lost all awareness of where they were. I guess I've always been drawn to stories because it takes me out of my world, and this is just a totally different level of the empathy created by doing that. It's that next level.

Nikola Todorovic: I also think it's such a psychological thing with our brains. Habituation, when our brains get used to activities, is a big problem. That's why story is so precious. If you make a good story, you can move and inspire someone, or get someone to understand how kids in Africa live or how refugees in Syria feel. You have to make a really good story, because we see these worlds on the news all the time, and after a while, our brains become adjusted to it as normal. We can't really feel that much empathy. Maybe for a second we'll stop, but you see violence all the time on television. When you see someone getting killed on a TV show or a film, it really doesn't affect you that much because you've seen it a thousand times, so you don't understand how it looks and feels in real life. I think VR is so new that our brains are tricked into believing that it's real.

John Bucher: With other types of visual storytelling, be it theater, be it film, television, even video games, we experience those stories in a dark room with strangers or on the couch with family members or in an audience sitting next to people. With VR, presently, you have an HMD strapped to your head, and you're very much alone in these environments. Can you talk a little bit about how you think the role of social VR will change storytelling?

Nikola Todorovic: That's *Ready Player One*, pretty much.

Tye Sheridan: A much more glamorous, attractive world. You can pick and choose who you want to hang out with—the world you want to live in. *Ready Player One* is based on a novel by Ernest Cline, and in it, you see all of these kids who live on different planets based on their desires and likes, whether they like arcades or they like roller coasters. You can literally go to the amusement park planet or the sports planet. There are so many different options, and why would we live in a world where the limitations are restricting us from doing the things that we love to do all the time? If you can have that at your fingertips, then why not?

Nikola Todorovic: Then comes the danger that I think that book speaks of so well—you can get lost.

Tye Sheridan: You can totally get lost in that world. That's one of the major themes in the story talks—staying true to reality and embracing it, because at the end of the day, it's the only thing that's real.

Nikola Todorovic: I remember when everyone first began doing chat rooms. It changed the way we related to each other. Now, talking on the phone is getting weird, because we're texting. You call someone that you've just met, they're like, "Why is this guy calling me? Why doesn't he text?" I think our kids are going to say, "Ha, you guys used to text. How ridiculous was that?" We lie to ourselves that it's not moving as fast as it is. I'm not as scared about technology as many people are. I think we need to accept it. I think it will be good. There's always the need for moderation.

Tye Sheridan: I have a 16-year-old little sister, and in the past two years, I've seen a lot of that change represented in her life and the way she interacts with everyone and the way she's evolved as a person. Back to *Ready Player One*, it touches on that a lot. It's one of the major themes. If you get so comfortable being someone that you're not, you start believing that you're that person.

Nikola Todorovic: I do think social VR and gaming's going to be way bigger than entertainment VR. I think we're going to be watching entertainment inside of these social experiences. For that reason, I don't think people will be building avatars as often. They are just going to be themselves, I hope.

John Bucher: Tye, how do you think VR is going to change the acting profession? Actors have been used to knowing, "This is my frame, and this is where I'm moving within a frame." As that goes away, how is that going to be for actors?

Tye Sheridan: That's a great question. In recent years, I've become very technically aware. I believe that it allows me to do my job better when I have an awareness of what the frame is. I always ask to see the frame before I step into the shot or what lens you're using, because when I have an awareness of the frame, it becomes clear in my mind. The easier that makes it for the cinematographer, the director, the gaffer. We can all start to work as one. We all understand each other's job and we all understand the way the camera works and the way the set is supposed to function. With Virtual Reality, when you're shooting in 360-degree video, it's also super important that you stay technically aware because of issues like eye lines. It creates a new challenge for actors, but it's also a new opportunity. In some ways, it's more like stage acting.

Nikola Todorovic: We shot a scene that was really hard recently. Someone who Tye's character loves dearly is getting killed in front of his eyes and he cannot move. He's tied up, so he's screaming and crying. That's really hard as an actor because he needs to keep that emotion going for the entire period. We can't cut away. I think a lot of VR is going to be shot on blue or green screen for that reason. Then you will be able to do scenes like that with multiple takes.

Tye Sheridan: There's so many things to focus on. I know it's also super difficult to direct.

John Bucher: The two of you have formed this VR company. What are you hoping to bring to the VR space that will be unique?

Tye Sheridan: I think there's a huge lack of really strong narrative and story in Virtual Reality. People are getting distracted by the medium, and it is cool, but what's the story?

Nikola Todorovic: I always tell Tye, you ask yourself if you made this and put it on YouTube as a regular video, not in 360, would it be good? Story is story. It doesn't change when you watch it on a different medium. Kids are watching multimillion-dollar movies on the iPhones. If you have a good story, it really doesn't matter where you watch it. I think that's one huge thing that we're [Aether] focusing on. It's story ahead of everything else.

Tye Sheridan: Right, you can't get distracted by the technology, just take us through the story.

Nikola Todorovic: Once you call attention to the technology, I realize I'm experiencing something. I'm no longer in your story.

John Bucher: It breaks the immersion.

Nikola Todorovic: It totally breaks the immersion for me. I've seen experiences that were done in 180, and they're great. I don't always even need the entire 360 if the story is there.

Case Study: Baobab VR Studios
Eric Darnell, Chief Creative Officer
Maureen Fan, Chief Executive Officer

FIGURE 8.1 Courtesy of Baobab Studios

FIGURE 8.2 Courtesy of Baobab Studios

Established in 2015 by Maureen Fan and Eric Darnell, Baobab Studios is a VR animation studio, creating dynamic narratives and story lines. *INVA-SION!* was the studio's first VR animated film, winning numerous awards including Tribeca Film Festival's 2016 VR Selection of the Year, Cannes

"Next Marche de Film," and Toronto International Film Festival. Maureen Fan has held leadership roles in film, gaming, and the consumer web. She was vice president of games at Zynga, where she oversaw three game studios, including the FarmVille sequels. Previously, she worked on Pixar's *Toy Story* and at eBay in product management and user interface (UI) design. Her most recent collaboration, *The Dam Keeper*, directed by Dice Tsutsumi and Robert Kondo, was nominated for the 2015 Oscar Best Animated Short.

Eric Darnell's career spans 25 years as a computer animation director, screenwriter, story artist, film director, and executive producer. He was the director and screenwriter on all four films in the *Madagascar* franchise, which together have grossed more than $2.5 billion at the box office. He was also executive producer on *The Penguins of Madagascar*. Previously, Eric directed DreamWorks Animation's very first animated feature film, *Antz*, which features the voices of Woody Allen, Gene Hackman, Christopher Walken, and Sharon Stone.

Focused on animated VR content, Fan explains why this medium has been their emphasis. "We believe that deep down inside, there's still a dreamer inside everyone, and we know it's true because it's the reason that we go to the movies to this day. It's to experience characters and stories beyond those that we meet in our common lives. And we believe that animation does this better than live action, because live action is still constrained by reality, versus animation, which is constrained only by the creativity within the director's head. Animation, to us, it's our emotion. It takes you to completely different worlds. It makes the world feel so real that you think you could reach out and touch it. The last two sentences that I just said, which is that it takes you to a different world and makes you believe it's real, are the definition of Virtual Reality, which is why we think animation and VR were made for each other," she said.

Darnell concurs. "We're focused on interactive storytelling in Virtual Reality, and leveraging off of one of storytelling's great strengths, which is the capacity to elicit profound, emotional experiences through the development of empathetic connections with the characters within the story. This is what storytelling has been doing for thousands of years. Storytelling has evolved with the human race. It's in our DNA. Really, it's what it means to be a human being, and it's one of the reasons why these classic forms of storytelling, like literature and movies and TV and plays, can elicit these really powerful emotions in all of us. We're talking about these powerful emotional journeys."

Baobab has won over some of the most significant voices in visual storytelling. After seeing their content, Alvy Ray Smith, cofounder of Pixar, compared the protagonist bunny in their film to the power of VR itself. "It gives you the opportunity to believe that a character really exists, and really matters, and then be able to act on that behalf. You just can't do that in any other storytelling medium. You know, if you look back at the movies, it's remarkable how you can just sit in that room and it can elicit these really powerful emotional responses. It can make grown men cry, make an entire audience gasp in unison, lovers clutch others' arms and children instinctively cry out for their mothers," he said. Darnell agrees that story will be the key to VR's success. "Through storytelling Virtual Reality, I believe we'll be able to have the same kind of deep and profound emotional experiences that we have at the movies, and these experiences have the potential to be even more profound because of the fact that we're actually living them.

"VR is not a movie. It's not a game, at least the direction that we're taking it. You know, there's no camera, there's no screen, there's no rectangle. There's no fourth wall to break, so when a character looks at you, they're just looking at you. You are in their world," he said.

Baobab plans to continue to focus its efforts around character-driven storytelling. "One thing that's definitely true in film and certainly true in VR is that having great animated characters are always worth it. This is what storytelling is all about. It's about connecting with these characters that you are in the world with, that you understand, not what they're, not just what they're doing, but you understand why they're doing it," Darnell said. "We need to know, we need to see what that character is thinking. Before they take an action, we all decide to take that action. We need to see that, and if you can deliver that to the audience and understand what's driving these characters from the inside out, that's what's going to give you the ability to really connect with them, understand them, and empathize with them," Darnell concluded.

Storytelling in VR through Journalism
An Interview with
Sarah Hill, CEO and Chief Storyteller, StoryUP

Sarah Hill is an Emmy-award winning, 20-year veteran of the interactive journalism industry. Before starting StoryUP, she built a successful TV feature franchise and the world's first interactive news program based on Google Hangouts. She has produced content in Vietnam, Guatemala, Sri Lanka, Indonesia, and Zambia and collaborated with companies ranging from Google to the NBA to the U.S. Army.

John Bucher: Tell me about how your professional interest in story began.

Sarah Hill: Telling stories became important to me early on as a journalist in my fixed-frame flat world. I got into television in the early '90s, and I did some stories about a few veterans that I fell in love with. We ended up opening up what's called an Honor Flight Hub in Columbia, Missouri. These were flights that take aging veterans to see their memorial in Washington, DC—physical flights. I got into Virtual Reality because a lot of these veterans were calling us saying they were too ill to travel on physical flights to see the memorial in DC, so we needed an alternative. We began using Google Glass to try to take them there. We were doing live streaming tours and then we would take laptops to the veteran's bedside. That had inherent problems with bandwidth and things like that. Someone suggested, "Have you ever heard of Virtual Reality?"

I tried Google Cardboard. I watched Chris Milk's TED talk and was totally blown away. I said, "This is the missing link, this is what we can do . . . Use it to capture these tours for these veterans." After we did that first experience for the veterans, I noticed they were overcome with emotion, far more than a regular fixed-frame flat video. After watching them react to immersive video content, I knew, as a storyteller, this was a very important tool that we could be using. In addition to good writing and good video, good production values, good characters, all those kinds of things—the technology of it is really ripe for storytelling to elicit an emotional response. From there, I quit my excellent job with a well-paying salary, and we opened our own company. We are an immersive media company. We have a brand studio and we have a journalism studio.

Primarily, our economic engine is working with foundations and charities to try to illustrate for people their problems so that they're able to then use that content to raise money or raise support among their donors. That's primarily the content that we do. We also do meditation and mindfulness experiences as well. Our app features a variety of stories, not only health-care stories, but experiences about what it feels like to experience stroke.

John Bucher: Talk to me a little bit about why telling a story in VR space is different—what sort of opportunities that affords the story-teller that are different from our traditional media.

Sarah Hill: It's different, but it's also the same. A lot of people think once they start telling stories in this sphere, "Oh this is great, there's no frame," and I was the same way. "Wow this is liberating. We can look anywhere," and then you get into writing the stories and you realize, there is a frame. It's just a frame inside the sphere and it's moving left and right and it can be confining to the storyteller, because for decades we had the control. We were the ones who decided what they saw through that frame, and now we don't have that control. The viewer has the control, and they have to decide where to look. As a storyteller, it's a power struggle for us because it's a different way of telling stories in that you don't know what they're seeing as opposed to what you're seeing. You have to use positional audio. You have to use narration. You have to use graphics. You have to use tracking objects in order to gently direct the audience's attention.

It's a different way of telling stories—a different way of expe-riencing them. We are not experiencing them any longer through the filter of the fixed rectangle. Storytellers had used flat words and pictures and video and still photos and all these media assets to try to place people inside a story, and now the technology actually exists that we can truly put you inside the story, which is an enormously powerful tool for a storyteller. We've actually done studies on the differ-ence between fixed-frame video and spherical video. There's higher viewer engagement. It's shared more. It's watched longer and it's also watched again. The reason why is that they think that they might have missed something in looking around in this sphere because they can look everywhere.

Which marketers love—the fact that people would actually want to watch their content again. There's also some very interesting things that happen in the brain between fixed-frame video and immersive video. We have a psychologist who works with us. His name is Dr. Jeff Tarrant. He's actually studying what immersive video does to the brain, so we give him our stories to work with. People aren't just watching the video, they're feeling the video, and so after you create an experience, you have to put it in the faces of a variety of individuals, even the most motion-sick-prone person in the room, and say, "How'd you feel watching that? Did this slight movement bother you? At any point did you feel queasy?"

John Bucher: Let's talk about the idea of narrative characters. We are familiar with the concept from traditional storytelling—plays and films and books. Can you talk a little bit about what you've brought from your traditional training and storytelling with characters and how you've brought that into the VR space?

Sarah Hill: In journalism, we were never allowed to stage anything or use props or a set or anything like that. We just had to capture reality, and that's what we're really doing here with VR. You will see a lot of filmmakers who are staging or telling people what to say. Or bringing in props. And ours is more journalistic storytelling and less moviemaking. As journalists, we learned how to find compelling characters for our stories. That was what drove our stories in the fixed-frame world. It was very natural for us to be able to translate that concept into the immersive world, because when we tell stories, you can't tell a story without a person. Sure, you can humanize around a tree or a dog or something like that, but you need characters, whether they be animate or inanimate objects. All of our stories are people driven, we call them CCCs, or central compelling characters in the story.

With immersive video, you really have to decide who is the camera in this scene in the story. The camera doesn't have to be one person throughout the whole piece. We learned that the hard way. We thought, "Oh, it's all these pieces, they have to be point-of-view pieces." Well, they're not, because when you do that, you don't get all sides of the story, and sometimes you totally miss the empathy. We thought, for instance, in our Zambia piece, the point of view we should adopt is the person on the ground and we should show that view, what that's like at all times, but if you show that at all times, you miss the very important view of what it feels like when one of these individuals was crawling towards you. You also have to have that third-person perspective as well, or your audience sometimes feels a little bit confined. Sometimes you want them to feel confined in experiences, but sometimes you really want them to experience all of those different angles.

Certainly, as a journalist, our default position is that we want the audience to experience a variety of different views. To answer your question from the fixed-frame world, as a journalist, what we carried over was the ability to find compelling stories. As journalists, this was how they trained us when there was no news going on. The assignment editor would say, "Go, get out of the newsroom and find a story." So that was what we had to become accustomed to, and if you ask any feature journalist out there right now, chances are they have about three stories in their mind that they could tell on a day when there's nothing really going on. Why? They talk to the people at the gas station. They talk to the people at the grocery store. They're volunteering in their communities and they're constantly asking people, "What's news to you?" They're constantly thinking about stories that they could cover.

John Bucher: Let's talk about the technical production of the pieces that you've done. In traditional, fixed-frame media, we've had the lower-third graphic that's come up under someone. You've moved the lower third out into the space to put it next to the person or put it somewhere we still can identify who that person is. Can you talk a little bit about that process of finding the sweet spot of how to technically achieve good storytelling in VR?

Sarah Hill: If you look at some of our early pieces, you will see that we did put it right where it's always been in the frame, because that was where our comfort level was. We quickly realized that was not always a workable solution because viewers can look all the way around. Why have it covering the speaker's body when it could be floating out to the side? When it could be embedded in a box that's next to them? When it could be put in the side of a mountain?

John Bucher: Can you tell us a little bit about where you're taking this and where you want to see VR storytelling go?

Sarah Hill: We have a project coming out with Empowered By Light and the Leonardo DiCaprio Foundation, and it's all about solar energy—how a lack of solar energy threatens to flood sacred lands of a certain tribe in the Amazon. These sorts of projects that make the world a better place are where I'd like to continue seeing us go. We're also shooting a project with Facebook and Oculus and a charity called Love Has No Labels. We're playing with cropping. We're playing with the sphere. We're playing with mirrors. We are looking at implicit bias, using 360-degree video to illustrate for people our implicit bias, and how if we're only seeing this much of a story or of a person, we're not seeing their whole picture. We're not seeing them fully, and we don't have enough information to judge that situation fully.

John Bucher: Finally, all technology takes us somewhere. It transports us somewhere. Where, in an ideal world, would you love to see this technology transport humanity?

Sarah Hill: I would like it to transport us back to our home videos. I want the ability to put my fixed-frame video of my second birthday with my mom in a VR headset and watch it again like I was there. I know that some smart person will come up with that idea, but I think that would be really great to see.

INSIGHTS FROM THE STORYTELLERS

Storytellers provide looks at life that range from our own backyards to the farthest reaches of outer space. The tools at their disposal are advancing faster than ever. Some storytellers work with characters and archetypes very familiar to their audiences, like Rob Bredow. Others, such as Sarah Hill, are making the decision of what real-life personalities will be the characters in the story with every project. Both storytellers use characters, but in completely different ways. Understanding how characters work, as discussed in detail in Chapter 6, helps creators identify one of the most basic building blocks of narrative. We feel empathy for characters and the situations they find themselves in, not for environments or lifeless objects, such as costumes, important as those elements are. Bredow more specifically identifies emotional resonance as the sort of empathy he looks for in creating stories. Resonance suggests that two similar things share qualities. Emotional resonance would then speak to two individuals sharing qualities or emotions—the character and the audience member. Hill referred to these as the three Cs—central compelling characters. These are just the sorts of characters Tye Sheridan embodies when telling stories in VR. He models what is possible when an actor truly understands their role in the storytelling process. There's no need for us to consider or move on to storytelling structure if we don't have compelling characters in place.

While Baobab uses primarily animated animals in their stories, they demonstrate the same understanding of characters. They value the same empathy and emotional resonance that Bredow speaks of. There is a wide span between the sorts of stories told by Sarah Hill in Africa, Baobab in animation, and Rob Bredow in the Star Wars universe, and yet there is not. All the storytellers in this section understand that story begins with effective characters that people can identify with. All understand the power and even limits of the technology they are using but don't let that become the focus of their work. They create characters that embody the best (and worst) of who we are and who we want to be. We learn lessons from the characters' mistakes and take joy in their victories. Stories that are true, loosely based on real events, and completely fictional all have a place in the narrative universe, and certainly in the world of VR, as long as they hold the tenets of storytelling that have served humankind for thousands of years—characters, conflicts, and resolutions.

A number of storytellers in this section and in this book mention that VR will not be experienced by only a single person at a time for much longer. As social VR experience becomes available, the emotional resonance experienced through the technology will be held by an entire audience together, much as it is in a movie theater. Social VR experiences and stories will hold the capability to engage the smallest audiences of two or three, as well as the capability to tell stories to literally thousands of people at one time. These potentials will undoubtedly change the ways stories are crafted in VR space as they develop. These changes will make it increasingly important to rely on and implement the elements and methods that have seemed to work across centuries and mediums. As Eric Darnell stated, "Storytelling has evolved with the human race. It's in our DNA." There's been no indication it will not serve us in all the same ways it has throughout our evolution.

THE TECHNOLOGISTS AND PRODUCERS

Nonlinear Storytelling in VR
An Interview with
Jonathan Krusell, Google Daydream Producer

Jonathan Krusell is a creator with more than ten years of experience leading production, creative, and strategy for interactive entertainment. His career has included roles ranging from VP of production to studio director. Awards for some of the games he has worked on include IGN People's Choice Award 2012 (*Avengers Initiative*), Best Family Game at E3 2009 (Disney's *Guilty Party*), and GameSpot Best Use of Zombies at E3 2005 (*Stubbs the Zombie*). Other significant properties he has worked on include Disney's *The Haunted Mansion, Charlie and the Chocolate Factory, 50 Cent Bulletproof: G Unit Edition*, and *Spiderman 3*. Currently, he serves as an executive producer at Mindshow and a producer for Google's Daydream.

John Bucher:	Tell me about your background in gaming and how that led to VR.
Jonathan Krusell:	I've been doing games for 15 years—console, PC, and mobile. Games are what I set out to do, actually. I went to film school, was interested in movies, but to me, I felt like movies had peaked in the late '70s. I don't know if I was right about that, but I wanted to get into something that was still on the rise, so games are where I was focused for a long time. The thing that I find interesting about VR is that previously in games, the user is pointing things into a controller, the controller takes those signals, puts it into a system, the system interprets that and then triggers animations, right? If you think of the player as a performer and the avatar as the presentation of that performance, there's a lot of layers between them. A lot of those layers collapse now with VR. On the high-end systems, and even the medium-level systems in VR, you basically have consumer-grade motion-capture systems. The HTC Vive has the lighthouses that capture your motion. Oculus has cameras. Daydream has accelerometers. They're all capturing motion, but it's actually your motion.

Some games let the player directly drive the characters. That means that all those layers have collapsed now. What that means is that there's this opportunity now for improvisation. You can do things that no engineer ever thought of. Previously, engineers, designers, and artists had to think about everything ahead of time and invest it all into the software so that you could trigger it. They don't have to do that anymore. You can't do *everything* yet, because it's not full-body mocap, but it's still pretty robust. In the near future, it will get more and more robust as newer technologies develop and converge. Things like that exist right now, but just on separate devices. As those things come together into a single device, it will be more and more robust.

John Bucher: What were you able to bring over from the gaming world that works well in VR? What did you have to transcend?

Jonathan Krusell: The biggest thing I think I bring to VR is just a stomach for software development. Software development is a very nerve-racking thing. Things are constantly evolving, and it's hard to predict where it's all going to end out. The first three times you work on developing a project, it's terrifying. Eventually you get a stomach for it and you're like, "Okay. Everything's probably going to be okay." I'm also comfortable with nonlinear storytelling. Actually, I'm super comfortable with it and prefer it to a three-act structure. A three-act-structure story means you're taking agency away from the user. Video games tried to do that for so long with movie audiences. We were just trying to recreate a movie in a game. Nonlinear storytelling has served me very well in VR. I used to run a motion-capture studio. Similar to a theater in the round. We were constantly thinking about 3D volumes and 3D spaces and thinking about storytelling where you don't know where the user is. *Half-Life*'s always done that really well. There's a narrative happening with dialogue that's preprogrammed, but you can move throughout the space and they react to you. On top of all that, I love the idea of immersion—trying to find ways to get the player to be engrossed in the experience. Not many other mediums have immersion at the level VR does. Books are the most immersive thing in the world, but they're a particular medium that doesn't include an audio/video experience or haptic feedback.

John Bucher: In VR, we have a deeper level of embodiment. In some VR experiences, I can look and actually see my hands. Can you talk about embodiment?

Jonathan Krusell: That's something that is actually different from video games. The tropes that I'm used to from games—they're evolving. They don't apply the way they used to, whereas a third-person action game previously felt like you were driving an avatar, right. But now, a third-person experience in VR feels like me and you. There's a character, and I'm a different character, and we're working together to do something. That's very different.

First person is even more different. Previously, first person felt like I was in the action, but there was a barrier between me and the world—the screen. But now with VR, that barrier is dissolved and I am actually surrounded by it. It can be jarring and shocking for some users. As a designer, you have to ask, how uncomfortable are you willing to make the user, and does that become a barrier to other things you're trying to accomplish?

With some of the applications I've worked on, you could embody an alien, or you could embody a woman, or you could embody a man with completely different proportions, right. In all those cases, there's going to be moments of, minutes of, or never-ending discomfort. Female characters in video games are super popular. But I wonder if in VR it will be a bigger barrier for some males—to embody a female character and get comfortable with that. You have to be thoughtful about when and how you're going to do it and also to prepare the user for it. It can be jarring to suddenly be in a new space and have a little micro–identity crisis about what's going on. That's one area where it is very different than games, and there is still lots to figure out and learn about.

John Bucher: You have developed content for Disney before. We often think about VR as being something that people 16 and up really engage with, maybe 16 to 40, actually, being the target demographic. When we think about putting a headset on children, do you think there are going to be different ways that we approach VR for different-age audiences? Obviously, content is going to be an issue, but do you think there will be differences in how we design or tell stories?

Jonathan Krusell: Yes. I think there's different ways that you would consider the ideal-use case—thinking through session length and intensity. I think Google Cardboard is something that is okay for a ten-year-old, because it's not as intense. It's something that's easy to remove. It's something that's made with short sessions in mind. I think *Expeditions* is a great example of how you can make content that is only doable in VR—taking big field trips together. My kids are pretty young. I hesitate to put them in any VR, but I certainly wouldn't put them in an HTC Vive, because it's just too intense. I had a weird experience showing my mother VR. She's over 70. I didn't realize until it was on her how ridiculous it all looked because the Vive looks like you're piloting a drone or something. It looks military grade.

John Bucher: What do you think are going to be the ongoing challenges that storytellers in VR will continue to grapple with?

Jonathan Krusell: When you're in software development, the thing is that you never get comfortable. The technology's always changing. You have to get used to that sort of cadence. I think that's going to be challenging for people coming from other industries that are now learning the ins and outs of software development. At some point, there's going to be some pretty big moral content decisions. Right now, it's a pretty tight-knit community, and there's some unspoken territory to stay away from. It's not going to be like that forever.

John Bucher: If I become comfortable having the experience of killing a very human AI, I've experienced the feeling of murder. What do you think are the ethical issues that we would do well to think about now? Most people agree, you can play video games and you can shoot people all day, and you're not going to really want to go kill a human being. But at some point, with artificial intelligence in Virtual Reality, you're going to feel like you've *actually* shot someone. How do we navigate it?

Jonathan Krusell: Yeah, I agree with you. In the past, there was the barrier of the screen that arguably made everybody realize it was fantasy. That doesn't exist anymore. How do we regulate that? I don't know. How do current channels with lots of power self-regulate? Because, ideally, there's some sort of system that *self-regulates*. I can't immediately think of a system like that that works well. These are important questions to ask because they're inevitable.

John Bucher: I want to circle back to nonlinear storytelling. It can be argued that with all of human activity, we make sense of the world through narratives.

Jonathan Krusell: We layer story on it, constantly.

John Bucher: Absolutely. When we talk about nonlinear storytelling, are there narrative shards that we pull from a structured story where we say, "Well, it's not a linear story, but we still have a good guy and a bad guy, or we still have this conflict"? How does nonlinear storytelling work? Can you tease out that a bit?

Jonathan Krusell: There's different kinds of nonlinear storytelling. If you think of the film, *Clue*, it has multiple endings. So does the board game. Nonlinear works well in the mystery genre. Where the board game Clue is simply context and progression, there's the context of a game board, and there's a context of the clues and the characters, and then there's the progression as you move through and make your own deductions. The game doesn't know what choices you're going to make. The game doesn't tell you how to perceive the clues that you find and make the deductions that you make. Now, the game does know who is actually guilty. It's in the envelope. That doesn't change the story that you're telling.

It's all nonlinear until the end, because the ending is decided. But you're able to create your own story in your head by the breadcrumbs that you pick up and how you interpret them. To me, that is nonlinear storytelling, which is like context plus progression, having choice in the matter, and being able to interpret and deduce what you believe. That's what I think I'm really excited about in VR is the idea of mystery games. When you talk about Alternative Reality games, the murder mystery is the oldest Alternative Reality game there is.

John Bucher: In video games, most stories have an end—you can conquer the game. There's exceptions—world-building games that just go on and on. Do you see, with VR experiences, somebody entering a space where there's not a clear ending or objective? Do you think that's going to get frustrating for people, or do you think just being able to constantly explore will have the same effect as, say, a *World of Warcraft* that can just go on forever? What do you think we need to be designing experiences toward? Do we need to guide people towards an ending or just endless exploration?

Jonathan Krusell: Well, I think it's going to evolve as the medium evolves. I think, right now, an ending is fine. I think right now there's going to be a lot of single-player experiences that are finite in length, maybe even episodic. These are all experiments right now, to learn about what is ideal. Then as it evolves, it can go in any number of directions. I definitely think that multiplayer or shared experiences are going to be huge. I think that taking on different characters, like in a murder mystery, where there is improvisation, will be effective. Let's do it in a castle. No, let's do it in a Victorian manor. That sort of thing, that allows people to customize the experience for themselves. Then, ultimately, I do think that these things would exist in some sort of shared universe where it's looped within loops. Where you complete one loop and it just reveals a bigger loop. Which is just basically creating some sort of simulated reality. But a simulated reality would define rules. What matters the most, though, is what the promise is to the user when they're going into it. Is there promise of an ending? Well, then you better give them an ending. Or is the promise a universe? In which case, you have to establish the rules and then let them make whatever choice they want within those rules. That's where the real potential is—shared universes.

John Bucher: Do you think rules are going to be necessary in order to ground Virtual Reality and cause people to actually have a truly immersive experience?

Jonathan Krusell: I think rules are inherent. That's why if you make something look photo-realistic, then you are setting a bar that everything else has to match, so the physics better be realistic, the lighting better be realistic, and the rule set better be realistic. Whereas if you make something that looks like VR *Super Mario*, then it's a totally different rule set.

I think it's not a question of do we have to create a rule set; people expect rule sets and they take in what they see and they make rules already. They try to figure out what the rule set is in a scenario, and hopefully you meet that expectation. If you make a decision to dramatically surprise them with a rule they didn't expect, that's a risky move, because it could blow away immersion. If something did look photo-realistic, but then I couldn't pick it up, I'm upset. In video games, you get away with that stuff because the expectations are different. You get away with a lot of things in video games that I don't think you can get away with in VR. You have to be very deliberate. That's why for right now, stylized content is a little safer, because then you can communicate the rules to the player as you go. I like starting small and then layering complexity on top of it. That's just my style, because I think you can get to something more consistent that way.

John Bucher: You brought up multiplayer experiences. In the history of VR, it's been a very singular experience thus far. I put on the glasses and I'm alone. I'm figuring this all out myself. That will obviously change in the near future as we begin to have these multiplayer experiences with friends or family or strangers. How does storytelling change when we go from a medium for individuals to a group dynamic?

Jonathan Krusell: I think it's going to be like LARPing—where we all agree to live in this fantasy and we do our best to support each other in that fantasy, and if you break it, there's some sort of social repercussion for that. I mean, we're all doing that right now, every moment, in real life. It's just not as fantastical. The trick with the VR, though, is going to be matchmaking—which is a really big deal. You have to have a critical mass of players at a certain time, at a variety of skill levels, that you can set up quality matches where everyone has fun, and then they show up again later. That's how things are with console games.

Now in VR, at least in my opinion of the immediate future, you're looking at drastically shorter sessions—like an hour or less. How do you reach critical mass so that you can have a quality multiplayer experience? It's tricky. It has to be very event driven. It has to be super event driven where there's a reason. It's like now with Netflix and all this streaming media where you can consume anything at any time. Now there might be this new VR event system where it becomes water-cooler talk. "Oh man, were you there last night?"

There's two things that are exciting, to me. There's the shared fantasy, and then there's the creation tools. I am intrigued by shared fantasy—role-playing. Then things like Google's Tilt Brush that allow you to create in a way that you can only do in VR. If you can combine those two things, that's the magic.

John Bucher: Can you speak about what VR could look like as a storytelling medium once we are able to get away from the HMDs? Once it becomes truly augmented reality across the board, what is storytelling like then, and how thin does that line get between narratives and just actual reality?

Jonathan Krusell: There'll have to be some sort of visual language or some sort of adaptive density of fantasy where it can figure out the mental state you're in and dial it in to what you need at that moment. When the technology is that seamless, it's going to get real weird. Is there some sort of centralized service that is making sure that we're all not in conflict, like our fantasies are harmonious, or at least reinforce each other? That we don't walk off cliffs or something like that? I think that barring any extinction-level events, it will eventually get there, and that's where we'll need AI to help out a lot, if they don't enslave us first.

Horror-Based Storytelling in VR
An Interview with
Robyn Tong Gray, COO and Lead Designer, Otherworld Interactive
Andrew Goldstein, CEO, Otherworld Interactive

Robyn Tong Gray is an interactive media designer who weaves new media together to explore narrative and empathy. Her projects have been featured at venues including the Independent Games Festival, IndieCade, and the Sundance Film Festival. Robyn is the director of *Sisters*, Otherworld Interactive's horror franchise revolving around a pair of spooky twin dolls and their haunted home. She and Andrew Goldstein founded Otherworld Interactive, a Virtual Reality content studio located in Culver City, CA. Their company has been featured in publications across the industry, including a significant profile in *PC* Magazine.

John Bucher:	How did you become interested in VR? What brought you into immersive space?
Robyn Tong Gray:	Andy and I both finished our graduate degrees over at USC's Interactive Media Program. They have a really high concentration of professors who came out of VR. When we were there, Mark Bolas was still on faculty. He's now working on the Hollow Lens at Microsoft. We also met Scott Fisher. Both of these guys worked at NASA on some of the first early, practical VR in the 1980s.
	When I first started in the program at USC, I was a research assistant at the Mixed Reality Lab, which, at the time, Mark Bolas was the director of. I loved storytelling in all mediums. Interactive is particularly fascinating to me. Game markets were flooded, but there's this whole new thing with all these new opportunities to actually make something that people will see and has a chance of standing out—and that was VR.
Andrew Goldstein:	Robyn had been making some Virtual Reality projects and had a lot of knowledge there and looped me in, saying, let's see if we can push this forward and start a business. It was great because, at the time, we were one of the few people out there making VR, and we basically have rolled that into a company.

John Bucher:	Let's talk about your most successful horror project, *Sisters*. How did that project come to be?
Robyn Tong Gray:	*Sisters* was originally a two-week project. I love horror movies, and obviously, VR is a lot about tapping into players' gut reactions—something horror excels at. So we thought, why not make something spooky? I would say with *Sisters* we play a lot with tropes. We're not really treading new ground when it comes to the scares there, but I think that's actually important right now in VR—to make people understand that this is something they are familiar with on some level. Even if they don't recognize the media they've suddenly been placed in.
John Bucher:	Did your classic story training and the storytelling tropes you mentioned translate well to VR?
Robyn Tong Gray:	I think it translated really well. With *Sisters*, it was taking a lot of the stuff you learned about when you make games. A lot about indirect control and then also a lot more pushing audio, for example, which is often ignored in games. I came up with the script really early on. I decided the interest curve we want, and that we don't want to have too many plateaus in there where people lose interest. I think from there, it was mainly fine-tuning things, figuring out a good distance for the dolls to pop up from, the timing, and things like that. Also, playing around with jump scares. I love jump scares. They are really easy and cheap, but I love them. We also wanted to move beyond jump scares to incorporate details that might tell a little bit more about the story and that might give you a hint that there's something beyond this two-minute, linear narrative.
John Bucher:	Let's talk about the idea of agency in VR. It's one of the things everyone is trying to figure out—what's the perfect mix of giving the viewer a sense of local agency as opposed to giving a sense of global agency? Do people want to make the small decisions of figuring out what weapon they are going to be able to carry, or do they want to make the decisions that drive the entire

narrative? Are you having those sorts of discussions in the things that you're designing?

Robyn Tong Gray:
We've taken a lot of what we've worked on so far from the traditional gaming world. We are asking if we want to make branching narratives. Do we want to make this linear? As a player, I always want to feel like I have these awesome choices that I'm really going to affect the world that the story's taking place in. On the flip side of that, I feel like nothing I've seen has done that in a way that makes me really satisfied about it in VR yet. I think it's often to the detriment of the story at the moment.

Even with *The Walking Dead* experience by Telltale. They really tapped into people's empathy, really made you feel like you were struggling for these choices, but if you play it a second time around, you feel like nothing you decided on mattered because the other people got axed later. That's horribly dissatisfying. Clearly, there was a story there that whoever made it really wanted to tell, and anything that diverted from that main vision didn't feel great as a result. For us, we've been setting tone for this global story. We want the players to feel agency in that. They might not be able to alter the huge overarching fate of the world, but they can make decisions for themselves that feel good and feel like they did the best they could, just like in real life under those circumstances.

Andrew Goldstein:
Robyn brings up a really important point that Virtual Reality is about environmental storytelling. It's not always about linear storytelling. Your job as a Virtual Reality creator is not always to create the best linear story possible. That's sometimes the job of the film the experience is based on. Sometimes, our task is to create the best environment possible that adds to that story. A lot of times we reference things you embed in the environment that may be interactive, that you might catch, but add a slight level to you being in the space. They're not necessarily linear pieces, but they add to the overall ambiance of being there.

It's creating a new language and new canon for the media. That's where I think a lot of people don't quite understand that Virtual Reality is not the next step in film or the next step in games. It's its own separate thing, and we're still tinkering with how to make it good. Specifically, with that, there are genres in Virtual Reality that play much better than other genres. Horror, sci-fi, stuff that's really heavy on *being there* to understand it does so much better than comedy and drama. People who initially start out trying to do comedy have a lot tougher goal getting something out there because comedy is really specific with timing, or else you kind of miss it, whereas horror is completely ambiance. It's about feeling scared.

John Bucher: Let's talk more about challenges. For several years, people have said the biggest challenge to VR storytelling were things like frame rates or latency—those types of technical challenges, which certainly still exist. But aside from the obvious technical challenges, what are you finding are the biggest hills to overcome?

Robyn Tong Gray: I think it's really about setting expectations. With a lot of traditional, say, inventor games, you have the expectation very quickly knowing that something's purple, which means you can interact with it. You can grab it. Other things are not purple, so you can just ignore them. With VR, you're putting people in this place, and if you've done it really well, then their expectations will be that *everything* is interactive in the world.

It's really about how you frame expectations to the user so that you have formed this version of reality in their mind with nothing that breaks that even on a subtle level. If they see a pencil setting on a table and want to pick it up, they need to be able to do that. And if they can't, it's really disappointing. On the other hand, things like physics are much more powerful, too, as a result. There's not the expectation right now that you can bounce a ball, but if you can, that's really delightful.

John Bucher:	Can we talk about the potential future of VR once HMDs are not the only way that everyone is experiencing it? Have you started to give thought to how your properties will work in AR environments?
Andrew Goldstein:	Every company in VR has to think about AR. You can't be locked into this one specific genre. AR adds a whole new level of that storytelling. But if you're doing it right in VR and the AR platforms come out, you should have no problem transitioning stuff over there. If you want to be an AR company as well as a VR company, you have to start figuring out how you tell stories that work in both worlds.
Robyn Tong Gray:	It's very specific. It's just like you wouldn't make a computer game and expect it to run in VR, necessarily. Some of our stuff would translate really well. For others it would be very different. I personally think VR is the superior storytelling medium. I think there are very specific stories you'll be able to tell in AR, but, personally, just the way I use technology in my everyday life, I want AR to give me all the practical things.
Andrew Goldstein:	We have a lot of internal conversations about how VR is a superior entertainment platform but AR is a superior tools platform. If you look at the disruptions in technologies over the years, the most disruptive things are tools platforms. That's what becomes ubiquitous in daily life. We can use tools platforms as world builders. And, obviously, world building is wrapped into environmental storytelling.
John Bucher:	In one sense, my mind can't tell the difference between the environmental storytelling that is happening to me digitally and somebody really scaring me in real life. Is that something that you think about? Does it go into the design process at all?
Robyn Tong Gray:	Definitely. That is why we like working in the horror genre. Because like I said, it's really about empathy, and one of the easiest emotions to provoke out of people is being uncomfortable and being scared and

not feeling safe. We're playing on all those instincts all the time. We try to keep people constantly primed to be on their toes. You've removed the 2D screen from the equation, so now they don't know what direction they're safe in. They're not safe on their couch anymore. Things could be behind them. That was definitely a very intentional choice. This genre automatically taps into that.

Andrew Goldstein: Virtual reality tricks your senses because you've added that visual fidelity and added spatial audio. When you actually feel that you're there, when you can actually walk in any given direction, you can feel and touch things—that's when this completely new and different medium has come into its own. Right now, we're just tricking.

Robyn Tong Gray: And even though we are not quite there yet, we talk about the memories you make in VR being much different than the memories you make with a linear, 2D story. When you experience something in VR and you close your eyes later, you can really remember that the ceiling was a certain height. That distinguishes VR as a completely different medium alone.

Andrew Goldstein: The example we always use in presentations is that if you watch a movie and you see a really key scene, you can't say how large the room it took place in was. There's so many visual tricks that are going on. You can guess, but you were never there. You never saw it for yourself. But if you were in Virtual Reality, you can literally say it was 8 feet. I was actually there. Your brain processes that in a completely different way, and stores it in a completely different way as a memory, too.

John Bucher: One of the things that has continued to make the world of gaming really take off has been the ability to experience games socially—to play with other people in other parts of the world and build community within that gaming world. How important do you think the social aspect of VR is going to be to storytelling? Will it look like it does in the gaming world, or do you think we're in for something really different?

Robyn Tong Gray: I don't know if it's important to its overall success. I think it's going to be a huge thing. I don't think it's necessarily going to be make or break, because a lot of the people who desire these VR experiences are just people who desire just to see something new, whether or not that's with other people. I think the more it becomes integrated, the more people will want other people to accompany them.

Andrew Goldstein: I would say it's the direction of the experience. If content creators create great content that is meant to be social, then it'll enhance the experience. If they create content that's meant to be experienced as an individual, it'll be really interesting to do that, too.

John Bucher: We have first-person experiences in VR, and we have third-person experiences where we're a ghost in the room that's observing. Do you approach projects differently, or are you doing everything in first person or third person?

Robyn Tong Gray: We stick with first person. Third person, where you are a ghost observing, is interesting to me, but I feel like it misses the point of VR. We really do love messing with first person and playing around with who you are in the experience. It's definitely something we consider a lot. For example, with one of the upcoming projects we've been talking about, we were saying that we don't really see mom characters in games enough. There's been this huge surge of paternal characters, but you don't really see moms. I like the idea of having people, especially within our demographic, that's often men, having to step into the shoes of someone completely different. In this case, maybe a mom. You'll get these people who could never actually be that in real life now forced to confront small parts about this character's life and how they might think differently, or how they might therefore have to think to solve these puzzles or go through this story.

Andrew Goldstein: Character identity is central to Virtual Reality because you now assign that. You're not just a fly on the wall. You have to make sure that your character identity works with the narrative that you're telling. Also, you have to be careful not to break the experience. The character's role is essential in terms of helping to provoke a narrative. I'm really excited when there are games where you aren't actually assigned a character, and you grow or become one out of that. It's going to feel even more different because it's actually you being in there, not just you having a relationship with an avatar. You're not looking at an avatar, you are the avatar.

Case Study: Light Sail VR
Matthew Celia and Robert Watts
Managing Partners and Producers

FIGURE 8.3 Courtesy of Light Sail VR

Light Sail VR has been responsible for creating some of the most innovative content on the market. Their experiences hold one element above all others: story. Matthew Celia explains, "Storytelling, in my opinion, hasn't changed since the dawn of mankind. Storytelling in its very nature is a linear process. It is someone who says, 'Let me begin, let me tell you the middle, there's conflict, there's character, and then there's a resolution.'" Light Sail has used this methodology to craft VR experiences including the *Paranormal Activity* VR Experience for Paramount Pictures, *Reggie's Garage* for baseball Hall of Famer Reggie Jackson, and *Fowl Seas*—a VR pirate adventure for GoPro.

Robert Watts says, "For us, it's all about motivating who you are in the scene and why you're watching." Each decision made in the stories that Light Sail tells is based on presence, which they define as how you exist in space.

"If I'm watching a VR experience and suddenly I think I'm a person, but then I'm lifted up high into the air, and I'm like, 'Well, who am I? What just happened?' Suddenly I'm no longer present in that scene. Suddenly I'm thinking I'm in a game or an app. Suddenly I'm no longer actually in that world. I'm in a game, and it reminds me that I'm in a game, and for me, that takes you out of presence," Celia said.

In their *Paranormal Activity* experience, the team was challenged with hiding cuts in the postproduction process. Taking a cue from Alfred Hitchcock's *Rope*, they hid the cut in a place that was organic to the story. "We put a flickering light in and hid the cut in the flickering light. It still feels seamless. It still feels like you've never moved, but we have been able to give you that seamless experience and make that part of the story effective. There's a ghost, so of course the ghost is going to mess with the electricity. It's all story driven," Celia explains.

Watts agrees. "It fit in the world. In the *Paranormal Activity* universe, the camera flashes out, so we can use that to hide the guts behind the technology."

Light Sail continues to find innovative ways to use the language of cinema in storytelling. Discussing the use of close-ups to establish emotional intimacy in traditional filmmaking, the team discovered that the same trope in VR actually made audiences uncomfortable and disoriented. However, having the actor look directly into the camera, breaking the fourth wall, from a slightly greater distance, had a similar effect as the close-up. "There's a piece we did for Go Pro where we do a lot of eye contact, and that makes you feel very connected in the scene." Celia said. Light Sail ran into similar problems using voice-over in some projects, pointing out that audiences sometimes spent the first few moments of the piece searching for the source of the disembodied voice and often missed a key story beat.

Watts and Celia also have continued to experiment with the effectiveness of various run times in their VR films. "I don't think the length ultimately matters. It depends on how much you connect with the characters onscreen and what their emotional stakes are and what they're going through. We are exploring short-form series, because right now, we're dependent on the headset technology. Someone might not want to wear it for more than 15 minutes at a time, but it doesn't mean you can't do a whole TV series worth of content. You can still build your emotional arcs over that series length.

You just have to pepper it in at the beginning to get people hooked, just like a normal TV pilot would," Watts said.

Celia added, "I also think that audiences have matured in the way that they view and consume content. We're much more a serialized society than we were 20 years ago. Twenty years ago, it was all about the feature film. I'm not saying feature film is dead, far from it, but I'm saying right now, the golden age of television in my mind is really due to the fact that audiences are craving deep emotional characters that they can identify with and that they feel connected to. I think you're not going to have those watershed moments in VR until we start seeing more stories where people can relate to the characters onscreen."

Presence and relatability continue to be the two big issues the team discusses with every project, considering how the audience will connect with the lives and nuances of the characters on screen. When scripts are crafted, the process and format look similar to that in traditional scriptwriting, with several notable exceptions. Actors will always be on screen on VR, so giving them business and motivation throughout every moment of the scene has been a useful technique, similar to the approach used in theater. "In a film, you cut away to the shot of the friends in the café and leave your other characters, and you forget about them for a second. In VR, you need to make sure you deal with them, because the characters are always on the screen, so you must give them entrances and exits that are story motivated. It's a really important tiny nuance," Celia said.

Expanding their stable of writers beyond just traditional scriptwriters, Watts also suggested that comic book writers have been successful at writing for VR because of their abilities to describe environments and build worlds.

Combining strong writing with the talents of a strong director aptly describes the creative approach that Light Sail is pursuing. Celia explains, "It needs the strong point of view of an artist to guide the audience on a story. It needs a storyteller, and that audience can't be the person. Something I'm very passionate about exploring, and I believe strongly, is that I don't believe that you as the viewer can be the protagonist in the story. I think it's impossible. I think you can be the antagonist, I think you can be an observer, but I don't think you can be the protagonist because there's nothing for you to latch on and identify and relate to."

Celia and Watts are quick to point out that all that they believe they have learned thus far about VR could change as the medium evolves. Watts said, "Just in general, I think people are still trying to figure it out. I would say beware of people who say that you can or can't do this, because someone just hasn't figured out how to do it yet, so in every piece we do, we try to explore a new way of telling the story and making it effective."

Storytelling in VR through POV
An Interview with
Tai Crosby, Founder/CEO, SilVR Thread

Tai Crosby is the founder and CEO of SilVR Thread, specializing in first-person POV Virtual Reality technology. With its patent-pending camera systems, SilVR Thread created Lionsgate's *Nerve* VR Experiences, which allow the viewer to embody the stars' characters in action scenes that transport them onto a skateboard tied to the back of a moving police car and onto a ladder suspended between two New York City buildings.

John Bucher: Why is storytelling important to understand in VR?

Tai Crosby: At the fundamental core of storytelling is how we transfer knowledge. It's survival. It's how we as a society stay whole. If you look at where we are as a human race, we have more knowledge than ever to transfer, and we have accessibility to more knowledge than ever, but how do we keep the focus on what is important? How do we get back to experiential knowledge? Experiential knowledge is different than just, "I read it in a textbook." How do you build wisdom? At SilVR Thread, we're able to essentially capture a memory and experience, package it up, and allow somebody to experience that again as if it's truly occurring for them. It's the ultimate visualization tool. It's a very specific place in learning, and it certainly doesn't eliminate or change the teacher. The teacher's more important than ever. It's how we experience things we normally wouldn't encounter.

John Bucher: Talk about how story fits with the POV approach that you're taking to create VR. How does it change the experience for the viewer to be the protagonist, as opposed to putting on a headset and just observing a narrative playing out?

Tai Crosby: We believe it's huge. It is the very core of our company. This is what we were created to be. Our core design philosophy began years ago with my experiences as a fashion and travel photographer. I was traveling through the Himalayas taking pictures, told a friend, "Oh, this is so cool, the photo's so great, but if only you were there with me." The photo speaks a thousand words, but it's not enough. You have no idea what it was actually like to have dinner with this group of people that had never encountered anybody else and were completely off the grid in the middle of the jungle in India. You had to be there and to actually have somebody hand you that meal.

In this little village I visited in India, the women aren't allowed to touch the food, so they slide it to you with their foot on the ground. That's considered polite. These are those moments you just have to experience. It's not just seeing it, it's going. To embody somebody in the experience changes the way I believe we relate to these things, and it takes us away from being able to step out of it, and forces us to truly feel what it's like to be human in that scenario. From day one, we never set out to build a 360 camera. We're not a camera company. It was always about how we capture the human experience and replay that for someone.

John Bucher: Tell me about the *Nerve* VR experience, which was originally a feature film—a traditional narrative experience. How did your team walk through that process? What was the philosophy behind taking a traditional narrative and creating a VR experience?

Tai Crosby: I think a lot of this is very market driven right now. I think this is something that we're all pioneering. Everyone in this space has seen this evolve daily. A lot of it has to do with forming a critical mass of consumers. We've seen inventions be adopted swifter and swifter. If you go back for how long it took for the original radio to catch hold, it was almost a decade plus. Even cell phones had a seven- to ten-year adoption rate. We're seeing it move quicker and quicker. The good news is there's more and more VR headsets in people's hands, but having said that, the paid gigs, the actual revenue where people are writing checks still involve a lot of marketing material.

It can be concentrated delivery. It ties directly into another asset, and at this point, it's still promoting other assets to make more money for the film. Now, from the storytelling place, we love this, because it enables us to go out and produce this great stuff—to produce these stories. We're in a place (Los Angeles) where we can bring a lot of these traditional film elements in and apply them to this new medium and advance the medium much faster than if we were somewhere else in the world.

We did two pieces for *Nerve* originally, both about what's it like to be in the body of this teenager. We flew to New York City. We were on the set of the film and had our team of seven and we go in, a little surgical strike force, and rig up the stunt members 12 stories up. They put a ladder between two windows, between two apartments, in an apartment building. We've got the stunt woman rigged up, and we were quite literally recording her experience. She had to cross the ladder.

John Bucher: Just like the scene in the film.

Tai Crosby: Just like the scene in the film. We captured that scene, produced that, did everything behind the scenes, Lionsgate loved it so much, they said, "Hey, this is amazing. Can you do another one on top of this for the same property before it comes out?" We did another piece where we explored what it was like to ride a skateboard behind a cop car. It's a great piece, everyone has to try it. I recommend experiencing it in VR over doing it in real life.

John Bucher: Good suggestion.

Tai Crosby: You look at great storytelling in great movies. The best movies are the ones where you walk away and say, "I didn't even realize it was in the theater. I was so immersed in the story." This is just a new tool that does that.

John Bucher: I watched a piece your team created where my body changed over the course of the experience in the VR world. I was a DJ one minute, and then I was someone else a few minutes later. I was really surprised at how that didn't cause me any problems. I very easily transitioned. Actually, I enjoyed transitioning from this character to that character. Can you talk about the thought process behind that? I have to believe that didn't come by accident.

Tai Crosby:	Trial and error. Lots of error. Lots of failure along the path of success. Everything we're doing right now is pioneering, and everything that we as a community are doing is pioneering. One of the core things with our technology is we're constantly pushing to have the most realistic perception of your own body in the actual world. All of our footage is in true 3D. This isn't algorithmic, but it's true stereoscopic, which is just how we see, and we've got some secret sauce that, as you look around, makes you realize it's not just 360, but you're looking with a natural field of view of a human.
	What it does is, by being in a body, make your brain feel comfortable, and that actually alleviates a lot of motion sickness. We can do things with SilVR Thread technology in a movement sense that other 360 cameras just can't do because the body doesn't feel like it's right. The moment you're in a body, the brain feels very safe. The ability to jump between different characters is a thing that we've been looking at for a long time. It feels right.
John Bucher:	It does.
Tai Crosby:	The second you look down, it's like, "Oh my God, this is incredible. What is it like to actually be in this beautiful girl's body in a bikini partying on the other side of this incredible party scene?"
John Bucher:	I saw the scene differently at that moment.
Tai Crosby:	Exactly right. That's where you go, "Hang on, this changes the game." Telling the story from a POV is exactly what we're doing. By definition, that is what we're doing. It expands your experience as a whole because you're seeing it from multiple angles as multiple people. How did that person experience it? Tons of fun. There's so many other things we're working towards, such as being able to navigate dynamically through things. It's not just to choose your angle, it's truly choosing whose perspective you want to be in as you're experiencing this.
	One of my favorite classes back in school was the study of the gaze. Are you the watcher or the one being watched?

John Bucher:	Laura Mulvey's theory?
Tai Crosby:	Exactly. From the storytelling perspective, how do you determine the behavior of the viewer? How do you influence the behavior of the viewer? Where are you empowering the actors and the other characters? This is now embodying that in a completely different way, because *you're* embodied. You are there.
John Bucher:	Let's move to the future. This technology is moving really quickly. VR experiences are headed towards a mainstream saturation like we've never experienced before. I'm not asking you to guess what the future holds, but what ideally would SilVR Thread like to move this VR world towards? Where are you guys driving the ship to go?
Tai Crosby:	It's a wonderful question. Our core has always been POV VR and always will be POV VR. We're constantly not only allowing that to be possible but trying to increase the fidelity of the experience and at the same time make it easier to produce so that more content can get out there, more experiences. Beyond the business, there are so many humanitarian tales that need to be told. We live in an age that's more polarizing than anything, I think. We have a project we're working on with a former world leader. He was president of a major country and he's devoted his entire life now to kids. He set up a foundation, and he teaches a couple hundred thousand kids about leadership. They call VR the empathy machine. Well, if VR is the empathy machine, SilVR Thread is the way to inject it into that personal experience through POV VR. I think it's remarkably powerful, and I can't wait to see what lots of great artists and thinkers and activists do with this technology.

Storytelling in VR through Game Design
An Interview with
Adam Orth, Creative Director, Three One Zero

Adam Orth is a former creative director at Microsoft. He now heads up Three One Zero, an independent video game and digital entertainment studio. Their first title, *ADR1FT*, has been nominated for numerous awards and lauded as one of the top narrative experiences in VR.

John Bucher: Tell me about your initial pull into this sort of storytelling.

Adam Orth: Video games were actually my second career. My first career was a musician here in Los Angeles. I was a songwriter telling stories. I grew up playing video games and I was always a gamer, but when I began to focus on games, professionally, I got a job working on a James Bond game for the PlayStation One. The game industry was like the wild west at that time. I liked hanging around the studio and started being a game tester and realized very quickly that I could learn about and touch all the different disciplines of game development. I wanted to be a game designer because I love to tell stories, and this is a way for me to create interactive stories.

I ended up getting a job at Sony and worked on *God of War.* Then I went to EA and worked on the *Medal of Honor* series. Then I got an opportunity to go and be the external creative director of Lucas Arts. I really wanted to go make good *Star Wars* games. I'd always been drawn to telling a really good, quality, emotional story built around good characters. I ended up working at all of these big places where there's huge teams working on giant products, and it was really hard for me to fit into those environments, because I really wanted something small and personal, but wrapped in that kind of super glossy triple-A production packaging.

After I left Microsoft, I had this space idea, and I realized, I can make this cool small space game and talk about some of the difficult things I've been through. I approached the storytelling like songwriting. I had something to say that was really personal and very meaningful to me, but I buried it behind some very thin metaphors, I think. When I was a songwriter, I always wanted songs that had meaning but were also accessible to a wide audience. That's kind of how I approached the story of *ADR1FT*. I wanted to talk about normal life things that people experience. My goal was hoping that people would find some kind of common parallel there. Really, at the biggest level, my only goal was just to strike a chord in someone somewhere. *ADR1FT* is not a big multimeaning, circle of life kind of story. I just wanted you to put the controller down when you were done and go, yeah, I can relate to that. That's how I approached it.

I started thinking, there is a traditional way I can tell the story, and I embraced that, but there's these side stories that are a bit nontraditional, and they're all connected. The first thing I thought when I sat down was, most games tell a story—A to Z. You get to the points along the way, and there's this arc of storytelling in video games that's very stiff and requires a lot of hand holding. It's very overt and very neat and tidy. I just didn't want to do that. The idea of *ADR1FT* is really about minimalism. We're a small team. We have limited time, limited budget, and we can only do so much.

John Bucher: The chord that resonated in me while playing is that *ADR1FT* is inherently about loneliness.

Adam Orth: Yeah, I wanted you to feel that, not only were you in a bad situation, but that virtually by hearing all these other stories that you're a part of from people who are now deceased—it's a very lonely feeling, because you find out, you matter to these people, or you didn't matter to them. It's almost like reading someone's diary in a way. You feel weird doing it, and it makes you feel all these emotions.

Anyways, I didn't want to do the story traditionally. So I thought, if you were actually in that scenario, you wouldn't possibly get a perfectly linear story. It would be messy, and you might only get 10% of it just based on the fact that you're not going to stick around and smell the roses. Instead of telling this really fleshed out narrative, I approached the narrative bits as seeds. I just wanted you to get this little chunk and then to start growing whatever you think it is until you get to the next one or the next one. I think it was successful in that way. That's one of the things in the game that I'm really proud of. It does have that feeling of this hollowness, because you're learning that this is your fault in a way. Everyone knows what it feels like to mess up. Everyone knows what it feels like when you're left out of the gang or just not included in something. I wanted you to have that feeling, and I feel like it's there. Although I'm a little desensitized to it, just from playing it and making it, but many people have told me that that's what they got out of it.

John Bucher: Can you talk a little bit about your approach to characters?

Adam Orth: Yes, so first of all, every bit of narrative in *ADR1FT* comes directly from my life. Every single thing. Some things might be twisted around to fit the fiction. But I talk about addiction. I talk about cancer, relationships, parents, all of those things. Everything, those stories all happened in some form to me. That's why I think those characters feel authentic.

When I decided to make the game, I also said, "I'm going to make it totally raw. I'm going to just put it all out there." I feel like those characters are interesting. I hope that they are more interesting because they're not totally fleshed out in the experience. They are fleshed out for me as the creator though. I wrote all of those characters' life stories and then just cherry-picked some stuff to include in the game.

John Bucher: I am really fascinated by the idea that you took people and situations and elements from your life and worked them into the story for this game. I think a lot of creators desire to do that, and I think the toughest thing to figure out is, when do I stay true to what happened in my real life, and then when do I need to not do that?

Adam Orth: That's a good question. It's not something I struggled with, but I recognized it when it was happening. My thought process was, stay true to the character. Because you're already putting them in this fantastic goal situation, and because the more true it is, the more real it is. That was my mantra when I was creating the game, just be true to the characters and be true to what you are trying to say. There is nothing wrong with mindless entertainment, but I just feel like if I have the opportunity and the audience, why not say something true?

John Bucher: Can you speak about the relationship between external conflict and internal conflict? One of the things that I think's really great about the game is there is this level of internal conflict going on that connects to the external conflict.

Adam Orth: A lot of that has to do with the environmental storytelling. You have these mechanics that are working against you, and you have this beautiful world that you want to explore, but it's dangerous to do that and it's risky and you have to make bets. You know you're in a bad situation and have to get out of it, but then there's also the wonder of the entirety of humanity right there. The setting being in Earth's orbit in that way, and being alone and having this totally beautiful but mangled environment that is also your enemy and your friend at the same time. There is some nice juxtaposition in those things.

John Bucher: Why does story matter when creating games?

Adam Orth: Well, because you're asking people to buy into a fantasy. You can do that with just the environment, and you can do that with mechanics, but it's not really a full experience until you have story. There are games and experiences where it's just about walking around the environment and checking stuff out, and that's awesome. I love those things. But do you want them to *create their own* story or do you want to *tell* them a story?

I kind of like to try to be in the middle, because the agency that you have when you are doing something interactive can be important, and that *does* tell a story. I just think that, if I'm going to ask you to go fight a dragon, you want to know why, and I want to know why.

When you play a game and there's always twenty-five different side quests, those characters matter too. It's not just that the goblin is terrorizing the village. Go a little deeper. That goblin used to be my brother and now he's a goblin, or whatever. It's important to me, and I think video games often get characters that are shallow. I don't want to see that continue in VR. Now, I think there is a risk of giving so much agency in a VR experience [because] you are turning loose of the reins of really directing the experience. It can be the beauty of the experience too. Turning loose of those reins.

INSIGHTS FROM THE TECHNOLOGISTS AND PRODUCERS

The most effective technologists and producers understand the elements and methods used in storytelling. They understand that the technology is a means to an end and that in its highest form, it is invisible to the end user. Jonathan Krusell mentions that there was a time in the past when audiences were more aware of the fantasy elements in well-told stories. We knew there was a screen that separated us from this other world. Technology has now allowed us to cause the audience to feel as though that screen has disappeared, fully immersing us in the worlds of our fantasies. Robyn Tong Gray agrees with pushing the audience into the new medium as far as possible and suggests that audiences be provided something they are familiar with on some level. That something might be familiar characters, genres that follow rules audiences have come to expect, or even environments that they have positive associations with. Successful VR experiences tend to embrace a mix of familiar elements and those completely new and foreign to the audience.

Robert Watts suggested that the key to this mix is communicating to the audience who they are in a scene and why they are watching. His partner, Matt Celia, believes that it is exactly the moment that the audience begins to question either of these concepts that the immersion is broken and the experience begins to fail. Krusell, Gray, and her partner Andrew Goldstein all agreed that the environment crafted by the creators of an experience plays a major role in answering these questions for the audience. How realistic or nonrealistic an environment appears to be provides different sets of rules for the world the user is immersed in. Tai Crosby and the creators at SilVR Thread approach VR exclusively from the first-person lens, allowing them, in a sense, to capture a memory, move through an environment, and then allow a user to experience it. Other creators throughout this book mention connections between memory and VR storytelling—a topic that deserves further exploration and consideration.

Krusell discussed the challenges with creating VR both now and in the future. These challenges range from the discomfort a viewer may feel when being forced to embody a gender, body type, or experience they are unfamiliar with to the ever-changing technological nuances of the coding world. In many ways, technical producers of VR stories, games, and experiences are put in the position of bridging the worlds of artistic storytelling and scientific practicalities, all while managing to create an emotional experience. Adam Orth stated that throughout the development of his project, his biggest goal was to strike a chord with someone somewhere and process his own loneliness. While not always possible, when creators do have the opportunity to create or work on projects that resonate with them personally, either emotionally or biographically, there does seem to be a level of energy in the final product that can't be manufactured otherwise. All the technologists and producers in this section and throughout this book are united by the motivation and drive to share experiences with an audience. Tai Crosby spoke specifically about his experience of being in the Himalayas and wanting to bring his friends along so that they might all be able to see what he saw. When producers are able to work from a place of clear motivation, such as this, it gives the creator a metaphoric North Star for their future work.

THE ARTISTS

Storytelling in VR through Fashion
An Interview with
Angela Haddad, VR Artist and Producer

Angela Haddad is a VR artist and producer who got her start in the industry by producing story-like animated 360 videos out of hand-painted art under the handle One Third Blue. The studio creates original VR art productions for fashion brands and magazines, including *Marie Claire*. A VR Producer at SilVR Thread, Angela creates first-person POV stereoscopic VR experiences that inclusively capture the human body for moments that replicate the in-body human experience in its truest form. At SilVR Thread, Angela has coproduced VR experiences for Lionsgate's movie *Nerve*, where three stunts from the film were recreated to be experienced by fans in POV VR, allowing for transformative, total human body presence. Angela has judged and spoken at 2016 LA Hacks, has been featured at SXSW, in WGSN, Mettle's Blog, and is an active member of the SH//FT and Women in VR communities.

John Bucher: Tell me about some of your early experiences with art and technology.

Angela Haddad: I grew up in a very tech-oriented family. My dad was a tech entrepreneur his entire life. I reached college, and I felt like I needed a bit of a change and so I studied political economies and focused on the Middle East. I ended up with a concentration on the underdogs of Lebanon. I grew up drawing, and when I graduated college and started working in tech, I realized there was something missing. My dad always told me you need to get a hobby that keeps you creative, a hobby that makes you money, and maybe a hobby that keeps you fit. I really felt like I was missing that hobby that kept me creative.

I picked up my brush, my pencils, and my calligraphy inks again. One day I was looking through Tumblr and found this fashion illustration that I wanted to print and frame on my wall, but I couldn't because it was too low resolution, so I decided I was just going to draw it myself. From there I got hooked on fashion illustrations.

John Bucher:	Fashion is, in many ways, another form of storytelling. Can you talk a little bit about some of your underlying observations about the psychology of fashion and story?
Angela Haddad:	When we wear something specific, we feel differently about it, about ourselves, compared to when we're wearing something else. Ultimately the fashion industry is not just selling you clothes, they're selling you dreams and they're selling you a story. The thing is, a piece of clothing is very rarely a piece of clothing by itself; it usually comes in a collection, and that creative collection is inspired by a creative story. When you look at, for example, Valentino Fall 2014, you really can see the collection is inspired by Greek mythology. Everything really does have to come with a story. Very rarely do you see a collection come down the runway without an immersive environment around it that can really put everything together. You're really immersed in this greater environment. You're immersed in a story, and the clothes are a part of it, a big part of it, but really, ultimately, just a part of it.
John Bucher:	You've got a very clear voice in your VR art. It's very distinct and it's a very feminine voice. It's someone who's speaking from a woman's point of view. Can you talk a little bit about the voice of women in VR, art, and story?
Angela Haddad:	Looking back at the history of fashion art, it began as basically a way to illustrate *Vogue* covers. The earliest *Vogue* covers were not photographs. They were actually fashion illustrations. The earliest fashion illustrators were all men. Now, if you look at the top fashion illustrators, for example—Megan Hess, Megan Morrison, Katie Rogers—these are all women and they're doing fantastic, fabulous work. Very few top fashion illustrators are men. I think that it's always critical to keep women's voices in mind, just as it is critical to keep it in mind with the tech industry. Right now, with the VR bubble, I think we're all doing a fantastic job about keeping women involved and making sure that women have more and more of an equal opportunity. The Women in VR group is really strong. Women lend a different voice.

John Bucher: Tell me about your initial experience with VR. How did that come into your world? What's been your journey with it?

Angela Haddad: My first experience with VR was with an Oculus DK2. My brother brought it home and said, "You have to try this." I put it on, and my first demo was one of the default demos, and it was simply this 3D house that you could walk into. I remember that I had heels on and I had to take off my heels because I felt so off balance. The level of immersion was just insane. After that, the first thing I could think of was what if we could replay our memories in VR? What if we could, for example, record our wedding days in VR and our really special moments in VR and replay them for later on? Because of that, I set out to learn how to stitch 360 video. I took a class and I kept practicing, and then I released my first 360 video, which was monoscopic at the time. My first video was of me illustrating art around a 360-degree space. I put five easels around the 360-camera rig and I went around the rig and I drew a fashion illustration on each easel.

Once I released that, I started thinking about what else I could do. I started thinking of ways of taking that to the next level. I played around for two months with various programs and software to figure out how I could incorporate my art into 360 videos. I didn't want to just animate, I really wanted to animate in 360. The more and more I played, the more I figured out how to more easily build those environments, and eventually there came a point where I thought, okay, well, these animations have to tell a story now, and so now each of my videos is truly a cohesive story. They're not just characters running around being animated in a software program.

John Bucher: Can you talk a little about some of the things that you learned along the way?

Angela Haddad: To me, the most critical thing in my 360 videos was the trigger points. What is going to trigger you to look around and move your head around 180 degrees to look at that other thing that I want to show you? In the beginning, that was really difficult for me to figure out. It didn't come easily. For example, with my first 360 video, it was a live action, and I was going around the camera and drawing, and I wanted people to easily understand that I was going to stop at a certain easel, then I'm going to move to the left. I literally put arrows around to help guide the viewer. That to me was a good first try, but it wasn't interesting enough. When I moved into creating art in 360, I really wanted to have something that wasn't an arrow. Whenever I wanted you to look around, I wanted to make sure that it was part of the story. For example, with one of them, I have lipstick flying around. It's flying around the walls, and the lipstick's job is to paint each of the illustrations on the walls different colors. That was part of the story.

With a recent piece for *Marie Claire* magazine, they wanted me to illustrate the three summer cover girls— Selena Gomez, Blake Lively, and Amy Schumer. What I did was draw each of these girls on their own set, within the 360 video, and the one cohesive point that made you look around the 360 was this table that moved around from set to set. It was the same table, but in each set, there was a different object laid on it. In the first set, I think it was flowers, in the second set, it was a different object and it was the same table, and that was the trigger point that made you look all around. This is applicable, I would say, to almost any 360 experience. With live-action experiences, for example, the most common trigger point would be like an audio cue. That is where 3D audio comes in.

John Bucher: How do you come up with a trigger point like the table? Do you just brainstorm or do you talk to people or do you write things out? Talk a little bit about your process.

Angela Haddad: Usually the greater story comes first. For example, with the *Marie Claire* piece, the general theme that they gave me was the three summer cover girls. I played around with different ideas, and once I set out to build three sets within those 360-degree spaces, that's when the question starts coming in. It's usually about, I would say, a quarter of the way through the storyboard. It goes hand in hand with what the animation process is like. What is the story on each set? Where does the animation start? Once I figured out that this is what Selena Gomez needs to do, this is what Blake needs to do, this is what Amy needs to do, then the table idea came through. I would say it's usually a quarter of the way through the storyboard for almost every project. It is a really critical point, so it does have to come towards the beginning. It also goes hand in hand with how much a viewer is expected to look around. Do you want them to just look around 180 degrees? Or do you really want to take advantage of the full 360? Yes, it's really all about the story.

John Bucher: Let's bring AR into the conversation. Some people are being introduced to VR initially through AR experiences.

Angela Haddad: I think AR has a bit of a longer way to go than VR right now. I see a lot of uses for AR in fashion, especially in retail stores. For example, being able to see what the clothes look like live on you in AR before you purchase them without having to go into a fitting room.

John Bucher: Let's talk a little bit about the future. There's plenty of talk in the VR space that eventually we'll probably get away from HMDs and have a contact or a chip or whatever. What do you think are the advantages and disadvantages of creating a completely immersive experience for people? Is this going to cause problems? Are we going to have people that never want to leave their immersive environment? Can you talk about how you see the future of VR?

Angela Haddad: Regardless of what I think, I think our society is ready for that kind of thing. I think when VR tried to break its way through a decade ago, our society was just not ready for that yet because we were not stuck to our smartphones twenty-four-seven. We wake up and for most of us, it's the first thing that we do. As a society, we're ready for technology where we're completely immersed in it and completely lost away from our actual reality. I think that is inevitable.

John Bucher: Why is story important when we're working with technology?

Angela Haddad: I think that's the only way you can relate to people. I think it's the only way you can resonate with somebody. If you don't have a story, then what are you sharing? If you're just sharing sound bites, for example, that's not going to stick with them. That's not going to be a memorable feeling. I think that if you want to create a true memory, you have to tell a story. Especially when we're talking about something like Virtual Reality. If you throw somebody into a virtual experience and maybe there's a lot of really cool effects and maybe there's a lot of really visually intriguing things going on all around them, it's very difficult for them to remember what they watched in a year or two years or five years or even ten years if there isn't a cohesive story.

Storytelling through Immersion
An Interview with
Annie Lesser, Immersive Theater Director

Getting to Know You

(A)partment 8

(B)arbershop

Annie Lesser is a writer, director, poet, and photographer. She has been recognized as one of the top creators of immersive theatrical experiences in Los Angeles. Her work has been recognized by *LA Weekly*, the Hollywood Fringe Festival, and the National Foundation for the Advancement of Arts. Several of her immersive theatrical projects are in development as VR experiences.

John Bucher: Give us a little background on your creative development.

Annie Lesser: From a young age, I was always making skits and putting on
                 shows for my parents. I was very much the kid that played
                 make-believe. I wrote a lot of poetry. I did anything I could
                 do that was creative. When I was nine years old, I said "I'm
                 going to be a big screenwriter one day." You know how
                 when you see an eyelash, you blow it and you make a wish?
                 I always wished I was the greatest screenwriter in the world.
                 It's such a force of habit that I didn't even think about it.
                 When I went into high school, I started to get a lot more
                 into writing theater. I wrote student plays that were in some
                 theater festivals. I did a lot of slam poetry. I was a finalist
                 in the Chicago Louder Than a Bomb poetry slam competi-
                 tion with my team from school and won some other poetry
                 awards. I was a National Merit Poet from the National
                 Foundation for the Advancement of Arts and an Illinois
                 Merit Poet. I did one interactive class in college, where we,
                 as a group at the end of the semester, put together a walk-
                 through adaptation of Raymond Chandler's *The Big Sleep*.
                 I graduated NYU with an Excellence in Television Writing
                 Award and had two of my plays in festivals. So, I was pretty
                 busy. But when I came to LA, I was having a lot of trouble

breaking into the industry, so I became a freelance photographer. It gave me a lot more freedom and flexibility to write and produce work on my own. I'd wanted to do some interactive theater for a while, so I began with a piece called *Getting to Know You*. It involved eight audience members and eight actors.

John Bucher: Had you seen anyone else do interactive theater before?

Annie Lesser: I always loved cheesy dinner theater growing up. My bat mitzvah was a murder mystery theater bat mitzvah. I have always been really supportive of Mick Napier. He always told me really nice things. Mick Napier is the founder of the Noise Beater. He's an amazing improv, sketch comedy guy. He directed *Highway 53*, with Amy Sedaris, Stephen Colbert, and Paul Dinello. I saw *Hotel Savoy* at the Goethe Institute in New York. I loved just getting in there, and the freedom of relating to the actors, and trying to talk to them without there being the consequence of the rest of the real world. I wanted to create something like that, where someone feels something like I felt.

I wanted to create something where someone asks "Was that person really hitting on me?" Or "Was that person really upset by what I said?" I wanted to create those moments. Obviously, I've seen *Sleep No More*. I've seen *Then She Fell*. I'd seen a couple things around LA. I'd been to two different versions of *Delusion*. I was at this point where I was like, "I want to create something, where someone feels that feeling that I had when I went to see the *Hotel Savoy*." Because it was such an amazing feeling. I want to create that in people. I also really wanted to create things where people are introspective about themselves.

John Bucher: With *(A)partment 8*, you moved out of the theater into an actual apartment. Can you talk about thinking through the idea of bringing people into an immersive space? How was that different than approaching something that was just in a standard theater?

Annie: When I came up for the idea of *(A)partment 8*, I just wanted to create something in my apartment, since it was a location I already had access to. It gave me a lot more freedom in what I was able to do and when I could rehearse and when I could work with my actor. I have a vision in my head about what would evoke emotional response for me. I also go through the experience the audience will have first. I start acting like different worst-case-scenario audience members and then see how my actor reacts. I always worry that what's going on in my head and what we're actually doing aren't the same thing, so I just have to hope and pray that people relate to it. Because people could say, "That didn't make sense," or "That was really pretentious."

I began with what would make me feel something. I started with a nugget. I started with the nugget of a dead actor in the bathtub, covered in blood. Then I write around that. I go into the space, because I write for the space, and add elements from that. Right now I'm dealing with the fact that I don't trust a lot of people. Let's make this a piece about trust, and how other people control our lives the way that God does. Let's do that. I really have a lot of faith in Carl Jung and the collective unconscious and that we all have these similar emotional reactions to certain stimuli. I want to try and tap into that.

John Bucher: One of the big buzzwords in immersive experiences with Virtual Reality is this idea of agency being given to the audience. So, with your experiences, the audience has different types of agency, depending on the experience. With *(B)arbershop*, it felt like the audience had the most agency. In *(A)partment 8*, the agency is very different.

Annie Lesser: It's internal for them. People react different ways. I basically try, with all my pieces, to create an internal agency more than an external agency. It's placing them in a situation where you are creating this bond of trust. We are trusting you with our artwork, and you are trusting us that we're going to keep you safe. I also feel if I'm good enough at my job, I create an emotional intimacy and trust with you and the actor. You should feel like this is something that is real, and you should have some sort of emotional relationship to the actors around you. I feel like 95% of the audience does what they're supposed to do.

John Bucher: Many audience members are used to watching a performance and not having agency. How do you guide people through the introduction of that power without forcing their hand?

Annie Lesser: It's always hard when someone doesn't know what's going on. Or even when someone does know what's going on, but they want to take charge in a way that the piece wasn't meant to support. I try to set a tone with actors asking the audience questions right away. They (the actor) might have a monologue, but within a minute or so, they'll start asking you questions. They direct it at you, and they guide you to follow them, or things like that. For *(A)partment 8*, there's a little bit of an intro where we say it's okay to feel your own feelings. It's okay to feel the feelings of the person whose skin you're inside. It's okay to draw on your own experiences. I feel like I try to do things that engage you right away.

John Bucher: In Virtual Reality, one of the things that people are trying to wrap their head around concerns the camera. Previously, we've been able to use cinematic language like close-ups that force audience perspective. Being a photographer, as well as someone who works in immersive space, can you talk about the relationship between the two?

Annie Lesser: Well, the forced perspective comes from the actors and comes from the language. I'm not forcing you to pay attention to a certain visual, but I'm forcing you to pay attention to a certain concept. It's more like making sure that there are aspects of that littered throughout. In *(B)arbershop*, in the background, we had *The Bachelor's* rose ceremony playing, and *Bachelor Pad, Bachelor in Paradise*, which you wouldn't normally even pay attention to, but they are there. It plays to the theme of what's going on. We choose where you're sitting, and we place that. We create the whole tone of the space. You're controlling the space. You're trying to make everything fit with those themes you want to touch on. In the same way, when you're reading a novel, you have all these little things that are symbolism and subtext, and you try and create an entire space that has that symbolism and has that subtext and has these ideas.

You're just trying to create an entire space where the actor is engaging enough that they're holding your attention. There's suddenly a knock at the door, and you could choose to pay attention to the new audience member entering the space or choose to pay attention to the actor, but you're paying attention to that dynamic. With *(A)partment 8*, you could be looking anywhere. You could avert your gaze from Keight (the actress in the piece), not wanting to look at her, but you have her presence in the words that she's saying to you. You have the image of when you first open your eyes, you're like, "I get it, there's a dead body here. This is a bathroom." You have that. You have the intro of the audio beforehand, priming you for this experience. You hear something, and you go into it. You're asked to meditate a little bit before you take off your blindfold and headphones in that piece. That prepares the audience. You've internalized yourself. You're now in this space the way that you want to interact with it, but I have placed all these things that, hopefully combined, will elicit a certain emotional reaction. I think that's what's also interesting about the ABC project is that I'm looking for these spaces that lend themselves to that. I'm writing a piece of theater for this space that I think is the best way I can utilize that space to create and elicit an emotional reaction by adding things to it. But still, everything in this space, I try and use as much as possible.

Case Study: Jaunt Studios and the *Invisible* VR Series
Doug Liman, Director, *The Bourne Identity*, *Edge*
of *Tomorrow*, *Swingers*
Melissa Wallack, Writer, *Dallas Buyers Club*, *Mirror Mirror*
Grant Anderson, Head of Studio
Tom Vance, Head of Content
George Kliavkoff, CEO and President

FIGURE 8.4 Courtesy of Jaunt

Jaunt VR was created in 2013 after one of the founders returned from a trip
to Zion National Park and wished he could return for a brief *jaunt* at any time
from any place. Focusing on realistic cinematic content, the company has
produced the highest-scale, big-budget VR experiences available. Partnering on content from creators ranging from Paul McCartney to Disney, Jaunt
focuses on developing stories that match the production quality of network
television and film studios. Head of studio Grant Anderson explains the
company's model as having four main buckets: narrative, sports, music, and
travel/adventure. "We've experimented with a broad range of content from
the very beginning with different types of experiences, but narrative is what
people want to see. Whether that's in sports, or it's in music, or it's in travel.
Since we are in the very beginning of VR, there's a lot of experiential stuff,

FIGURE 8.5 Courtesy of Jaunt

FIGURE 8.6 Courtesy of Jaunt

FIGURE 8.7 Courtesy of Jaunt

which was interesting, because it was the first time we've seen it in VR. But now, even in those genres, we need to have story. That's what really keeps things interesting. We really wanted to expand on the type of narrative work that we're doing and really bring even stronger narrative to VR," he said.

Jaunt is betting that success on a large scale in the VR market will be in telling stories that combine elements of cinema, gaming, and interactive theater, as well as elements specific to VR that are still being discovered. "It's about bringing all those parts together that's really going to create this amazing experience. Video games have been trying to do this for 20 years. How do you tell a satisfying narrative where the viewer still has some sense of control? It's a really interesting problem, and it's what drew me to this, because I was a video gamer. I worked in 3D. I worked in visual effects. I worked in production, film. This is a combination of all of those, so it's a really exciting challenge for how we tell these amazing stories that you can feel in your gut. This will be the way of the future in how we experience stories. It's not quite what we've had in just linear narrative," Anderson said.

Recognizing the value of what the tradition of cinema can bring to VR, Jaunt has been especially interested in tight narratives, the use of three-act structure, strong character development, and rich worlds—all of which have been staples of filmic storytelling. They have searched for writers who are comfortable with using these elements in nonlinear story environments while crafting their content.

One of the storytellers Jaunt has partnered with is Doug Liman. Liman has directed big box-office fair ranging from the indie cult classic *Swingers* to action tentpoles like *The Bourne Identity* and *Edge of Tomorrow*. His first project with Jaunt is a five-part VR series called *Invisible*. Liman brought in Melissa Wallack, nominated for an Oscar for *Dallas Buyers Club*, to write the project.

Tom Vance, head of content, explained the working relationship between Jaunt and Liman as a true creative partnership. "What makes Doug so remarkable and why he ended up being such a phenomenal partner is his willingness to take on a challenge, whether in *The Borne Identity*, completely upending and reinventing the editorial style of feature film, to *Edge of Tomorrow*, which is something studios just aren't making—ambitious standalone original sci-fi movies. Doug brought all of those things to the table for us," he said.

George Kliavkoff, CEO and president of Jaunt, agrees. "Doug's unique process, in terms of shooting and editing in real time, was incredible. The whole process was a living document until we found the story. We knew what the story was going into production, we had a script, and that story is the story that ends up in the show, but in an effort to actually execute the story, we put the show together and broke it apart a number of times before we actually felt like we were communicating what was on the page when you're in a headset. That process itself was amazing."

Jaunt became interested in Liman when they heard he had been experimenting with VR on his own. The team knew they wanted to work in the genres that he excelled in. Vance is excited about working in genres with wide international appeal. "I think 45% of our total audience is global, so we're not thinking about developing content for a territory-specific audience. Sure, there're going to be pieces that are catered to some sort of geo-location, but with our high-concept and tentpole content, we want to make broadly appealing commercial concepts. We are asking, who are the internationally relevant actors? Who's the biggest star in China that is forward thinking and wants to be part of a big kind of tentpole VR series? How can we bring those people together and create what is not just a show for North America and Europe but for the global audience? That's something that we're contemplating today, because the audience already is global," he said.

Jaunt is looking ahead to the future, incorporating social VR narrative strategies on upcoming projects. "This bridges the cinematic VR space and the gaming VR space. Being in a film together with your friends will be a way that stories are told in the future. We plan to be on the cutting edge of that," Anderson said.

Storytelling in VR through the Artist's Lens
An Interview with
Mark Cordell Holmes, Art Director, Pixar

Mark Cordell Holmes has worked for 25 years as an art director and visual storyteller. He creates original narrative, interactive, and VR experiences. A significant amount of his work has been at Pixar, where his credits included *A Bug's Life, Monsters Inc., The Incredibles, Ratatouille, WALL-E, Toy Story 2, Toy Story 3, Cars 2,* and *Brave.*

John Bucher:	Can you talk about your philosophy of VR storytelling?
Mark Cordell Holmes:	The interesting thing about VR is it's a merger of different storytelling disciplines. It's a new way of looking at this stuff, and so there's going to be a limited value any one group can bring to it. There has to be almost this whole new art form or storytelling form that's going to be a combination hybrid of these things in some sense and a still undefined combination.
John Bucher:	That's exactly what I would love this book to be— the marrying of all these disciplines to figure out what storytelling in this discipline looks like.
Mark Cordell Holmes:	I can share with you how I learned to apply design to conventional visual storytelling through emotional storytelling both in a narrative context and interactive context, although I have less experience at that. VR definitely seems like a place where it's definitely the merger of narratives and interactive experiences, immersive experiences. I definitely see people approaching it from either the narrative standpoint or the interactive standpoint and each falling short. I'm fascinated by that gap in between those. I think that's where the sweet spot will be.
John Bucher:	Tell me about your background and what has brought you to the point you are at now with story.
Mark Cordell Holmes:	I've had some time to think about it because mine has largely been a career of circumstance in high

school and college. I loved reading. I was a big reader. I loved science fiction and fantasy. I was a big movie fanatic. I was already loving stories. Probably around sixth grade, I stumbled into role-playing games with some friends. The thing that I fell in love with, though, was the dynamic storytelling and I just love the idea of creating worlds and characters and possibilities. It was like a vehicle for me to explore stories. I think that was more interesting to me than maybe the game mechanics themselves.

I was also, was a voracious comic book reader. I loved early anime stuff. I just was always consuming story content in one form or another. I wanted to be a comic book artist in high school. I would even take my little portfolio with me to comic conventions, and I would always chicken out and not show anyone anything. It was a fantasy that I could be doing that, but I didn't really have any idea how it could be possible to do that for a living. It was almost just always like a side project. I didn't know what I wanted to be when I grew up. My mom was practical. She wanted me to maybe be in accounting. Once I got into college and I looked at course catalogues, it blew me away that you could actually study these things, let alone get a job in it.

I was not a great student. I didn't appreciate school, but my first week, I got a job as a paid graphic artist. I had to learn how to use a Mac and from there, it was pretty much my first job. I was already accruing skills that made me competitive. I ended up dropping out of school because I decided my job would be my education. My career would be my education. I found I was far more motivated if I was at the risk of being fired than I was of getting an F or a low grade. I got swept up into Silicon Valley. There were not many people that were trained on the computers or on the software, and I fortunately had been exposed to enough that not only did I have the drawing skills, but I had enough software knowledge to be competitive and get work. Then it just bounced around. I was always trying to find work that involved creating characters or worlds or a fantastic context or something was more interesting to me. I wasn't really a big gamer per sé, but again, it was almost like those early role-playing game days. I was immersing myself and visualizing these fantasies.

Again, I was just lucky enough that there was always opportunity. Right before *Toy Story* came out, I ended up getting a job at Pixar and working with their commercial group. I didn't even know that they were making an animated feature. I just thought they were making commercials. I was working in the back office with a handful of people. I didn't realize there was a warehouse filled with animators and technical directors. Then shortly after the movie came out, I was pulled into the feature group. The Pixar opportunity was far more fulfilling for me because I really love story. In college, I'd wanted to be either a filmmaker or a screenwriter.

Pixar was definitely a step closer to what I wanted to be doing. I really wanted to be a story artist. I really wanted to be helping with the stories. I took some story classes while I was there, and I had a screenwriting mentor for years. I was a better artist and writer and was able to learn to contribute to the stories in a different way in a visual context, especially as I went from being a production artist, where my focus is on the nuts and bolts. How do you make something work? How do you design a character's environment so that they can fit through the door and so that it could accommodate the action and the storyboards and all that stuff?

To then get to art direct and production design where you're responsible for not just the look of the film to support the story. That for me was really magical, and it began to give me a real fulfillment, because I felt like I was contributing to story in a very meaningful way. Then after a while, I'd been there long enough where I wasn't growing in the ways I wanted to grow and then helped start up a game company, where I was able to take my learnings from Pixar and try to apply them to an interactive experience with a computer game. I'd been out of games for 16 years, and so it was like starting over but seeing it through a new light. I couldn't map the learning between the techniques in a direct one-to-one way, but there were definitely places where it could apply. There were places where it didn't apply where it challenged me to think. In a film, we would use lots of cameras on certain things. Here, we don't have that control. It's up to the player to explore. How do you create either the probability for things or communicate things where you are not reliant on composition?

That was definitely a great learning curve, and I feel like I was just scratching the surface. Unfortunately, after we put out a game, our publisher had a strategic shift, and they ended up dropping the developers, including us. As a startup, we didn't have any other financial backing, so we had to dissolve it. I was very excited at that point. I really wanted to get into VR just because it seemed like the perfect laboratory environment for how do we bring all of these assumptions we have and techniques and learnings we have of storytelling and these different disciplines, and how do we bring them together in a new combination? A new way to create a totally unique immersive experience that's still fulfilling but fulfilling in a whole new way.

John Bucher: Where does game theory apply and where does narrative theory overlap, and how do we tease those apart?

Mark Cordell Holmes:

In terms of immersive entertainment, there's a couple of perspectives to which I'm seeing people approach it. Google is trying to repurpose the traditional narrative experience into their medium, and there is a whole host of challenges that come with it, of course. Each of the films they've done presents a different approach and different learnings and different failures, and they are all wonderful.

Some others rely on novelty, but after a couple of viewings you go, okay, there's nothing very substantial to hold you in or to make you want to go back to it. Other people are doing the games approach, so they are doing a first-person shooter. Where it seems like the obvious way you would use medium but to me it's not pushing the medium, it's not taking advantage of it in a way that's different from how you experience forward. It's almost just like watching a movie with stereoscopic glasses on. It gives you the illusion of immersion, but it's not fundamentally shifting the experience in a way.

I hate the idea of the helmet. I think you look stupid when you're wearing it. It feels isolating. It's like you have to have a huge space. There are a lot of barriers to entry to the experience that to me are a big turn off, and also I get motion sickness pretty easily. The discoveries will be made across different people trying different things, but eventually if the success is a little bit still down into more of a craft.

John Bucher:

Some have suggested there are two schools of philosophy for VR. One being the viewer as observer versus the first-person shooter where the viewer is actually participating or being active in that. Do you think those are geared towards different types of people or that different types of people will gravitate to one or the other, or do you think one will eventually win out the format? What are your thoughts on where that's going to go?

Mark Cordell Holmes: My instinct is that there is going to be many, many different kinds of experiences. These are our reference points right now. Third-person shooters, a third-person observational narrative experience. You can still have top-down VR experiences. You're going to have the same reference points for how people experience things that will probably evolve in some capacity. I think some will be more successful than others because maybe they will lend themselves to the medium in a way better than others. There is going to be a process of natural selection that certain things will win out over others just because they are more engaging or more satisfying or what have you—more effective.

John Bucher: The word that seems to be on a lot of people's tongues when it comes to VR is "empathy." You were associated with a company (Pixar) that has had the corner on the market on storytelling empathy—across the board. Obviously, you're someone who knows something about communicating empathy from those experiences. Can you talk a little bit about empathy? Is how you've seen it working in the past the same as how that could work in VR?

Mark Cordell Holmes: It's interesting. My guess is that there is going to be different ways that you would use to create that but maybe not. From the Pixar standpoint, they are making stories. It's narrative storytelling, and it's actually quite a long process. It's in the writing. It's in the storyboarding. There's a very iterative process there. At a certain level, it's like there's the writers, the storytellers. There's a degree of themselves and their characters, or their own humanity is somehow going into it at some level. Whether it's a direct personal experience or again it's just, they are bringing their own empathy to the characters. There has to be a love for the characters.

I think one of the differences between Pixar's stories and other stories that maybe come off as being less empathetic or maybe less successful is that Pixar consciously enables the story iterative process to continue to the bitter end. If there's time to make a change to make something better, they will do that. It's expensive, and there is a lot of throwing out of work.

As you go to the process of putting characters through their paces and bumping characters against each other and you have conflicting goals and obstacles, you start to learn things about them, and your ideas about them change, and you get into the process. You always get to the process where the story starts to write itself where you have to trust the process and let go of your preconceptions. What happens too is that until all these pieces come together towards the end where you have a context now. You've been with a character long enough that you're starting to get to know them in a way where they are starting to reveal this dimensionality, and it's even surprising to you—where you as the creators are starting to be surprised by these characters. It's almost an unconscious thing.

I think that Pixar allows themselves to get to that point where they have all this context, they've lived with the characters enough and there is that last little bit of evolution that starts to give them that real dimension. I think a lot of other studios, what they do is they want to lock the script early. The script is locked and let's just make it. They didn't allow themselves to have the time to be with the characters, to see them evolve, to give them space to evolve, and to surprise themselves. The result is that they have a cheaper movie with probably a higher profit margin, but it may not have the same humanity, the same depth of character that will stick with people for generations to come. The empathy I think comes from characters being believable and dimensional and of course being flawed and vulnerable. There is a lot of other craft sides of what you can do to make a character sympathetic. I think there's a lot of important ingredients.

John Bucher: I think it is interesting when you look back to the early days of filmmaking, we see the mistakes that they made, is there anything just intuitively that you're feeling at this point, that people want to avoid as they are looking at interactive or immersive-type storytelling in this medium?

Mark Cordell Holmes: If I'm understanding you correctly, you are talking about how there are mistakes early in the process, and the history of the storytelling craft. The first thing I would say is that there really are no mistakes. I'm going to go for the low-hanging fruit here. One of the iconic early pieces of filmmaking that literally helped to catapult the medium into the mainstream was *The Great Train Robbery*. Everybody ran out of their chairs because they thought the train was coming at them. We look at that now, we look back at that, and you think, God, you guys were idiots. It just seems so juvenile, but it's when you look at the nativity, they were all experimenting with the medium. This was a brand new medium. There were no rules. They are taking baby steps and they would fall down and then get up. Someone else takes a different baby step and they fall. Eventually as there's collective learning, each generation of storytellers or filmmakers takes the little bit of pieces that work and string them together, and then they make their own mistakes and they bring their new learnings to it.

I feel VR right now is like we are making trains that are flying out in your face and straight at you. That's all we are doing. It's all novelty to an extent. You even look at the advent of 3D animation not that long ago. When you look back on them now, they are just these tacky, cheesy things to laugh at, but they were such milestones and it took those steps to lead to the next steps. Until you get this guy named John Lassiter whose job it is to make a text demo and instead of making a text demo, he makes a story about lamps or about a bee stinging a guy's face.

He was able to elevate beyond the novelty of the technology or the novelty of the medium to use it in a meaningful way as a form of expression, artistic expression. It then becomes truly empowered in a way that has relevance to people's lives. You could look at a shiny ball and go, "That's neat," but then you're going to forget about it. You go, "What am I going to do with that?" If you come up with this little lamp bouncing on the ball, that's going to stick with people, and then they care about the medium. Everyone thinks that they know what they're doing, and they do to an extent, but it's such a brand-new field that people should be throwing all kinds of stuff at the viewer or trying all kinds of things. Hopefully, in five years, ten years, it could be three months for all I know. At some point, enough of what works and what people are responding to will connect.

Honestly, we won't know for a while because we don't have any mass adoption of the technology yet, and there's still a lot of barriers to entry. I think in time, though, we're going to be discovering things that none of us could anticipate now that are experiences we just have never had before. That we have for the first time in this medium and it just blows us away and creates that into an art form or a new storytelling form or maybe as just some completely different application we can't even imagine that becomes the new internet or the new way of doing things. Anyway, it's a super-exciting idea. We're still taking baby steps right now.

INSIGHTS FROM THE ARTISTS

Those bringing training and experience from other disciplines will continue to be important contributors to the field of VR storytelling. Artists with understanding of immersive principles in their respective fields can teach VR creators what has worked and what has failed in their experiences and potentially create significant VR work themselves. Angela Haddad's background in fashion and design was useful in thinking through new ways VR could be expressed. Annie Lesser's work with moving audiences through immersive drama has served as a basis for her beginning work in VR, AR, and MR. And of course, Mark Cordell Holmes's talents with animation made for a natural bridge into creating experiences in which digitally produced characters engaged with the audiences in VR. All of these artists also share a common characteristic: a gift for knowing how an artistic element will impact the audience emotionally. Haddad called these elements trigger points. In her work, they are the elements that cause a viewer to turn their head and look in the direction she intends.

Artists in any medium, but especially in VR space, must become familiar with the tools at their disposal for moving an audience's emotions and experience. Jaunt Studios chose to work with Doug Liman because of his ability to move an audience through a wide range of emotional space—from comedic moments to breathless suspense. Jaunt is transcending the traditional film studio model, creating both the technology that makes its product possible as well as the talent and understanding about how to tell stories in immersive space. Similarly, in her field, Lesser is meticulous about where she places actors interacting with the audience. She is aware that space itself is a tool the creators must use wisely. Liman demonstrates a parallel understanding of space in *Invisible*, placing his camera in positions and angles that defy traditional cinematography. His canvas had changed, and it became important to change the ways he used his tools. Lesser uses the location of her artwork as environmental storytelling, never missing a chance to let the objects in the room play their part in telling a story. Many of the immersive principles discussed in Chapter 4 unpack the ways that artists like these approach space.

Holmes compares the artistry in VR to the earliest works of filmmaking, relying often on novelty and not yet pushing the boundaries of the medium, which does take time. Most creators featured in this book stressed the importance of experimentation and risk taking in VR, recognizing that this path is the only way to keep moving the medium forward. It could be argued that the film industry has slowed its development as a medium due to the lack of commercial opportunities for films that push the artistic boundaries forward in ways that do not reinforce what audiences are already comfortable with. Lesser mentions the importance of symbolism, subtext, and thematic exploration as ways of pushing a medium forward along with the technological. Many times, these methods are more accepted by audiences simply because it gives them handles to grasp while trying to make sense of the new experience. Haddad relies on a similar approach with her work. Many experimental films use a few of the basic elements of traditional cinema in order to give their audience familiarity on some viewing level. Remembering that the experience of the audience is paramount will continue to be a guiding principle for creating VR stories.

THE VISIONARIES

Storytelling in VR through World Building
An Interview with
Larry Rosenthal, VR Pioneer and Producer

Larry Rosenthal is a veteran of the VR industry, working in the field since the late 1980s. Currently he owns Cube3, a company focused on building virtual worlds and experiences.

John Bucher: Let's start by talking about what world building means to you.

Larry Rosenthal: In today's world, it's an interesting concept because everyone has an idea now of what it means. It's a buzz-word. With certain properties like the Marvel universe, the money is there now to really build worlds. The lexicon has also moved on from Virtual Reality to virtual worlds back to Virtual Reality in a sense. I did a seminar in 1995 called "Places not Pages." I was trying to get people to understand that the virtual world was going to be a bunch of social places more than home pages. At that point, everyone was trying to put a brochure on the internet. No one understood that it was a spatial relationship through Virtual Reality with a screen.

World building is mediation. There's nature. There's a tree, the sky, the ground. There's the man living in the cave who gets wet when he walks out. The minute you start to mediate the world by putting something over his head, going back into the cave with his wet hand, and putting it on the wall, it's creating a mediated world. That's what we did as humans. World building for us is mediation of the natural world. The nature of God as the world builder depending on your beliefs, full of every-thing we've been thrown into. World building to me always sets up an interface for the world. It can be used for all different sorts of things, often selling agendas. It can be used for entertainment. It can be used for teach-ing and learning. It's a way of modeling.

John Bucher:	There's a lot of people who say VR is the ultimate empathy machine. Why might that not be true?
Larry Rosenthal:	Because it's the ultimate emotion mediator, but it's not an empathy mediator.
	It's an emotion machine, but empathy is up to the user to figure out. Someone was posting yesterday on Twitter the same thing. They said something like empathy is what you may feel compassion for but look at what you actually do. There's no doubt that VR is the so-called last medium. One of the reasons I've stayed in it for so long is not just because I don't want to be on the streets and broke. It's because this is the atomic bomb. This is the third act.
John Bucher:	You talk about some of the uses of story and narrative in VR. Can you talk a little bit about what has been the history of story in VR, and more importantly, what you think is the future of how story will be used in VR?
Larry Rosenthal:	I like the term "narrative" better than "story." The simplest form people understand is the "Choose Your Own Adventure" book. It began with the paper medium, and because we numbered it, we ordered it, we allowed people to basically skip ahead and branch off, and it only cost paper. They were books that were targeted for kids, but basically it's where almost all the narratives in the digital industry come from. You had to let go of the attention. You had to let the viewer be a user, the star of the show, for lack of a better term. 3D games have already covered a lot of this. There's no doubt in my mind that the people who are dealing with the worlds of RPG games and 3D games and theater outside of gaming are the most into what this will be. It's their lessons that are going to work. The ones that are driven by a lot of the character-based ideas are the ones that are going to find what doesn't work. They'll find it again as everybody tries to become the Pixar of VR.
John Bucher:	Why has the character-centered narrative not worked as well in VR?

Larry Rosenthal: Because they're not the star. You are. In other words, the audience, the viewer has so much of the weight that you have to be the one who's really driving the antagonism of the show. Otherwise, you're watching a cartoon. You're watching someone else do a performance, which is fine. The problem is right now and maybe for the foreseeable future that there are two things to consider: ROI and ROE. Everybody knows what ROI is: return on investment. But I've been using ROE for return on entertainment for just as long. That's why a lot of the web 3D stuff and a lot of multimedia stuff fails, because you have to jump over too many hurdles. It ruins the entertainment.

John Bucher: Just to build on that, why do you think our culture has become so hungry for experience as opposed to just entertainment?

Larry Rosenthal: I think they're both the same in some ways. We're in an interactive age. We've gone from ear-eye to hand-eye as a culture. In the 1980s we got the clicker, so now we have control over the media. We've got 500 channels and nothing on. That began to change us from the ear-eye of having to sit through whatever was on TV to now where you can interact. You get anxious if you aren't able to control your medium. The HMD, I think, is going to have the shortest lifespan ever as the mediation device, because I think within a decade, we'll have gone from these into the chip. Now that we're networking, acceleration factor, McLuhan, all this stuff kicks in. The kids will have the chips.

Storytelling in VR through Light
An Interview with
Paul Debevec, Senior Staff Engineer, Google VR

Paul Debevec has served as chief visual officer and led the Graphics Labora-
tory at the University of Southern California's Institute for Creative Technologies. He is a research professor in the USC computer science department.
He earned degrees in math and computer engineering at the University of
Michigan in 1992 and a PhD in computer science from UC Berkeley in 1996.
He directed a photo-realistic fly-around of the Berkeley campus for his 1997
film *The Campanile Movie*, whose techniques were later used to create the
Academy Award®–winning virtual backgrounds in the "bullet time" shots
in the 1999 film *The Matrix*.

At USC ICT, Debevec has led the development of several Light Stage
systems that capture and simulate how people and objects appear under
real-world illumination. Early Light Stage processes have been used by
Sony Pictures Imageworks, WETA Digital, and Digital Domain to create
photo-real digital actors in award-winning visual effects in *Spider-Man 2*
and *King Kong, Superman Returns, Spider-Man 3, Hancock,* and *The Curious Case of Benjamin Button.* The most recent Light Stage process based on
polarized gradient illumination has been used in numerous films, including
James Cameron's *Avatar, The Avengers, Oblivion, Ender's Game, Gravity,*
and *Maleficent.* In February 2010, Debevec received a Scientific and Engineering Academy Award® for the design and engineering of the Light Stage
capture devices and the image-based facial rendering system developed for
character relighting in motion pictures. He is senior staff engineer at Google VR and recently worked with the Smithsonian Institution to scan a 3D
model of President Barack Obama.

John Bucher: Can you talk a little bit about your philosophy of bringing
                humanity to these digital creations? It seems to be a value
                you hold.

Paul Debevec: I got into computer graphics pretty seriously in graduate
                school when I was at UC Berkeley. At the time, we didn't
                really know how to do photo-realistic digital faces. It was
                clearly a holy grail of the field. We didn't even know if it
                would ever be possible. Originally my work actually had
                more to do with architecture and lighting and digital

photography. That's where I found I could make contributions. As soon as it looked like we could bring human faces into the discourse of our research, with our first Light Stage, which was a way of reproducing the light of some other environment onto a human face, I knew that the work would get quite a bit more impactful.

Another part of that is the inspiration from the filmmaking side. Back in the '90s, I would try to do research in the fall to publish a paper for SIGGRAPH. Those were due in January. Their computer animation festival deadline was usually in April, so I had a few months to try to make a computer-animated short film that leveraged the technology and then have that be in the film showcase for the conference and get some good press marketing between the creative work and the technical.

I made these films, *The Campanile Movie* in '97 and *Render of Natural Light* in '99, and I was really enjoying the filmmaking process, but I realized my movies don't have any people in them. They were about architecture and lighting, and you can make an interesting two-and-a-half-minute abstract short that way but little more. *The Campanile Movie* technically did have a person in it, but that was live action. To go to the point where we could try to create a realistic, digital human face felt like the modern equivalent of the problem that painters had in the 1300s and 1400s and 1500s of getting to the point where a painting could show somebody that you felt was a realistic-looking person.

John Bucher: In your TED talk, we saw digital Emily on screen. It's difficult to tell if she's real or a computer. Do you believe that we are approaching an age where we'll be able to create digital actors and eliminate human presence in our films and storytelling?

Paul Debevec: That's a great question, and sometimes when we have an actor on one of the Light Stages, they'll ask, "So this is going to make it so we don't have to act anymore? Or they're not going to need us anymore?" If it looks like a character is giving a good emotionally engaging human performance in a film or video game, the reason for that is that a real actor actually supplied that engaging human performance, and through performance-capture techniques, it was mapped onto the digital actor. There are a couple instances where key frame animation techniques were used to create the performance. For example, the Michael Jackson performance at the Billboard Music Video Awards, where he performed a song in one of these reflective *Pepper's Ghost* images. We assisted with the project with the Light Stage. We didn't do the animation. I met the animators, and they actually provided the performance with lots of reference from the real Michael Jackson. It's incredibly well documented, so in a sense, it's his performance up there, or it's based on his performance. Lots of incredibly talented animators crafted it, so in that case, the animators are sort of the actors in that human element.

If you go to any Pixar or Disney 3D computer animation, it's the animators who are providing those very engaging performances of the animated characters. We're not eliminating the human elements at all, in any of these cases. When you get to VR, the question does become a bit different. Once you have one of these headsets that you can look anywhere, and you really feel like you're in a different world, a character that's in that world with you, or that you see there—you really feel a lot more like that person is actually there with you. Since you can interactively look around and explore the scene, you feel this is a much more present experience, so your expectations that that character will react to you and that you can converse with them are much higher.

Unless we're doing a telepresence situation, where it really is another person over there, and I hope VR will produce great technologies for that, then we do have to figure out a way for this synthetic human to interactively react to you. To do so in real time, and believably—that's something that is an area of research right now. It probably needs several years to get to the point where we're blowing people away with what's capable. I think VR, much more than the games, certainly way more than movies, is going to push the need for development of artificial intelligence technologies that can simulate engaging human behavior.

John Bucher: I love that you brought up *Pepper's Ghost*. If we look back at history and what people have been trying to accomplish with putting virtual presences in front of people, we must discuss *Star Trek*'s holodeck. Do you think VR is headed to a place where we take the glasses off and we experience this Virtual Reality in an even more realistic way?

Paul Debevec: The holodeck, for a lot of us researchers, was the shining example of what we wanted to create when we created virtual environments and the kind of content creation techniques you need to generate what the *Star Trek* characters experienced, and that was a very reasonable vision, because they're really these amazing 3D light field displays that can make you feel like you're in a different place in that way. I think of it like the CAVE systems. They were early VR experiences with six screens around people that are projected and you have to wear 3D glasses. That was more kind of like a holodeck sort of experience.

With this renaissance of Virtual Reality and the fact that now the screens are high enough resolution that you can make out a bit of detail in these environments and that the computation and the display is fast enough that it really feels like it's reacting to how you're moving your head in real time, I think within a couple generations of these headsets, we'll have things that are incredibly satisfying VR experiences, and we're going to say, "Holodeck? Why do you need a holodeck?" You can do this in VR. I don't think that we actually need to invent the large-scale, 3D light field displays that the holodeck seems to have.

John Bucher: You did a piece on the Parthenon. You've had an interest in Greek storytelling and what has come before. What do you think are some of the key things from our past we must remember and what we have learned over the last couple thousand years about story that's important for us to bring into VR space?

Paul Debevec: I love how, in our excitement about creating content for VR, we have thrown so much energy into the conversation of what is story, what is interactive storytelling, and how will we be telling stories in the future? I'm certainly of the camp that believes that with VR experiences, people feel like they're in the present, generally. When you have the ability to affect what is happening in the environments and with the characters that are around you, it feels like this is happening now and it doesn't feel like it's once upon a time. "Once upon a time," "in the past," I think that's storytelling. Stories are how we store information about history and the lessons that we can take from that history, allegorically. Maybe we should just call some of these things interactive experiences to differentiate it from storytelling—which is this whole other new completely amazing thing, where you feel like it's the present—you feel that you have agency within this world. We're only getting started with that. I'm so excited to be in this field for the next decade at least, because we're going to see brilliant people coming up with brilliant stuff. It's really even hard to imagine at this point as to what people will find fun and engaging to do in these virtual worlds.

John Bucher: You've been called "Hollywood's Master of Light." Can you talk a little bit about the role of light in storytelling?

Paul Debevec: I'm very happy that in my career, I have gotten to work with and talk to some of the great cinematographers in the film industry and learn a little bit of their craft. Lighting is incredibly important for setting the mood for a scene and the visual look of how wide the color space is, saturated or not saturated, the contrast you're not seeing contrasting. Is it hard light or soft light? I'm conscious of light a lot more than the average person from studying it, but I can remember back before when I just wasn't very conscious of light. I saw things in terms of objects and the colors of the objects rather than realizing that I don't actually see objects, I only see light reflecting from them, and that light changes remarkably, depending on how things are lit.

I find that lighting is a way to communicate directly to the subconscious experience. Take a look at Instagram, which is a multibillion-dollar company right now. It was founded originally on just taking a cell phone photo and altering the colors and the contrast in a way that it looked like a

Polaroid from the 1960s, for example, and it completely changes your emotional relationship to that material, and that was enough to launch an enormously popular company, which does much more now but began with that simple idea. I'm looking forward to seeing what cinematography means in the Virtual Reality world, and I hope to get to work with some of these folks and experiment in the space myself.

John Bucher: I would be remiss if I didn't ask you to tell us a little bit about the experience of working with President Obama in the project that you did at the White House. Could you talk a little bit about how that worked within the larger scope that you're doing?

Paul Debevec: That was an extremely exciting project, and it was nerve-wracking. It was basically like playing a really important away game for us, because we usually have people come to our Light Stage in Los Angeles, to our own space, and if anything goes wrong, we have everyone who designed everything around. In the case of the scanning we did at the White House, which we did at the invitation of the amazing 3D digitization office at the Smithsonian Institution, who were our collaborators and decided that, from some talks I'd given, that using our techniques for the front of Obama's face, ear to ear and down to the neck, was, at the time, the highest-quality 3D scan that could be done.

We had to customize our system to take it to the White House to take the scan, and we had a very limited time to do that. We'll have a major actor, like Tom Cruise or Angelina Jolie, for at least an hour, and in the case of President Obama, we had to make sure that we could do it in just a few minutes. One of the awesome things was, we were so fast, and the Smithsonian folks were so fast with their systems to get the back of the head and the shoulders for the 3D printed bust, that there was like 10 minutes left over, so he just hung out with us and we talked about the technology, and it was a pretty special time. I'm so glad technology happened to work flawlessly that day, and we were almost inappropriately exuberant afterwards in the White House once everyone had left and we realized that we got it done.

John Bucher: In a perfect world, what would be your ultimate goal or ultimate dream for Virtual Reality?

Paul Debevec: I think of VR and the content creation technology in general that I've been trying to help develop as enhancing the ability for people to communicate with each other and to tell stories to each other. I want it so that anybody, with anything that they want to show the world, to tell the world, can communicate that as realistically as possible, as fleshed out in terms of the environments and the characters as possible, and that we'll be able to make experiences on the epic scale of *Avatar* with a relatively small group of collaborators who are able to do the key creative things to get that stuff done.

Case Study: *Lucy* **VR Series**
Written and Directed by Matt Thompson

FIGURE 8.8 Courtesy of Matt Thompson

Matt Thompson created the VR series *Lucy* as an exploration of life's biggest questions. Why are we here? What happens after we die? "The idea of the afterlife and the idea of a story taking place starting at the point of death was really interesting to me. I'm particularly interested in spirituality. To me, spiritual stories are the stories, that started stories," Thompson said.

Following the loss of his father at a young age, Thompson had explored the theme of loss in his work for some time. With *Lucy*, he wanted to explore what his father's journey might have been like entering death. VR presented a new medium to explore this theme in.

"Virtual Reality is not the new film, it's just a new medium. For the afterlife, there's a lot of stories, a lot of narrative written, but there's never been an opportunity to step *into* the afterlife and be meditative about it. That's what I was looking to do," Thompson said.

The script for *Lucy* became an evolving document, changing as different scenes were crafted in virtual space. The dialogue for each scene remained roughly the same, but the capture process constantly presented new challenges as well as new opportunities. Combining VR computer graphics with two live-action sequences, Thompson storyboarded using five circles on a

FIGURE 8.9 Courtesy of Matt Thompson

page to represent the different angles available to the viewer in each scene in order to craft the narrative.

The production process leaned heavily on practical lighting and hidden microphones to keep gear out of the shots. "We coined the term 'DPP,' the director of pan-optic photography, for Matt, our cinematographer. We were intentional to adopt a philosophy that recognized it's not virtual cinema, it's Virtual Reality," Thompson said. "It's a lot more about context. When I walk into this room, I feel a certain way about you, and not because of how you're lit, although it helps, but it's because of the context that I know you in. That's what I started with to create the environment and world," he continued.

Because Lucy is a first-person experience about a protagonist that loses their body, Thompson decided to envision the camera as a *vessel*. "If people are going to put something on where they can now look all around, it is now inhabiting a body. You can make these experiences where you can still be omniscient and you're watching people, but I don't think that makes sense," he explained.

Logistically, tempo and pacing are among some of the most difficult elements to control, according to Thompson. The loss of certain editing techniques in the post production process forced the crew to think differently about how to establish a rhythm in the story. Audio became a driving force in the process. The audio team developed a spatial mix for the project for viewers on the Oculus platform as well as a standard stereo mix for viewers on more basic systems.

Future episodes will explore death experienced by a different person from a different place in the world, exploring their cultural, religious, or spiritual beliefs. The ongoing theme will examine how planet Earth thinks about the afterlife as a whole. "When you can experience it (afterlife experiences) side by side, I think you can get a real sense not only of perspective but empathy," Thompson said.

Thompson remains focused on simply telling good stories in VR space as opposed to crafting content around the medium. "I think that if I can just focus on making really compelling content, the brilliant engineers of the world will keep making the technology better and easier," he said.

Storytelling in VR through Agency
An Interview with
Brian Rose, Google VR Team, Community and Outreach

Brian Rose has worked as community and outreach manager for Niantic, creators of AR mobile app games Ingress and Pokémon Go. He's now in developer outreach and community for the Google VR team, working on AR projects such as Project Tango and VR projects such as Daydream.

John Bucher: Let's talk about some of the more philosophical ideas when it comes to Virtual Reality. One is the idea of agency. I've noticed that Google has been leading the path on providing agency to people, especially with programs like Tilt Brush. Can you talk a little bit about the way that you and your team approach agency when you're trying to design something for the end user?

Brian Rose: On the Google VR team, we're working on a lot of different projects. On the YouTube side, we have things like *Spotlight Stories*. One of the things that came out of the YouTube *Spotlight Stories* project was this idea of branch story lines. In normal Google Cardboard 360 content, you're essentially just stuck in one place and you can look completely around you, but a lot of our creators had asked for some kind of interactivity. Some kind of either look-based or gaze-based interactivity. We created animation with Aardman Studios that had something like forty-five different branch story lines or possible story lines. When I thought about a lot of narrative games which I really love—games like even *Life Is Strange* for example, or any Choose Your Own Adventure book, a lot of times I'd have a lot of fun in the process of reading the stories or playing through the games, but at the very end, it always felt like it always came down to this binary (a) or (b) path. Whenever I hit that end point, I don't know if I ever really felt satisfied with being able to choose, "Do I save the town or do I save my friend?"

So, because of that, what we decided to do on the *Spotlight Story* side was always have the same beginning and ending to the video, but how you get to that ending or the subplots or substories that you see along the way—those are the things that are different and can change anytime. It might be unique in the way I watch it or you watch it, but we'll always have the same beginning and ending. We have that shared experience, but the way that we get there could be different meandering paths.

I do think agency is very important. We created a narrative called *Pearl*. We had talked about a 2D version where it's just something that you could watch on a TV or on a computer. Or perhaps a 360 version that you could watch on mobile VR with the YouTube player. But on the HTC Vive, you get a greater sense of agency. You can actually walk around the car or stand up when the little girl pops out of the sun roof to catch the fireflies. That agency provides some powerful, emotional moments that come from that.

There's a difference between what I refer to as ghost stories, where the characters don't know I'm actually there, and stories where you have presence *with* the characters. In the first type, I'm essentially a ghost in the story. I'm just passively watching things happen as they happen versus actually being able to interact with characters in the story or affect the environment, affect the other characters in the experience. But those are both paths that we've been exploring.

We're doing so many things in VR. We try to do a little bit of everything to see what works and what doesn't. Also to see what works for specific platforms. There are some limitations that we have with mobile VR that we don't have with desktop-tethered VR. Being on the Vive gives us things like hand controllers that Cardboard doesn't, for example. Being able to use those hand controllers, being able to take advantage of room scale and figuring out how to incorporate those into the story in a natural way, they're all parts of things that we're working on with the Google VR team. I wouldn't really say at this point there's one right way or a wrong way to do it. There are certain things that work better on specific platforms, and because VR is so many things, we end up doing a little bit of everything.

John Bucher: As you and your team are looking at and designing experiences, when do narrative elements rise about "this character" or "this conflict"? Can you talk about what some of the conversations are around designing an experience when it comes to narrative elements?

Brian Rose: A lot of what we try to do is create tools to enable creators to tell those stories and then make sure they can reach as wide an audience as they want to. On our team, part of our thinking is that if we are going to create these platforms, it would probably also be helpful for us to provide some high-quality content so that we can show people, "These are the things that we're looking for." Or, "These are things that we think are possible on the platform." To that end, we do have a team in New York that's working on content. Jess Brillhart is our principal filmmaker, and she can talk much more in depth about her point of view or her direction in terms of storytelling and narrative in VR.

On the Google VR team, a lot of what we're focused on is the technical aspects rather than on trying to tell creators, "Here's how to or how not to create content." I will say though that with the hardware itself, I don't think it is what's most important. At the end of the day, although we are working hard to bring mobile VR to the masses of Cardboard users, we're working hard on bringing up Daydream with higher-quality mobile VR. Story is such a key part of that. As much as we can, we work with the community to figure out if there are tools that content creators need that don't exist today. If there are, please let our team know and we'll work to build those into the platform. Things like those branch story lines or things like interactivity through hand controls or gaze-based and look-based interaction.

Storytelling in VR—it's incredibly important. Those rich examples of the great stuff you can do with VR, really come down to creating compelling immersive stories. That's why we're so invested in trying to support this community.

The Future of VR Storytelling
An Interview with
Ted Schilowitz, Futurist, 20th Century Fox Studios

Ted Schilowitz was a founding member, first employee, and integral part of the product development team at RED Digital Cinema. He currently spends his time focused on the future of the cinema experience. He has a studio deal at 20th Century Fox as their futurist, working directly with senior leadership at the studio on the constantly evolving art and science of the digital age of motion picture creation. He advises and creates strategy on future technology and vision of cinema for the next generation of movie entertainment.

He has been featured in *Wired, Variety, The New York Times, The Wall Street Journal, The Hollywood Reporter,* NBC, *American Cinematographer, MacWorld, Popular Science, LA Times,* and in countless other trade publications and the mainstream press, discussing technology advancements in his areas of passion and exploration.

John Bucher: I'd love to start by talking on a macro level about VR. Why now? Why is it that we suddenly hit a breaking point in the adoption of VR, and what does that have to do with storytelling?

Ted Schilowitz: I think about this a lot. I think about what the many answers to that might be, much more than the raw technology itself. I think about humanity. We spend a lot more time touching technology in a more intimate way than in generations past. You look around this world and see how many people are holding a little piece of silicon and functioning to achieve things through that. Eight to 10 hours a day, right? Or maybe longer. With kids, probably longer. The question is, "Are we ready as a society for the next step in a visualization experience? For a more intense and modern experience than what a phone offers?" I believe that we likely are.

John Bucher: Perhaps a more embodied experience than what we currently have with the internet?

Ted Schilowitz: When we talk about the curving of technology and the use cases of technology, this becomes this very popular discussion, which I'm sure you've had many times, about what makes it "Virtual Reality." What takes us to a point of presence, to a point of awareness that our optic system, our brain, our limbic system, and our physical body are actually connected into that world? That's when you start to get into the world of the *Ready Player One* metaphors.

That starts to get into this interesting discussion of the dystopian or utopian universe. What I like to say, and I think this is a fairly popular point of view, is that humanity tends to find a way to drift toward more of a utopian future than dystopian future. The more and more powerful the tools get, the more and more chance that the dystopian part can actually be more powerful and more meaningful. You end up in this interesting ethics discussion about connecting all the different systems of our physical body as a new form of entertainment or a new form of communication. Do I believe it's going to happen? The answer is yes. I'm already seeing touchpoints every single day.

It's been a year, maybe more, the first time I did VR karaoke. I actually stood up in front of a virtual crowd and actually sang just like I was in a real karaoke bar, but it's virtual. So, my brain is being tricked. You get the same nervousness. You get the same amount of tension. You get the same performance anxiety. I've done a VR talk show where I actually sat with a group of people on a virtual stage just like it would be at a real event that I do at real places all the time. I interacted with them. Essentially we were all avatars at that time, but that's going to change as well, as far as body scanning and so forth. It's spatial. That's actually a big point of something we might want to talk about. The sense of what we call true spatial sense in Virtual Reality and augmented reality is fundamentally different than flat-screen media or all the media experiences that have come before it. I think it's not discussed or talked about nearly enough.

John Bucher: I'd love to talk about that.

Ted Schilowitz: What we see now is that the head-mounted displays that exist today do a really good job at surrounding our visual experience and firing our visual cortex. You're firing a lot more brain cells in VR than you are when you're watching a screen in front of you. You start to get that sense of believability. You start to attach the first step in the equation, now very commonplace, which is your hands. But you're still using controllers for your hands. It's a metaphor from the past, which comes from video games. You're still clicking buttons.

I think when you put your futurist hat on, where it really starts to go is what we refer to as the *ghost hands*—when you're not actually using a physical device. The sensors are just good enough that it can actually track what you're doing. If I was in front of a virtual panel, getting ready to go into a sci-fi adventure, I would move my hands around *Minority Report* style. If I was going to be in an active shooter game, as opposed to using a game controller, I would just literally have a physical prop, and that prop would be tracked in space. It would feel like it's a real gun and act like a real gun.

John Bucher: If you own a 3D printer, then you can easily create those props.

Ted Schilowitz: You see companies doing this now. None of this is exotic anymore, and that's when I ask, "Why is this now?" The confluence of all these things. We talked about humanity a bit. We also should talk about the fact that you can actuate and create things that deliver on that dream without having to go to huge amounts of expense or exotic tool sets to do that.

Now, the next step in the equation is when you actually start to make a choice to wear enough sensors on your body that you have what we would call full-body presence. There are a number of different companies that I'm very closely involved with that are touching this. Again, not all that exotic. You're talking about motion-capture tracking systems and wearing little balls. With enough of those data balls, which is like performance-capture equipment, but simpler, you get a sense that "I can see my own body in VR." If you think about it, what we've always been doing in entertainment are these magic tricks.

We're creating illusions, and the more you can blend technology into the illusion-creation system, the more of a chance you have to actually really fool people. It's no different than going to a magic show. The better magicians, you fully believe, and you're scratching your head going, "How the hell did they do that?" In the world of VR, there are moments that I have, even as a practitioner of this now, a conjurer in my own right, where the illusion is almost complete. You set the stage for "Wow, look what just happened to me. I started here, and I ended here." Historically, if you want to reference the practitioners of that, for a number of generations, they have been people that were creating theme park entertainment.

I've often made this funny little trite reference that now we have the ability to wear a theme park on our face. Take it with us in our carry-on luggage. Put it in our living room or our dining room or our game room. Whereas before I had to go to a real theme park to get a theme park experience. To get into a simulation ride or experience. Technology is now merging that with an at-home or mobile device, or anywhere I want to be in experiences. That's the real power. That's the lightning bolt. When you say, "I could only do this in a very exotic place." Now I'm moving to what I would call a semi-exotic place.

John Bucher: You've brought up theme park experiences. You've brought up viewing experiences. We certainly have gaming experiences. Let's talk for a second about the narrative elements that we find in all of those experiences. We are bringing together the world of gaming, the world of theme parks, and the world of film and television in VR. It's merging into this new medium. Can you talk about the narrative elements in this space?

Ted Schilowitz: Sure. I'll take this in a slightly different direction than a lot of people would take it. I have slightly different kinds of language points. Why do we like cinema? Why do we like gaming experiences? What are their similarities and what are their differences? This is interesting to me. You're watching something play out on a screen. The fascination is there, even though you know it's already been captured. It's been created. As you watch it for the first time, you are just a fraction of a step behind what we would call reality. That's what's so intriguing for us as humans. I'm watching a story play out in front of me, and I don't exactly know what's going to happen in the next moment. Now, I make all kinds of predictions about what could happen in the next moment based on the last 5 seconds, 5 minutes, 30 minutes, 1 hour. When it takes a sharp right turn or sharp left turn, and I didn't understand for a moment until my brain caught up why that happened, that's to me, the magic of cinema.

We can talk about why are twist endings so important. Why does the horror genre work so well? Why does action-adventure work so well? It's because even though you think you know what you know, they put a big twist in. It's that, "Oh! You got me" moment. That's storytelling. It's when you're always right on the razor's edge of thinking you know what's going to happen but not exactly sure what's going to happen. That's real life. That's the mirror of real life.

The part of our brain that gets stimulated from this passive entertainment where we know the choices have been made for us. We're actually not going to get to make any choices here. We're going to watch, and our brain is going to wander down the path as the story's catching up to us. There is a different part of our brain that actually functions in the decision-making process, which is a more active part of entertainment. Look at who likes games versus who likes passive entertainment and why there are not a lot of people that would say they're super passionate about both. It is because people that like to make decisions when they entertain themselves drift toward interactive entertainment. They drift toward console gaming, PC gaming, mobile gaming. They want to be an active participant in their own destiny.

John Bucher: They want agency.

Ted Schilowitz:	They want agency. Agency often gets misused a little bit in VR. It's like, "Well you have agency." Well. Not if it's not crafted right. You have pseudo-agency.
John Bucher:	Then you have global agency and local agency and all these other ideas with that.
Ted Schilowitz:	I think that's a super-interesting way to think about the world. It's interesting when it comes to the age dynamics of why we see that younger kids, at the end of their day, want to entertain themselves with a gaming experience versus people that are a little bit older want to entertain themselves with a passive experience. I have a theory on this. It's not proven. I just have a theory.
John Bucher:	I'd love to hear your theory.
Ted Schilowitz:	My theory is that as a young kid, you're not often asked from the minute you wake up in the morning to the minute you get home at night to make a lot of decisions. You sit in school and they're putting an educational curriculum out for you. You're asked to do things and stay on the path. Pay attention. We're going to deliver a lesson plan. You're not given a lot of agency. In the more creative schools, you get more agency. I think that's actually why the superstar kids come out of schools that have figured out that they need to be more interactive and more demanding on their students in terms of making their own decisions. Even with that being said, the end game is usually set. It's like, "Yes, we want to give you the illusion that you're doing this on your own and you're going to come to your own conclusion. But ultimately as educators, we think we know the conclusion."
	As a kid, you're not often asked to make a lot of decisions in the first 8 hours of your day. When you get home at night, the entertainment you want to do is more about wanting to be the master of your universe. You want to control because you didn't get to make 200 decisions from eight in the morning till five thirty at night. My mom puts dinner on. I don't get to pick. She just made

dinner. If I don't eat it, I go up to my room. When I get to break out, I want to get into the *Call of Duty* world. I want to get into the *Grand Theft Auto* world. I want to get into the *CS Go* world. I want to because now I have the ability to make my own choices. To hide or shoot. To get better at something. To activate with my friends in a certain way. It fires a completely different part of our brain. Now, on the flip side as grown-ups, you're often asked to be in an environment where you have to make decisions all day long that are affecting other people in your world, that are affecting your job, they're affecting money. At the end of the day, as a grown-up, you want passive entertainment. You don't want to make any more decisions. Which is why the appeal of a game, a console game, a PC game is much less so for someone that had to make decisions all day long. They now want to turn that part of their brain off. Kid's want to turn that part of their brain on at the end of the day. Adults mostly want to turn that off. Now, I would say, we're starting to see a conflict. We're starting to see a new generation of kids that grew up in that world of, "I don't get to make decisions here but I get to make decisions there" now becoming adults. They're blending those two worlds in a different way. They want to entertain themselves in a different way. They don't find the idea of sitting in an office all that compelling. They want to move around throughout the world and have agency in everything that they do. At the end of the day, they want theme park entertainment. They don't want passive entertainment.

John Bucher: I think that leads to a discussion on presence, because in a movie theater, that's a passive experience. We turn the lights off so that you don't even see yourself. There's no sense of presence.

Ted Schilowitz: The noise of your neighbor bothers you because now that decision-making process in your brain is turned on, unfortunately. When I see the light of a text message in that dark theater, I now have to make a decision whether to tell that person to shut that thing off or to try and ignore it. It throws you out of that passive relaxation of entertainment.

John Bucher: Everyone is going for the deepest sense of presence and immersion that can be accomplished in VR space, but there are some who would say, "We're actually trying to move towards AR world rather than taking you out of the present reality." A sense of presence changes as we move to AR because we're here. There is presence. How do you think we are going to deal with presence in an AR world?

Ted Schilowitz: I'm doing a lot of VR and I'm doing a lot of AR. I actually think it's two different forms of art. I think VR is literally creating a universe that is trying to include as much of the real world as possible and take you to another place. That magic trick is all about trying to convince me that I have left the real world. With AR, it's a blending of worlds. In a world where we're playing a mobile game on a screen, the real world is kind of there with me. I have to multitask a little bit. As I start to wear it on my face, that changes.

If I was wearing some sort of AR glasses, in the future, if I don't have time to go to another world but have five or seven minutes to kill some aliens in the parking lot I'm walking through, I can do that. That's fun. I don't have to leave my world to augment my world. HoloLens is doing it. Our friends at Magic Leap are doing this. There's a lot of companies that are starting to figure that out as a form of entertainment. I think it's extremely powerful. I also think it's actually very different than VR. They're almost two different artistic pursuits.

John Bucher: How does gaming figure into VR and AR from a storytelling perspective?

Ted Schilowitz :   Games have figured out another way to tell stories. People sometimes don't think gaming is a storytelling medium, and I violently disagree with that. Everybody's played *Pac Man*. I don't care how old or how young you are, at some point in time, you've played *Pac Man*. You have agency in *Pac Man*. You have a device that allows you to make choices in *Pac Man,* and you have to run away from ghosts. It's a flat metaphor that is telling us a story. You got to get away from the ghosts, hide, eat some food, and then progress to the next level in life. It's a story.

John Bucher: It really is a story.

Ted Schilowitz: It is, right? In the most basic understanding, I just told you a little story. Okay, so here's a story. You're going to be this creature and you have to find a way to survive and ghosts are going to chase you. Well of course it's a story. *Space Invaders* is a story. *Galaga* is a story.

John Bucher: *Pac Man* is like the oldest story of humankind. I'm going to hunt for food and try and get away from ghosts. That's like a caveman's story.

Ted Schilowitz: That's modern storytelling, too. What I find really interesting in the world of Virtual Reality is the intersection of the cinematic type of story and the interactive story of any of these game references. With Virtual Reality and Augmented Reality, you get to take those two areas of pursuit and combine them together into one. Anybody that plays games enough knows what a cut scene is or a cinematic scene. For a very long time, you would play the game at a various state of fidelity. Then when you got into the cut scene, the fidelity would go up. You wouldn't get to do anything, you just now have to watch. The controller has no function right now. It's an achievement, and it's propelling the story forward. It always was a bit of a weird break point. If you're activating and making decisions in a game, when suddenly you're asked to make no decisions for two and a half minutes, the two sides of your brain conflict with each other. It's hard to tell a story if you need to interrupt active storytelling with passive storytelling.

Whereas, in the world of VR, once I've brought you into that world, I can blend those things in a much more nimble and effective way. I can point to story elements and capture you without having to remove you from the interactive moment. I can have a character start to address you and give you some narrative and propel you

| | in a certain way. That's hard to do in a console game. It's innately perfect to do in a VR game because you're asking to create reality. Theatrics. Magic. The chemistry's better. |

John Bucher: What are the big challenges that we've got to overcome in VR to tell better stories?

Ted Schilowitz: Getting the storytellers up to speed on understanding that this is a new medium, a new way to tell stories. I'll correct myself. I wouldn't actually say it's all that new. I've made reflections into the theme park world—into what Walt Disney saw when he was making movies and realized he could do more than make movies. He realized he could actually bring people into a world. That's actually the physical space of a theme park. Everything about that is a creationist's world. The minute you walk through that gate. The minute you go down Main Street and the minute you go into Frontierland or Adventureland or Tomorrowland, he's created a spatial sense of entertainment where you drop into things. He and the people in Imagineering had a realization that you could break those boundaries down. They recognized that the illusion is not just a screen. The illusion is every single thing about what happens when you get into an environment. Now we can do that artificially. We can create new environments in VR. That will enable us to begin to craft better stories.

INSIGHTS FROM THE VISIONARIES

In any discipline or medium, we must have those who look past the current state of the craft to the future. Those individuals act as lighthouses in the storms of experimentation. We need their forward thinking for direction and guidance as we attempt to transcend what we know to be possible and look to what instead *might* be. Anyone in the world-building arena of VR likely has some amount of vision. However, leaders will always emerge that point the way toward what will likely lie ahead. Larry Rosenthal compares world building to our relationship with nature, saying it is simply mediation. Matt Thompson's VR experience, *Lucy*, is certainly a mediation with what an afterlife experience might be like. Paul Debevec's work equally strives to create a mediated experience with the viewer, aiming at making that mediation as transparent as possible. All of the visionaries in this section and throughout the book take the responsibility of mediated experiences between the creator and the viewer very seriously.

Branch storytelling was mentioned by Chris Milk in Chapter 5 as one concept that will likely be important in the future of VR storytelling. Brian Rose speaks of the idea in similar terms. The team at Google continues to look for ways to explore the potential of combining social VR with branch storytelling within the confines of current technology. While the limits confine the process now, creators are confident that these barriers won't exist forever. They want to be ready with these more complex stories that allow the audience even greater agency, as soon as engineers and scientists are able to solve the tech issues. Rosenthal is confident that the progress the gaming community has made with branch storytelling will likely initially inform the early VR efforts. This reminds us of the importance of working with those both inside and outside of immersive communities in pushing forward VR techniques and methods.

Ted Schilowitz stated that humanity tends to find a way to drift toward more of a utopian than dystopian future. The more and more powerful the tools get, the more and more chance that the dystopian part can actually be more powerful. The section on ethics in Chapter 5 could not be more important in an age when our technology could quickly take us into uncharted waters we never dreamed possible. The stories we tell ourselves about who we are and who we might become take on even greater significance when our mediums of storytelling become more transparent and indistinguishable from reality. Our technology must continue to drive us toward a greater capacity for good, empathy, and humanity. Anything less leads to a reality that is not only emotionally empty but potentially bankrupt of that essential quality we desire as people journeying through life—meaning. Virtual Reality has offered us a new way to share our thoughts and experiences. It is a new canvas for artists to create with. Paul Debevec suggested that stories are how we store information about history and the lessons that we can take from that history, allegorically. The stories we craft within VR will remain a record of who we were on a great number of levels for generations to come.

Glossary

360-Degree Video

360-degree video keeps the viewer in a fixed point surrounded by approximately 360 degrees of video. This approach is considered less immersive than traditional VR, where the viewer can actually move within the world that has been built. Although often referred to as VR, 360-degree video in and of itself is not considered Virtual Reality.

Accelerometer and Gyroscope

Accelerometers are used to detect the orientation of the device they are placed in, such as a mobile phone, tablet, or HMD. The gyroscope adds another dimension to the information calculated by the accelerometer, tracking the rotation of the device.

Agency

Agency refers to the interactive capabilities available to a user in a VR/AR/MR experience. Most developers agree that the greater the agency enjoyed by the viewer/player, the higher the degree of immersion, thus the more real the experience will feel.

Ambisonic Audio

Ambisonic audio involves recording in the full sphere, including sound sources above and below the listener, providing a more immersive auditory experience, as opposed to more traditional recording techniques that only record on the horizontal plane.

Antagonist

The antagonist refers to the opponent of the protagonist. A well-constructed antagonist often wants the exact same thing as the protagonist (to win the game, to get the job, to rule the universe, etc.), but their reasons for wanting the same goal are vastly different. Antagonists should have compelling but flawed reasons for doing what they do.

Apollonian Approach

The Apollonian approach refers to the philosophical idea of reason-based thinking. Apollo was the god of rationality in Greek mythology. This philosophy is often juxtaposed with the Dionysian approach, which relies chiefly on emotion and instinct.

Artificial Reality

Artificial Reality is another term for Virtual Reality or interactive immersive environments. The term comes from a 1983 book by Myron W. Krueger, which focused on his ideas about his work in the field, dating back to the 1960s.

Augmented Reality

Augmented Reality is related to a larger idea called Mediated Reality and is designed to enhance one's current perception of what they see, through some sort of hardware such as a display or glasses, as opposed to creating an entirely new experience, as is the case with Virtual Reality. The surrounding world of the user is interactive in Augmented Reality and able to be manipulated digitally. Allowing a user to click on the costume an actor is wearing in a film and then purchase the same outfit would be an example of Augmented Reality.

Avatar

Avatars are digital representations of computer users in virtual space. The term originated as a reference to the many varying incarnations of Hindu deities.

Backstory

Backstory refers to the events in a character's life that occurred before a story begins. They may inform the present psychology, philosophies, and fears that character experiences.

Binaural Audio

Binaural audio uses a recording method that uses at least two and sometimes multiple microphones to simulate a realistic 3D stereo sound experience for the user. The technique accounts for the fact that human ears are found on each side of the head and creates a more immersive experience for the user.

Binocular Omni Orientation System (BOOM)

Binocular omni orientation systems are VR displays that served as forerunners to head-mounted displays. Users hold the viewport to their eyes and aren't required to support the weight associated with HMDs.

Branching Narrative

Branching narratives refer to the use of nonlinear story structure that allows users options that progress the story along. Options continue to be offered to users until either each option is given an ending or a series of options eventually leads to the same ending as a series of other options. Many users associate branching narratives with the "Choose Your Own Adventure" novel series.

Cave

CAVE is an acronym that stands for cave automatic virtual environment. It refers to a VR theater or environment where projectors are directed around a room-sized cube. Users then experience an immersive environment inside the cube.

Character Arc

Character arc refers to how the protagonist changes over the course of a story. In every good story, a character grows, develops, learns something, or realizes some truth by the end of the story. However, it's important to remember that these elements are part of a character's internal journey and not something the audience can experience directly like the external journey.

Cinematic VR

Cinematic VR is created from cameras that create either VR images or images that can be stitched (see the following) together to create VR in postproduction. The term can be confusing in that it does not refer to VR created through animation or in another graphical fashion, even if those images are used to tell a cinematic story.

Dionysian Approach

The Dionysian approach refers to the philosophical idea of instinctual or emotionally based thinking. Dionysus was the god of irrationality and chaos in Greek mythology. This philosophy is often juxtaposed with the Apollonian approach, which relies chiefly on reason and rationality.

Dramatic Conflict

The need to increase conflict is one of the most common problems a story can run into. While there are many ways to raise the stakes in a story, three of the most useful are to (1) compress the geographic space between the antagonist and protagonist, (2) condense the amount of time the protagonist has to achieve their goal, and (3) add an additional character who opposes the protagonist as they pursue their goal.

Empathy

Empathy refers to the ability to understand and share the feelings of another person.

Energy

Energy can refer to a variety of different definitions, depending on the context or use of the term. In immersive communities, energy often refers to the transmission of feelings, emotion, or some other force between the user, the creator, and the created experience.

External Goal

The external goal is what the protagonist spends most of their time trying to achieve. Regardless of whether the protagonist likes the goal, the goal should be imperative. It should be the thing that drives them. The ending of a film should always reveal whether the protagonist achieved their goal, and sometimes, it's more effective when the protagonist does *not* get what they want in the story but instead gets what they need.

Eye Tracking

Similar to head tracking, except the users' eyes control the alignment as opposed to their head.

Field of View (FOV)

Field of view refers to the depth of visual immersion the viewer experiences when looking around them. It is usually referred to by the number of degrees a viewer can see around them at any one moment in time. The viewing angle, or field of view, for the human eye is roughly 200 degrees.

First View

First view is often referred to as the front view or the initial view that the viewer experiences when a VR scene begins.

Fish Tank VR

Fish tank VR is a term coined by Colin Ware that refers to a small VR environment of high-quality visuals that is self-contained, more easily controlled, and can exist within the real world. An advantage of fish tank VR is the speed of the rate with which objects can be oriented in space.

Formats/Platforms

Formats and platforms refer to the particular software and coding used to access VR/AR/MR content. Leading formats presently include Samsung's Gear VR, HTC Vive, Oculus Rift, Google Cardboard, and Open VR. The term "platform agnostic" is also frequently used in the industry and refers to not believing in the strict use of a single format or a nonpreference among the available platforms.

Gesture

A movement, usually of the hand or head, that expresses an actionable desire in virtual space. Often, gestures are made with controllers and tracked with sensors in current VR technology.

Global Agency

Global agency refers to the viewer/player's ability to affect the overall narrative experience through world building and affecting the experience and potential success of other viewer/players.

Habituation

Habituation refers to the reduction of psychological or behavioral responses to the same stimuli over time. This condition is of concern to VR creators since some evidence suggests that users inside experiences stop responding in anticipated ways once the experience is no longer new.

Haptics

While encompassing a variety of nuanced meanings in various technological fields, this term in the world of Virtual Reality refers to a sensory experience such as touching something that's not there or actually occurring in physical reality. Haptics are usually experienced through some sort of controller.

Head-Mounted Display (HMD)

A key piece of hardware delivering VR experiences to users, HMDs are typically goggles or a helmet. Some HMDs have sensors for head tracking (see what follows), which allow images in the viewing experience to be manipulated to match the position of the head.

Head Tracking

This term refers to a technology that uses sensors to keep up with the movement of the viewer's head and move the images being displayed so that they align with the position of the head. In certain VR experiences, this technology allows the viewer to see the world that's been built above, below, and around the viewer as they turn their head.

Hypermediacy

Hypermedia is a term defined by theorists Bolter and Grusin as a style of visual representation whose goal is to remind the viewer of the medium. It refers to a user's desire for immediacy (see definition below) in virtual space.

Immediacy

Immediacy is a term defined by theorists Bolter and Grusin and refers to the erasure of the gap between signifier and signified such that a representation is perceived to be the thing itself. Immediacy involves the removal of the evidence of the "screen" between the user and the experience.

Immersion

Immersion refers to the deep mental involvement a user experiences while participating in a particular piece of media.

Inciting Incident

Story gurus have called the inciting incident by many names over the years, but regardless of what they call it, they all agree you need one. The inciting incident is the moment that starts your story. It's the moment when the pro-tagonist becomes aware of their external goal. Think of this as "the phone call that changed your life." After the inciting incident, nothing should remain the same for the protagonist. The inciting incident forces the protagonist to make a decision about whether to go on the journey.

Interactivity

Interactivity refers to the concept of two things working together, having influence with, and responding in some way to one another.

Interface

Interface refers to the point at which two things interact and communicate with one another, usually a human and a computer. An interface in VR may refer to the portal that a user enters or navigates VR space.

Internal Goal

Internal Goal refers to the achievement or intention that a character has but may never tell others. Finding love or acceptance are common internal goals for characters. These differ from external goals, which are usually explicitly stated in a story and are photographable.

Interpupillary Distance (IPD)

Interpupillary distance refers to the distance between the center of the pupils of the two eyes. This measurement must be precise in order to create an immersive experience in an HMD.

Intradiegetic

Intradiegetic refers to a narrative where the narrator of a story exists, is fully present, and is participating inside the world of a particular text.

Irony

Irony in cinematic storytelling refers to the ending of a story and the relationship between the external goal and the internal need. There are four types of endings:

1. Positive—the protagonist gets both what they want and what they need.

2. Positive irony—the protagonist gets what they need but not what they want.

3. Negative irony—the protagonist gets what they want but not what they need.

4. Negative—the protagonist gets neither what they want nor what they need.

Judder

Judder refers to the strobing or smearing of image inside an HMD in a VR experience. It occurs because of latency issues in the experience and can cause simulator sickness.

Kinesthetic Dissonance

Kinesthetic dissonance occurs when what the body does in reality and the sensations involved in such locomotion are not echoed in virtual space through haptic feedback.

Latency

Latency refers to any delay in the movement of the environment as a user moves their head or eyes. Since this never happens in the real world, the viewer is usually removed from the immersive experience of the environment when latency occurs. This technical difficulty is different from judder, which is "a combination of smearing and strobing that's especially pronounced on VR/AR HMDs" according to Oculus's CTO, Michael Abrash.

Local Agency

Local agency refers to the viewer/player's ability to affect the narrative experience through personal choices such as what weapon he or she might employ or what direction one might look.

Ludology

Ludology refers to the study of games and (video) gaming. Ludologists support that stories are only a subset of games and that games should not be analyzed primarily in terms of narrative.

Metadiegetic

Metadiegetic refers to a secondary narrative told by a character inside a story.

Metaverse

Metaverse refers to a shared virtual space or environment, where users can interact with one another. In some contexts, it refers to the sum of all virtual worlds.

Mixed Reality

Mixed Reality refers to the combining of VR and AR principles and elements. A VR landscape with the ability to augment or control elements within that landscape would be an example of Mixed Reality.

Multiverse

Multiverse refers to a hypothetical set of possible virtual universes.

Narrative

A collected account of connected events, either written, spoken, or experienced. "Narrative" is often interchangeable with the word "story."

Narratology

Narratology refers to the study of stories and storytelling. Narratologies support that games and other similar media are a subset of stories, and thus subject to primarily narrative analysis.

Navigation

Navigation refers to locomotion or movement from one place in space to another.

Payoff

The payoff refers to the emotional relief an audience experiences when an element referenced earlier in a story is completed or referenced again in some way.

Photo-Realism

Photo-realism refers to the technical qualities or resolution of an image or graphic that equals that of a photo or, in some cases, real life.

Point of View (POV)

Point of view refers to the perspective from which the user experiences a narrative. Common POVs include first person, in which a user moves through an experience as they would through their own eyes outside of virtual space, as well as third person, in which a user moves through an experience as an observer and goes unnoticed by others in the space.

Position Trigger

Position trigger refers to a point in space or interaction where a user's presence or action motivates a predetermined reaction.

Presence

Presence refers to the level of realism a user experiences in virtual space. The higher the degree of presence, the more the user feels as though they are truly in the environment and experience.

Protagonist

The protagonist refers to the character we feel the most empathy for in the story. They are usually the main character—sometimes called the hero or heroine. This is the character through which the entire story unfolds and develops. The protagonist usually has a very specific external goal they must pursue over the course of the story as well as an internal conflict that needs to be resolved. A protagonist must be a person capable of making a believable, proactive choice at the end of the story in order to reveal to the audience that they've completed their character arc.

Refresh Rate

Refresh rate represents how quickly individual images (or frames) are updated on an HMD or traditional display. Higher frame rates create a more immersive environment for the user and cut down on technical difficulties such as lag as well as unpleasant user experiences such as nausea. Frame rates less than 60 frames per second increase the chances of both of these issues.

Remediation

Remediation is a term defined by theorists Bolter and Grusin and refers to paying homage to, rivaling, and refashioning previous media forms. For example, film is a remediation of theater. Some consider VR a remediation of film and video games.

Resolution

The resolution of the story is the revelation of the answer to the problem the protagonist has been trying to solve—did they or did they not achieve their external goal? A good resolution also addresses the world in which the story took place—is the world now a better place after the protagonist has completed their journey?

Reversal

A reversal occurs when something unexpected occurs in a story. This tool can be especially effective if the audience is expecting a character to make one decision and they make the opposite choice. This idea can also refer to the changes of fortune that occur between the protagonist and antagonist as the story progresses.

Sandbox Experience

Sandbox experiences refer to virtual spaces or activities in which users may gather and engage in various games or interactions together.

Setup

In many ways, stories are greatly about setups and payoffs. A setup is narrative information that the audience will need later in the story. Sometimes, a setup will not feel greatly important to the audience until it is paid off.

Simulator Sickness

Simulator sickness refers to nausea caused by technical issues such as latency or balance and navigational orientation problems experienced by users in VR experiences.

Social VR

Social VR refers to immersive virtual experiences where users may interact with one another and share activities, ideas, environments, and media.

Spatial Navigation

Spatial navigation refers to how users move through space within a virtual experience.

Stitching

Stitching refers to the postproduction process of taking footage, usually but not exclusively from multiple cameras, and combining them to form a larger continuous immersive experience. For example, the footage from multiple GoPro cameras might be stitched together to create a 360-degree video.

Tele-Existence

Refers to the concept of the presence experienced by a user when they are given the agency to jump from space to space without necessarily experiencing the journey between those spaces.

Uncanny Valley

Uncanny valley refers to the phenomenon that occurs when a computer-generated figure or artificial intelligence shares nearly identical qualities and behaviors as a human being but causes a sense of discomfort or repulsion in the human interacting with it.

Virtual Reality

Virtual Reality refers to an entire field of computer technology in which environments, individuals, and experiences are replicated and presented for user interaction. The term is widely used and can encompass a great many ideas. However, all concepts seem to circle around the idea of an artificial yet realistic experience through technology.

VR Surfaces

Aside from HMDs, other surfaces are available for VR/AR/MR experiences. Current surfaces include VR caves, VR domes, and VR tables. The number and types of surfaces that one may experience immersive content in grows each year.

Index

JOHN BUCHER
@johnkbucher
tellingabetterstory.com

John Bucher is an award-winning writer, narrative consultant, and cultural mythologist based out of Hollywood, California. His work centers on the intersection of art and technology, as well as the power of story to change the journeys of individuals, communities, cultures, and nations. He is the author of books including *Master of the Cinematic Universe: The Secret Code to Writing in the New World of Media, Storytelling by the Numbers*, and *The Inside Out Story*.

His work can be seen regularly on LA-Screenwriter.com, in *MovieMaker* Magazine, and at HBO.com. He cohosts *The Inside Out Story Podcast* and *The Westworld Watch Podcast* and currently teaches at the LA Film Studies Center, where he leads courses in Virtual Reality storytelling and filmmaking. A popular speaker, John has given talks on five continents and is completing a PhD in mythology and depth psychology.

Lightning Source UK Ltd.
Milton Keynes UK
UKHW020627201118
332633UK00013B/195/P